BOISE STATE OF
MIND

BOISE STATE OF
MIND

THE EMERGENCE OF COLLEGE FOOTBALL'S
GRITTIEST UNDERDOG

JOEL GUNDERSON

Sports Publishing books may be purchased in bulk at special discounts for sales promotion, corporate gifts, fund-raising, or educational purposes. Special editions can also be created to specifications. For details, contact the Special Sales Department, Sports Publishing, 307 West 36th Street, 11th Floor, New York, NY 10018 or sportspubbooks@skyhorsepublishing.com.

Sports Publishing® is a registered trademark of Skyhorse Publishing, Inc.®, a Delaware corporation.

Visit our website at www.sportspubbooks.com.

10 9 8 7 6 5 4 3 2 1

Library of Congress Cataloging-in-Publication Data is available on file.

Cover design by Tom Lau
Cover photo credit: AP Images

Print ISBN: 978-1-68358-252-6
Ebook ISBN: 978-1-68358-253-3

Printed in the United States of America

To my wife, Katie.
My children Isla, Nash, and Stella
And to my parents Jackie, Ron, and Keith

TABLE OF CONTENTS

INTRODUCTION: CIRCUS

NICK SCHLEKEWAY couldn't take the stress anymore; vomit, from deep inside, now covered his jersey.

Just hours before, as his school's marching band had pranced across the playing field; as a nation was plopping onto their couches preparing to tune in with curiosity; and as those in attendance stood with hands over their hearts, singing along to the national anthem, his jersey had been a pristine shade of white.

Now here he was, with streaks of visible fatigue laced across his chest. It took all of the energy from Schlekeway, a defensive end for the Boise State Broncos, to not topple.

Standing frozen 59 minutes into the football game, he could barely feel his legs, let alone summon the ability to walk.

Breaths came in fits and spurts. Up to this point, the bout between his Boise State squad and the Oklahoma Sooners—in what would be derived as perhaps the greatest college football game ever played—had taken its toll: not just on him or his teammates, but on the entire legion of fans that poured their heart and souls into the school.

"We were just *exhausted*," he says now, reflecting back on the moment. He doesn't specify, but the "We" may as well have been the 13.7 million viewers who had tuned in to watch.

The date was January 1, 2007. The location was University of Phoenix Stadium in Glendale, Arizona. The event was the Fiesta Bowl.

Put in a blender, the Broncos and the Sooners were the quintessential ingredients for this match-up; Boise State, the plucky group of misunderstood underdogs from Idaho. Oklahoma, blue bloods of the sport.

Regardless of what would happen over the final minute of the game, Schlekeway and his teammates had proven their mettle. They hit Oklahoma with all available left and right jabs, and they had taken the counter punches. The Broncos had nothing left to prove. They had done more than anyone outside the state of Idaho had believed was possible.

Pacing the sidelines, Chris Petersen—who was in his first year as the Broncos' head coach—could see clearly the physical condition of his players. Despite their inspiring play up to that point, Boise State was not cut out for much more of this fight. The talk from media and fans alike heading in was that Boise State was built to compete, yet ultimately succumb to the physical superiority of the Sooners. That's what the Broncos had been told, time and again, generation after generation. Now, after taking Oklahoma further than almost anyone had expected, logic said it was time to give in to the enervation, roll over, and go home with nothing more than a moral victory.

However, that type of thinking never crossed Petersen's mind. It didn't cross Schlekeway's, or anyone else's on the roster, either.

What had gotten the Broncos to this point—the 12–0 regular season, the contempt and dismissal from their opponent—was irrelevant in this moment.

On the prior series, Jared Zabransky, the Broncos' oft-maligned quarterback, had thrown an interception which Oklahoma's Marcus Walker returned for a touchdown, giving the Sooners a 35–28 lead with just over one minute to go.

* * *

After the touchdown—and the back-breaking effects it could have—something snapped inside the head of Andrew Woodward, an offensive lineman for Boise State.

"I personally got crazy," he recalls with a half-chuckle, half-snarl. "I wanted to take and shake Zabransky because I felt, as a team, that we were together. The defense had been struggling, but as a team we were playing good. It was the offense's job to solidify that, and we didn't. I, personally, rely on our quarterback to get it done. And he didn't. I was pissed. . . . I was *extremely* pissed."

Although many felt Woodruff's frustration, no one took the interception harder than Zabransky himself. The senior quarterback had fought through canyon-sized low points in his career before that moment; one more porous decision, in his final game, now left everything feeling like it was slipping away.

When Boise State's offense trotted back onto the field after Walker's score, they found themselves 78 yards from the end zone, with 54 seconds left on the clock and two time outs left. The shock of the interception, and the touchdown scored off it, was visible, running cold down their faces. If the Broncos were trying to stave off the effects of the score, it was a spiritless effort.

A 36-yard completion from Zabransky to Derek Schouman on the first play of the drive put a crack in Oklahoma's mometum, but it was nothing more than a mirage. What followed left Bronco fans, who had descended upon Glendale in a fleet, feeling as though their moment in the sun had slipped away for good:

Sack, time out: 2nd and 18, 30 seconds left.

Incomplete pass: 3rd and 18, 23 seconds left.

Incomplete pass: 4th and 18, 18 seconds left.

"When Oklahoma scored, I think it really reset everybody," says Woodruff. Guys just weren't there. We were out of sync.

"To be honest, I sort of blacked out those first few plays of the drive."

That Boise State found themselves in a comeback situation was no surprise. During the regular season, the Sooners had been a dominant team. If they had been the beneficiaries of a good break or two, they may not have been playing in this game at all; the truth of the matter was that the Sooners should have been playing a week later for the National Championship. They were that big. They were that fast, and strong, and talented.

They were also that battle-tested.

On September 16, 2006, four months prior to the Fiesta Bowl, the Sooners were in Eugene, Oregon, to face the Oregon Ducks in a non-conference clash. It was as pristine a day as you could ask for. Not too hot. Not too bright. And if you were a Sooners fan, everything had broken correct for nearly 60 minutes of action. Oklahoma had lived up to their reputation as national title contender, waltzing into Autzen—person-for-person, one of the loudest stadiums in the country—and kept the Ducks at bay.

Running back Adrian Peterson (who would miss the final seven games of the regular season after breaking his collarbone in a win against Iowa State before returning for the Fiesta Bowl) was an almost unfair participant in the game, racking up 211 yards on 34 punishing rushing attempts. Paul Thompson, the Sooners' quarterback—who had taken over for the immensly talented, yet troubled Rhett Bomar—did his part to keep the Ducks' defense honest, posing just enough of a passing threat to give Peterson the room necessary.

With just under three minutes to play in the game, Oklahoma was squarely in control with a 33–20 lead. Even after an Oregon touchdown, cutting the lead to six, the Sooners looked poised to return home to Normal unscathed and in control of their title destiny.

Then, a blown call on Oregon's ensuing onside kick, in which the Ducks were inexplicably rewarded the ball, despite all evidence to the contrary. A touchdown immediately followed. In the blink of an eye, the Sooners went from up 13 to down one with less than a minute remaining.

Trailing 34–33, Oklahoma put themselves in field goal range following a long kickoff return, but Oregon blocked the game-winning field goat attempt, procuring the victory.

An Oklahoma win had been snatched away by both fate and terrible officiating; two weeks later, they would fall to their archrivals, the Texas Longhorns, 28–10.

However, after that second loss, the Sooners exploded. Over their final eight games of the season, they gave up just 100 total points (outscoring their opponents by 119 points in the process), defeating three ranked teams along the way—Missouri, Texas A&M, and Nebraska.

So, no—trailing by seven, and in need of a miracle, was not a surprise for Boise State. That they even found themselves in this position was the reason viewers were still glued to their television sets, calling friends and loved ones on the phone, frantically screeching, "Are you watching this?!"

When the Broncos were forced into that 4th and 18, with all hope circling the drain, a miracle was in order.

* * *

On the sideline, Taylor Tharp, the Broncos' backup quarterback, was incredulous.

When the play call came thundering down into his headset from high above the field, cataclysmic flashbacks raced through his head. Every week during the past season—usually on a Friday walkthrough before a game, and often with a child-like playfulness—coaches would have the offense run this particular play. It required a series of events to line up with precision; the timing from everyone involved, from the center on down, had to be perfect. If not, it would be a disaster.

The team ran it weekly. Not once did it work.

A missed route; an overthrown ball; linemen showboating if the ball bounced their way. Nothing from the fifteen weeks of practice—a zero-pressure situation—gave Tharp, a fourth-year junior and the man tasked with signaling it in, any confidence that it would work now, on the biggest stage of their lives.

But his job was not to question the call; it was to relay it in, as quickly and efficiently as he could, and let the chips fall where they may. So he did.

With 4th and 18 staring them in the face, just 18 seconds on the game clock, and the real possibility of blowing the biggest game of their lives weighing them down, Tharp began his task. Turning toward the field, he looked Zabransky—one of his best friends on the team, and a mentor in all things quarterback—right in the eye. He lifted both hands chest high, palms facing the sky, and began to juggle.

The play was sent in. "Circus."

For the Broncos to pull it off, all of the magic dust that had fallen over the program for the past twelve months had to tether in one nice formation. To make it work, to convert and score and live another day, would require perfect execution; not just from themselves, but from the Sooners, too.

"We didn't really want them to pressure us," Tharp says now. "If they blitzed us, it would have thrown everything off."

Tharp is laid-back, calculating. A true quarterback. Although he was born and raised in the high altitude of Boulder, Colorado, where his father was the athletic director at the University of Colorado, an almost California-like ease radiates off him. Sitting in the plush recruiting lobby inside the Bleymaier Football Center, which is attached to the north end zone of Bronco Stadium, his eyes pierce through his memory as the events leading up to the call come back, clear as the moment it was called. More than a decade has passed since the Fiesta Bowl, but every second of the game—every sight and smell—is vivid in his mind as if it happened just moments ago.

"The defense the Sooners were playing could not have been more perfect," he recalls. "It gave Zabransky the time to look elsewhere, the receivers time, so everything could line up."

Earlier in the game, when Boise State had jumped out to a 21–10 lead, with Oklahoma fans stone-faced and nearly catatonic from shock, "Circus" looked destined to be a celebratory play, one that would put the stake in the Sooners. The Broncos had turned what was supposed to be their own live beheading and flipped the script. Up until this moment, despite previous seasons of double-digit wins, the verdict on what exactly Boise State *was* had yet to be determined. Was this showing against Oklahoma, and their break-neck start to the game, a flash-in-the-pan? Did the Sooners so vastly underappreciated the Broncos that they themselves had allowed this to happen?

"They played well, we didn't, and that's the jist of it," says Rufus Alexander, the Sooners' star linebacker who was the team's defensive MVP during their Fiesta Bowl season.

Surely the Sooners overlooked the Broncos, though. There's no way they didn't.

Right?

"No. It wasn't hard to get up for them. I felt that if we came out and played our game, didn't turn the ball over, we were going to win," says Alexander.

* * *

The Boise State playbook—although expansive and imaginative—was not filled with plays designed to gain the yardage necessary to keep this partuclar drive alive. "Circus" was the only way to ensure that they could play on.

When Zabransky collected the snap and dropped back, three receivers flanked him to his right. Drisan James was the lone receiver to line up to his left.

Not wanting to get burned by a long pass, Oklahoma lined up in a semi-prevent defense with three safeties back deep. Within that coverage a pocket of space would be left open for the Broncos' receivers, conveniently, about 20 yards down the field from where Zabransky would wind up and let his pass go, two yards more than they needed.

And that magic dust that had been necessary?

Tharp smiles at the memory.

"It couldn't have been more perfect."

1

LYLE SMITH RIDES INTO TOWN

"Lyle Smith led this school to incredible successes
as a Junior College. Unmatched success."
—Tom Scott, Boise State historian

BOISE, IDAHO, EXISTS in a locale that the "hustle" long forgot. It's a place where folks saunter more than they rush; where they say "thank you" with sincerity instead of obligation; where they look you in the eye for reasons of comfort and respect, instead of condemnation or judgment.

While Boise flows with the feel of a big city, its subtle nature—and the down-home vibe of its citizens—belie the trappings that places of similar sizes fall under.

When Boise Junior College came into existence in 1932, it did so in the middle of town, parked squarely between family businesses and fast-rising conglomerates alike. Where most universities tended to trickle toward the outskirts, Boise set up camp in a spot where no mistake could be made: the university *was* Boise.

In 1947, Lyle Smith, at thirty-one years of age, became the head coach of the Boise Junior College football team. The program was entering their 12th season of existence (the school did not play from 1942–1945, due to World War II). Their record to that point—27–35–4—suggested nothing of a potential powerhouse; not at the junior college level, not at the Division II or Division I-AA level, and most certainly not at the Division I-A level, the highest in collegiate athletics. They were middling at best, bad more often than not and, worst of all, irrelevant. By the time Smith arrived, the school had already burned through three head coaches: Dusty Kline, Max Eden, and Harry Jacoby, whose stint sandwiched World War II.

Smith was a relative unknown when he arrived. Born in Colfax, Washington, his family would eventually settle in Moscow, Idaho, where Lyle would go on to star at Moscow High School in both basketball and football. While there, he would earn the coveted honor of being named to the "All-State Team." In the summer of 1939, he graduated from the University of Idaho with a Bachelor of Science in Education, while playing center for the football team and guard on the basketball team. After graduation, he accepted a teaching and coaching position at Firth High School; there, he married his college sweetheart, Maria Rappel, and set forth. He joined Moscow High School in 1941; for Smith, his life path was clear: alongside Maria, and the children that would follow, he would spend his days sculpting youthful minds. His afternoons would be for coaching; his evenings for family and friends. It was the dream he wanted.

However, reality was interrupted when, joined in force by thousands of men from across the country, Smith joined the US

Navy in June of 1942, as World War II took presidence. Smith would end his navy career four years later, where he primarily served as a physical education instructor. After his tenure, Lyle returned home to Moscow, and Maria, to complete his master's degree in education. In August of that year, 1946, as he was set to return to the high school level to continue, Smith suddenly resigned.

A different opportunity had presented itself, some 295 miles west in the city of Boise.

* * *

Harry Jacoby, who was in need of an assistant coach at Boise Junior College, had sought out Lyle for both his coaching acumen and his education background. Smith also brought a youthful enthusiasm that only exists with just enough inexperience.

The football program had yet to catch on in Boise, a town whose population hovered at just 30,000 citizens. It was not just that the program was relatively new; they had done nothing to ignite the fans' passion or provide a reason to engage.

If the only thing worse than being bad is being insignificant to a fanbase, that's what Boise was.

Case in point: when Smith entered the local barber shop for the first time after he arrived in town, he introduced himself, made mention that he was the assistant coach for the college's football team, and awaited the adoration that was sure to follow.

But as he sank into his chair, there was no exultation toward the coach. There was silence. The barber did not know there *was* a football team; he scarcely knew that there was even a college in town.

"When the barber doesn't know what's going on, it isn't a very big deal," Smith told *Sports Illustrated* in 2010.

Unfortunatly, during the 1946 season with Smith by his side, Jacoby's track record of mediocrity continued. After a combined 7–6 record the previous two seasons, Boise would stumble to a 2–4–2 finish. Jacoby—who also helmed Boise's men's basketball team—was the epitome of mediocrity as it pertained to coaching: his overall record in basketball, 24–21, verified his average abilities. Under his watch, both the football and basketball programs were struggling to find solid footing.

The Boise football program was hovering just above water. A change was in order, and there was one guy befitting of the job.

When the season came to its merciful end, Jacoby was out as the football coach; Lyle Smith, with just one year of assisting under his belt at the junior college level, was in.

Overnight, without anyone seeing the meteoric rise that was forthcoming, the fate of the Boise program changed.

* * *

In his first season, Smith took Boise from two wins to nine, posting a perfect record; the following year brought the same results. During his third year as head coach in 1949, Boise went a perfect 10–0, upping Smith's record to 28–0 overall. That season was the first time the school had played double-digit games, and they conquered them all. His squad would make an appearance in the Kern County Shrine Potato Bowl, the first bowl game appearance in the school's short history. When the team returned to Boise from Bakersfield, California, where the game had been played (after dismantling Taft Junior

College, 25–7), over 500 adoring fans awaited them outside the airport terminal. Children, their cheeks fire-red from the blistering cold that swept through the town, took in glimpses of their hometown heroes; chief amongst that status was Smith. From his first year, when not even the town barber knew of the program, he had brought them to the doorstep of a national championship.

"After that," he recalls, "we began to get a little notice in the community."

Lyle Smith was just thirty-three years old, sported a perfect record, and now the program was set to unveil a brand new 10,000-seat stadium. When he had taken over, the entire school was crammed together in a six-building unit in a small, previously vacant lot, inconsequential in the community with just over 700 students. Three years later, it was a steady-rising academic and football power.

He had the program and the community in the palm of his hand.

Once again his plan was derailed.

* * *

On June 25, 1950, the Korean War began. Smith—who would coach the first few games of the season alongside his trusted advisor George Blankley—was then called into duty, his military obligation taking precedence. Smith had won the first 33 games at the time of his departure, six more than the program had in its entirety before him.

Blankley would fill in for the remainder of the 1950 and 1951 seasons, accumulating an unofficial 17–0 record (he and Smith technically co-coached the first few games of the 1950 season, making the official records a bit blurry). Regardless of who claims the official Ws, the program had become the standard across the nation at the JC level.

The gameplan Smith laid out during his first season proved indestructible. It was so ironclad, in fact, that he did not even need to be in the country for it to succeed.

When he returned for the 1952 season, Smith picked up right where he had left off before his war exit. Boise rolled along, racking up wins, filling their luxurious stadium (by junior college standards), establishing themselves as the *crème de la crème*. Eluding them was a national championship, the last wall to fall in his takeover of the school.

It wouldn't take much longer.

In 1958, with his career record at an absurd 79–7, Boise claimed the NJCAA National Championship with a win over Tyler Junior College, out of Texas, 22–0.

The second half of Smith's 20-year tenure would prove to be just as fruitful as the first. By the time the 1967 season concluded, he had won 84.6 percent of the games he coached, posting a record of 156–26–6. Smith had coached 21 All-Americans, and had won a national title.

He also had a vision for the program, one which required a massive shift.

With that, after the 1967 season, Smith retired as the team's football coach, sliding into the role of the school's athletic director. His 20-year run was all he needed as the man in charge. Now as the AD, he took full control of entire athletic department. His fingerprints would be everywhere. And his first duty was finding a coach to replace him.

It was an easy choice.

2

TONY KNAP AND THE SECOND ROUND OF DOMINANCE

"With us as teammates, there was a common ground,
a common denominator. It's pretty much like a band
of brothers."
—Everett Carr, Boise State, 1975–1976

AS A PLAYER at the university of Idaho, Lyle Smith teamed with a young man by the name of Tony Knap. Anthony J. "Tony" Knap had played high school football at Riverside High in Milwaukee, Wisconsin, before heading west. He would go on to become a three-year varsity player alongside Smith, on top of his two-year run as a varsity baseball player.

Like Smith, Knap had joined the US Navy during World War II. After he returned to the states, he began a long and winding coaching career which included stops in high school, college, and the Canadian Football League (CFL). Knap had a stacked resume, and Smith knew that he could entrust the program to his longtime friend. It would take someone with big skills—and big cajones—to follow in the enormous footsteps Smith was leaving behind . . . especially when he would be just two doors down, running the show.

Along with transitioning to a new head coach—something the school had successfully avoided for the previous 20 seasons—Boise was also receiving a bump in stature. Thanks in large part to the run of success that Smith had taken them on, as well as the passing of a 1967 law allowing the school to make the leap, Boise Junior College would cease to exist beginning in the 1968 season. The junior college ranks were out; now they were Boise State College, a freshly minted four-year university. While the school sought out a permanent home conference to play their sports in, the 1968 season would see them play as members of the National Association of Intercollegiate Athletics (NAIA).

The nacent Boise State would face schools from five different conferences during their inaugural season as NAIA members— the Oregon Conference, Evergreen Conference, Rocky Mountain, and the Big Sky. While Smith's preference was for the Broncos to eventually buck into the Big Sky Conference, his patience in that quest would be tested; Boise State would be members of the NAIA for a minimum of two seasons. Despite his standing as the school's athletic director, Smith was as up in the air on the school's final landing spot as anyone else.

Perhaps puffing his chest just a bit, Smith made it clear— even if it was grand-standing—that the Big Sky would not hold the school hostage.

"We want to set our sights high," he told the Associated Press before the 1968 season began, "and we aren't sure that [the Big

Sky] is high enough. I believe we may go higher than the Big Sky Conference eventually."

Smith had slid into his role as athletic director smoothly, dreaming up visions far beyond what seemed realistic for a program still in its infancy. Forget one step at a time; he was looking two, three, *four* steps ahead.

* * *

After his hiring, Knap—who was coming over from Utah State—began the arduous but necessary task of rubbing elbows with the most vital people to the long-term success of a coach. The school's boosters, many of whom had sat front-row for Smith's wild ride, would be either his harshest critics or most important backers, depending on how things went. On February 15, 1968, at a small luncheon, aptly titled "Tony Knap Day," the fifth coach in school history—or, if you wanted to be literal, the first coach in "Boise State College" history—was animated about the situation in which he found himself.

"I feel I have inherited a legacy of great value," he told the assembled crowd, many of them getting their first glimpse at the new coach. "I appreciate the opportunity to follow someone with a program like Lyle Smith's. I have a stronger feeling about this job than I have had at any other school."[1]

The start of Knap's first season was still six months away, but already the buzz was palpable: the citizens of Boise had not experienced more than two losses in a season in more than twenty years; their status as a four-year school was the latest feather in their cap; and Knap was a known figure as the handpicked successor to Smith. Even with a daunting schedule ahead—including Eastern Washington State College, who had finished second in the NAIA the previous season—the feeling running through the streets of Boise was that the program would be in good hands.

* * *

When Knap's tenure officially began on September 21, 1968, against the Linfield Wildcats, his lineup featured 15 sophomores and 27 juniors, with the rest being freshmen. There was not one senior on his roster, giving him a wide net to cast. Not only would this season be a severe step up in competition, but he was also fielding a youthful squad still adhering themselves to both the playbook, as well as the physical nature of their opposition.

Unfortunately, it didn't take long for two realities to take hold: Knap, for all the excitement he brought, was *not* Lyle Smith; and the Broncos, despite boasting players who had tasted ample success, were in for a humbling experience. This was no longer the JC rank, where the school could pillage lesser teams; this was something all together different. Linfield crashed Knap's inauguration ball with a 17–7 win at Bronco Stadium.

Knap knew the big picture was the overall transition into the four-year university club, and not just this one game. Afterwards, he said the team's performance "gave us hope for the future."

The reputation of Knap prior to Boise State had been that of a master technician, who could teach the game in a nuanced manner that many others lacked. To do so in the proper manner would take time and repetition, and a deliberate attitude from both him and his players. The results would show in fits and spurts. At times it turned out well, like their week two win over Westminster, 50–2. Other times, like the following week when they were clubbed 44–3 at Weber State, the realization of how far they had to go would be apparent. However, as the season trudged on it was clear that Knap's message began taking shape.

Boise State would win their next two games following the loss to Weber State by a combined score of 69–0; included in that was Eastern Washington, arguably the toughest team on their schedule. The Broncos blanked the Eagles 20–0. They continued on, by defeating their next two opponents by a combined 30 points. They rounded out the season by outscoring Western State, Central Washington, and College of Idaho by a combined 118–14.

Knap's first season was an undeniable success, at 8–2. He deftly navigated the turbulent I-AA waters, and for his efforts he was granted a hefty raise, upping his yearly salary from $13,000 to $14,200.

He was secure. The Broncos, it seemed, were secure, too.

Now, the post-Smith era could begin in earnest.

* * *

In April of 1969, in an effort to strengthen the foundation of the team, Knap went out and signed two high school offensive linemen. Brothers Greg and Jeff Phillips were hulking, skyscraper-sized men whom Knap told the *Daily Herald* "will provide the foundation for a solid building program, upon which the football fortunes of Boise State College may rest for the next four years."[2]

He wasn't far off.

In 1969, the Broncos, in their final year of NAIA play—after officially being accepted into the Big Sky Conference for the 1970 season—went 9–1, outscoring their opponents by an average of 30 points per game. They steamrolled their opponents by such scores as 66–7 (Whitworth), 62–0 (Southern Oregon), and 45–0 (College of Idaho). They were dynamic on offense, relentless on defense, and fundamentally solid on special teams. It was impossible to deny that Boise State was Big Sky material. Now, they just needed to play there.

So, when they joined forces with Northern Arizona in jumping to the Big Sky the following year in 1970, their opportunity was at hand; and with it, the promise of immediate and unprecedented success—should they earn it.

Speaking in front of the Idaho Press Club following their acceptance, Knap laid out his aspirations: they wanted and expected to win a title. With all of the eligibility questions answered, Boise State entered the season with their biggest hurdle cleared.

"We were accepted with the understanding that we will be eligible to win the conference title next year," Lyle Smith told the *Daily Herald*.[3]

Or so they thought.

In order to be eligible for the conference title, Boise State was required to play at least four conference games over the course of the regular season. As January rolled into February of 1970, just eight months from the beginning of the season, they had only three scheduled. This quandry had a simple solution, one that made both geographical and financial sense: A game against the Idaho Vandals, a natural rival due to proximity, was something folks in the state of Idaho had long yearned for but had yet to see.

Should Idaho—already a Big Sky member—agree to a game, it would give the Broncos their fourth conference game.

If not, then . . .

"Somebody's going to have to bend to get us on their schedule," Knap told the *Idaho Statesman Journal*, "or we'll have to be permitted to count one other game as a conference game.

"Personally, I'd prefer to see Idaho drop Portland State and put us on the schedule."[4]

Knap's words, candid in nature, were taken as a shot toward Idaho, insinuating the state's land-grant university was either afraid to take on the newly minted Boise State College, or unwilling to budge from their status quo. Either way, newspapers across the state ran with it, making his comments the first in a long line of jabs between the schools.

Only, he wasn't finished.

"It seems to me Idaho could concentrate on winning the title rather than looking down its nose at its own conference."[5]

The identity that Boise State was carving out for themselves came directly through the irreverent attitude of their coach. At fifty-six years of age heading into the 1970 season, he still resided on the youthful side, allowing him to connect with the players on his roster. Yet his mind was fresh to the days when coaches took on roles of teachers and mentors as much as X's and O's savants. Like Lyle Smith, Knap had been both a teacher and coach at the high school ranks before his college career began. Molding the minds of adolescents as they traversed the waters from awkward, pubescent teens into men was something he not only believed in, but also thrived at doing.

Knap's teams at Boise were proving to be no different than his high school squads. The sophisticated offenses Boise State ran, the stout defenses, the academic successes—were all the byproduct of a coach who placed as much emphasis on the classroom and living room as the gridiron.

Later in life, as Knap and his wife, Micki, enjoyed the fruits of his retirement, he quipped to the *Lewiston Morning* this thought: "What is the most important thing in a guy's life during the time he is a student . . . obviously it isn't football. But, that's very easily overlooked. [Today] I'm afraid it's the unusual coach who tempers himself in his demands to be in tune with what is most fair to the player."[6]

Boise State College was also receiving a boon from an unexpected source—the local government. In the late 1960s, the state of Idaho had stumbled upon a sufficient and effective tax structure, resulting in a rather obscene surplus to the tune of $4.2 million, give or take a few cents. While many organizations around the state were in need of a financial pick-me-up—such as the Hospital South at Blackfoot, which had recently undergone massive layoffs due to economic downfalls—a major contribution was needed for higher education as well. Boise State, now two years into their run as a full-fledged university, was in no position to turn down an endowment of any size. So, when word came down that they would receive a gift of around $900,000, it was viewed as a major swindle for a school still seeking its footing.

Coinciding with the football team's move to the Big Sky, this represented the biggest uptick in finances and prestige the university had ever seen.[1]

* * *

---

1 The offseason before the team's 1970 campaign began had proven to be a busy one; on February 1, it turned solemn. On that date, The *Idaho State*

After the expansion of Boise State and Nevada in 1970, the Big Sky also consisted of Montana, Idaho State, Weber State, Idaho, Montana State, and Northern Arizona. The Montana Grizzlies, just two seasons removed from a disastrous 2–7

Journal ran a scathing article on the Civil Rights movements taking place in the state of Idaho.

According to the National Census, the city of Boise, in 1970, had a population of 74,990 people. Of that number, just 268 registered as Black, or 0.4 percent. Even smaller was the population of folks who identified as American Indian (160 people, 0.2 percent of the population). When the hearings went forth on Saturday, January 31 of 1970, racial dicrimination, injustice, and intimidation were brought forth by residences of the Bannock-Shoshone Indian tribes, as well as a representative of a Boise civil rights organization.

In the article, Rev. James Hubbard, a black chairman of the Citizens for Civic Unity in Boise, made mention of "subtle, sophisticated discrimination against members of minority groups in eight Idaho counties." Leading the charge were members of the Bannock-Shoshone tribes, with charges stemming from unfair working conditions, a lack of formal education, and unhealthy living conditions of tribes thanks to members of town not affiliated with the tribes.

Leroi Smith—a graduate student at Idaho State—spoke of the discriminations he witnessed as it pertained to black athletes, and the colleges and universities they attended. Smith had witenessed these conditions in his studies.

Boise State College was one of them.

"Boise State now owns thirty slaves," Hubbard said at the time. "There are now two of thirty willing to lay their scholarships on the line and speak up about the conditions. The fellows simply do not have the same rights as other students."

Over the following months, small protests would pop up at univesities around the state demanding equality, leading to a more cognizant approach to the conditions in which black athletes lived as it pertained to others on campus. ("Indians Level Charges at Civil Rights Hearing," Barbara Boren, Idaho State Journal, February 1, 1970.)

finish, had rolled through the conference in 1969 with a 10–1 record, while going 4–0 in conference play. Although they were not on the Broncos' schedule, the Grizzlies represented all that Boise State strived to be: they were the kings of the mountain, something Boise had been not long ago in the JC ranks.

Despite their most valiant efforts, and not-so-subtle hints, the Broncos failed to secure a fourth conference game. The three conference teams they would face—Montana State, Idaho State, and Weber State—had gone a combined 12–17 the season prior. Their first in-conference test would come in week four, with a visit to Bozeman, Montana, to face the Montana State Bobcats. It was a landmark day; just two full seasons removed from being a junior college program, they were finally on the doorstep of big-time college football.

They would announce their presence just as they had many times before: with a win. Their 17–10 triumph, served as a notice that the Broncos were at the appropriate level. Because they were not yet eligible to win the conference title, the season would become a long crusade to shake up the race for all others involved.

Although three losses would blemish their record a touch, including their final conference game against Weber State, 41–7, it hardly mattered. The 1970 season was about one thing: setting the tone for successes to come.

That's exactly what happened.

* * *

On September 11, 1971, in the opening game of the season and first in the record book for the rivalry, Boise State at last faced the Idaho Vandals. Before the game, Knap had commented on the significance of the match-up, noting to the *Daily Inter Lake* that a win would be "a stimulus for a very good year," and a loss would cause the Broncos to waste "a month getting back on track."[7]

On that day, 16,123 fans filed into Bronco Stadium. Although the game was originally set to be played in Moscow, it would be moved to Boise due to delays on the Vandals' new stadium, which was still being built. It didn't much matter; Knap's offense, wide open and carefree, ran circles around a stunned Idaho squad as the Broncos cruised to a 42–14 victory.

This, however, was not supposed to be the case: Idaho had entered the game as favorites—not just in the game, but for the conference as well. The Vandals were a loaded squad, and many pundits expected them to contend for the Big Sky title.

After the beating at the hands of the Broncos, Idaho would limp to a 4–7 record on the year.

Boise State, on the other hand, would finish 10–2, securing their first bowl game as a major university, where they defeated Chico State, 32–28, in the Camellia Bowl.

* * *

A 7–4 record the following season, in 1972, served as a stage-setter for a breakthrough in 1973. The school's first Big Sky title, and a berth in the playoffs, were well within striking distance. Alongside Montana State—the reigning conference champion—and Idaho State (another perceived favorite), the Broncos were seen as a viable title contender among coaches in the conference.

Boise State's offensive attack was once again a topic of discussion among conference opponents.

Knap, in a media call-in session before fall camp, attempted to water down the hype building around his team, noting that, "We'll be real good on offense and a question mark on defense. I'm a little concerned because you have to have a good defense in this league."

That part was true; it was also true that Boise State's offense could topple just about any defense thrown its way, nearly rendering their own defensive liabilities moot. The Broncos faced an unusual dilemma in that they returned the conference's top-two quarterbacks from a passing standpoint in Ron Autele and Jim McMillan. Together, the two had racked up 2,548 yards and 27 touchdowns the season prior. Even with just a month to go before play began, Knap knew as much as the public about who his starter was going to be. In all likelihood, it would hardly matter with as much talent that surrounded the both of them. Add to that the offensive line, which entered the season averaging a massive (for the time) 245 pounds, and either player at quarterback would be primed for immediate success.

A strong recruiting class would help ignite some much-needed energy into the defense. The year before, the Broncos had finished sixth in rush defense and fourth in passing defense in the conference. However, until those young players were ready to contribute, shootouts and nail-biters figured to be weekly realities.

For the second year in a row, the Broncos would open the season against Idaho; just as they had the year before, they took care of business, 47–24. Although Idaho was a big game, and one fans devoured, the Broncos had bigger things on their mind; namely, the following week, when the defending Big Sky champions from Bozeman would come calling.

The Montana State Bobcats had gotten the best of Boise State previously, and the matchup on September 22, 1973, figured to be the closest thing to a title game as could be expected during the regular season.

In front of 14,521 fans on a tepid Boise day, the Broncos—for the second week in a row—would topple a potential conference giant. Without their star receiver Don Hutt (who was out with an injury to his eye that he'd sustained against Idaho) Boise State relied on his little brother, Terry, who stole the spotlight, nabbing six catches, scoring a touchdown, and recovering a fumble. They would outgain the Bobcats 443–204, riding their surprisingly stingy defense in the second half. It was arguably the biggest win the program had experienced as a member of the Big Sky Conference; after four seasons of knocking on the door, and now two wins over top-tier programs to start the season, the Broncos were the clear-cut favorites to win their first conference title.

Two drubbings followed, with wins over Portland State and Weber State by a combined score of 98–14, before a road game at UNLV knocked them from the ranks of the unbeaten. At 4–1, the Broncos' offense was powerful, just as expected; however, it was the defense that was stealing the show. They were giving up just over 12 points per game and had displayed a level of tenacity that had lied dormant the previous season.

Two more convincing wins and a loss to Nevada left them at 6–2 with three games remaining.

In order to lock down the conference title, they had to win one game out of their final three. Stumble, and another offseason full of "What-if's?" would come calling.

Chance one of three came on November 10, as the team traveled to Pocatello, Idaho, to take on the Bengals of Idaho State. For the third year in a row, the two were set to lock horns in a game with the conference title squarely on the line. Two years prior, the Bengals had gotten the better of Boise State; last season, the Broncos returned the favor.

For the first 55 minutes of game action, it looked like Idaho State would again play the role of jealous sibling, snatching victory away from Boise State. After a back-and-forth affair, the Broncos took over on their own 9-yard line with just three minutes to play in regulation, down 14–17 and 91 yards from the end zone. Then Ron Autele connected with Don Hutt with 1:03 left to play, giving the Broncos the 21–17 win.

Boise State's ability to crawl out of a 17–7 hole in the second half was "a good example of why they deserved to be Big Sky champions this year,"[8] said Bob Griffin, Idaho State's head coach. "They deserve a great deal of credit."[9]

Autele had proven to be the differencemaker. Although his season had been marred by inconsistent play and a propensity for turnovers, his talent and athleticism was too good to ignore. "When he makes up his mind, he really executes. He has worked hard to develop his skills,"[10] Knap said after the win.

"It was definitely a classic."[11]

"Classic" may have been an oversell; historic was a better adjective. Exactly forty calendar years had passed since Boise Junior College first laced up and played a football game. Through all of the winning—156 wins in twenty seasons under Lyle Smith, and now an 80–14 record under Knap—the Broncos could irrefutably lay claim to conference champions at the Division II level.

The week two victory over Montana State had proven to be the de facto conference title game; the Bobcats finished 5–1 in conference play, the loss to Boise State their lone slip. Heading home for the final two games of the season, they awaited other dominoes to fall in determining their postseason fate (conferece titles did not automatically guarantee a playoff spot).

With Autele and Hutt suiting up for the final time in front of their adoring fans, and an undefeated and 4th-ranked Cal Poly Mustangs team in town, a celebratory and proving ground day was in order. "This is our biggest game of the year," Knap said as build-up began. "Now that we've won the title, the kids deserve a chance for one really big win."[12] After falling to the Mustangs the year prior, the Broncos could also take out a bit of venom as they ramped up for the playoffs.

They would.

Emphatically.

After falling behind 10–7 in the first quarter, and after a fumbled punt set up a Mustangs score, the Broncos steamrolled. Autele and Jim McMillan would throw for a combined 396 yards and five touchdowns. Don Hutt also scored a touchdown, and the team finished with 506 yards of total offense. They allowed just 216 yards of total offense, handing the Mustangs their first loss, forcing Knap to decry, "Our defense played better than it ever has before." As the teams exited the field, the Broncos, with smiles stretching from ear-to-ear, could overhear their coach—normally stoic and calculating—exuberantly singing their praises: "What a fantastic defensive effort!"[13]

The following week's narrow escape of UC Davis was hardly cause for concern. The Broncos were playoff-bound, set to host the South Dakota Coyotes in the quarterfinals. The Coyotes, co-champions of the North Central Conference (arguably the best in all of Division II), brought a tricky, wishbone-oriented offense that mixed in unusual passing concepts.

They were not a team that was easy to prepare for with an entire offseason to do so, let alone just one week.

"We are planning on playing our best game of the year on Saturday against them," Knap said the Thursday before the game. After a 25-point fourth-quarter rally in their finale against UC Davis, Knap could feel something brewing with his team. "[The comeback] makes me think that there must be greater things in store for us than a defeat at the hands of South Dakota."[14]

If Knap was worried about the Coyotes multi-faceted offensive attack, yet seeing "greater things" for his team, his gut feeling toward the positive would prevail. The Coyotes may have been unusual and difficult to prepare for, but they were, as it turned out, woefully inadequate in the talent department. Outside of running for 67 yards in the first quarter, keeping the Broncos' offense on the sidelines, South Dakota was outclassed in every aspect of the game; their 3–0 lead early in the game was an anomaly when looking back at the end. After Boise State's John

Smith returned the ensuing kickoff 85 yards for a touchdown, giving the Broncos a 7–3 lead, the rout was on.

Jim McMillan, hemming the offense for the Broncos after Autele injured himself the week prior, was lethal through the air. The junior quarterback, making his fourth start of the season, threw for 285 yards while completing 21 of 30 passes. Autele, who was suffering from concussion symptoms, played sparingly, including a two-play drive in the third quarter which covered 56 yards and resulted in a touchdown.

Before the game Knap told reporters he was hoping to hang at least 35 points on the Coyotes; that number, he said, should be enough to counter the offensive output he was expecting. His team obeyed, rolling to a 53–10 win. To the surprise of almost everyone in the stadium, most especially the Coyotes, the Broncos defense destroyed South Dakota mentally with every possession.

"We started great, but then the dam broke open," Joe Salem, South Dakota's head coach, told the Associated Press after the game. "Nothing went well after the start."[15]

The win set up a semifinals matchup against the Louisiana Tech Bulldogs, taking place in Wichita Falls, Texas. It was the longest road trip the Broncos had embarked on since their game against Hiram Scott in Nebraska in 1970.

Louisiana Tech's defense, known as the "Immovable Objects"—due to their freakish size and aversion to giving up points—would have their hands full: making the flight to Texas was the Boise State offense, which by this point in the season could lay claim to the best in the country. The Broncos had accumulated 2,776 yards in the ground and 2,805 through the air—an absuredly even split—and were scoring at a clip of 40 points per game. Bulldogs head coach Maxie Lambright knew full well the challenges that awaited his team. "It will certainly be our toughest assignment our defense has faced all year," he told *The Times* before the game.

Fortunately for Lambright, Knap could say the same thing; looking at the defensive stats for the Bulldogs was almost silly. At the very least, it could cause even the most God-fearing coach to reach for the bottle. Louisiana Tech had surrendered just eight touchdowns and 59 total points *during the entire season.* Although Boise State averaged 466 yards per game and would be going with Jim McMillan at quarterback after his late-season surge, Lambright felt confidence in his team's ability to break the Broncos.

"This is the best defensive unit I have ever had, and I'm not going to be the one to tell them they can't do it," he said.[16]

The Bulldogs had won 31 of their previous 34 games overall; Boise State, taking a giant leap up from their quarterfinal game, had to play near-perfect in order to advance to the title game.

In assessing the difference between their previous opponent, South Dakota, and Louisiana Tech, Knap was glib.

"It's kind of like jumping from the frying pan to the fire," he told the *Times.*[17]

In their first-ever semifinal playoff game, Boise State would be facing the best defense they had ever seen. Louisiana Tech was the type of challenge they clamored for when they first began sniffing around the Division II ranks. Now that it was here, the reality of the challenge was clear.

Although they expected few fans of their own in the stadium, upon their arrival to Wichita, Kansas, the Wednesday before the game, Boise State was greeted warmly from, as *Idaho Statesman* reporter Jim Moore put it, "a uniformed band and dancing girls, with cowboy-hatted members of the Pioneer Bowl committee."[18]

Dancing girls and cowboy-hatted well-wishers were nice; finding an answer for a defense that gave up 5.9 points per game would be nicer. When the teams kicked off on Saturday, December 8, that's what the Broncos did . . . for the first ten minutes, at least.

Two Jim McMillan touchdown runs in the first quarter put the Broncos up 14–0, sending shockwaves up and down the Bulldogs' sideline. In less than 15 minutes of action, the Broncos had almost tripled the scoring average of previous Louisiana Tech's opponents. Although the Broncos were unable to run the ball consistently, outside of McMillan scrambles, his ability to stretch the field vertically through the air was giving Boise State a chance.

A see-saw affair took hold for the remainder of the game, until—with just a few minutes remaining in the fourth quarter and Boise State clinging to a 34–31 lead—the Bulldogs, and their All-American wide receiver Roger Carr, got one last chance.

Needing 65 yards to clinch the win, the Bulldogs, after wearing down Boise State's vastly improved defense with 165 punishing yards on the ground, would rely on their star to deliver. With 12 seconds remaining in the game, Carr would do just that, hauling in a 21-yard touchdown pass from quarterback Denny Duron, capping off a dramatic, hard-fought win. In a matter of seconds, Boise State's first trip to the playoffs was over, a victory snatched out of thin air.

Game, and season, finished.

On the final scoring play of the game, Boise State—having used a blitz-scheme successfully at various points throughout the game—again brought everyone they could at Duron, hoping the extra pressure would force an errant throw or possibly a turnover.

"As I came out of the huddle I said, 'Help me, Lord,'" Carr said after the game. "I was praying they were in a man defense. And they were."[19]

In the locker room following the game, Knap defended the team's decision to bring extra pressure on the final play, knowing it would leave Carr alone with just one man to cover him. "We had blitzed them a couple of times and caught them with an inability to protect,"[20] he said. The error cost the Broncos a shot at their first national championship.

After playing out of their shoes for the better part of the season, Boise State's defense had cracked at the end, allowing Louisiana Tech to score at will for the last three quarters. The Broncos' inability to run the ball successfully—they netted just 40 total yards on 37 carries—was the nail in their coffin.

Their season had ended abruptly, but a new standard had been set; not just for Knap's tenure, but for the program as a whole. Their dominant run under Lyle Smith, and the national championship that had come with it as a junior college, was a small window into what they could be. Now, with one playoff run under their belt, the Broncos could see that there was something out there . . . something bigger.

* * *

The following season, 1974, saw the Broncos streak out to a 9–1 regular season record, tying their mark from the 1969 season. Unlike that year, when they were stuck in NAIA purgatory, they could fall back on their conference affiliation. Another conference title, and a return trip to the playoffs resulted in a first-round exit at the hands of Central Michigan. But back-to-back postseason berths had the Broncos sitting atop the Big Sky as the program to beat.

The only question, it seemed, was how long could the story last? How long would Tony Knap stick around before he was whisked away to a land of bigger paychecks and grander possibilities?

In an effort to delay that inevitability, Knap was rewarded another year of reappointment by the Idaho Board of Education, bumping his salary to $22,305—a pay raise of just over one thousand dollars from the year prior. After two consecutive Big Sky titles and two revenue-boosting playoff appearances, the program was as hot as it had ever been.

Knap, the maestro of it all, was reaping the rewards.

Adding even more intrigue to the program was the post-Boise State career of Jim McMillan. After taking over down the stretch of his junior season and putting forth a stellar senior campaign, McMillan was drafted in the 14th round of the 1975 NFL Draft by the Detroit Lions, capping off a remarkable turnaround. After serving as Ron Autele's riverboat sidekick for much of his first two years on campus, he had impressed NFL scouts with his ability to maneuver, scramble, and make throws in poor weather conditions. He also won a lot of football games, a desired trademark in any quarterback.

The 1975 season would move along much as the previous seven had under Knap: the team would win nine regular-season games, win the Big Sky, make the playoffs just to bounce out short of their ultimate goal. It was successful, it was directly in line with the goals set forth by the program . . . and, as it turns out, it was the end of yet another era.

The season concluded on November 29, 1975, with a loss to Northern Michigan, 24–21, in the quarterfinals of their playoff game.

On January 29, 1976, after guiding the Broncos to a 71–19–1 record under his watch, Knap was out, heading south to take the head-coaching job at UNLV.

3

FOUR HORSEMEN GALLOP TO TITLE

"Jim Criner was the kind of guy who would walk into
your office, if you were working after practice, and he
would say, 'We're not reinventing football. Go home,
go see your family. Get out of here.' He was the guy
everyone wanted to be around."
—Scott Criner, former Boise State assistant coach

THE VACANCY LEFT from Tony Knap's departure was a
double-edged sword: on the one hand, between what Lyle
Smith and Knap had accomplished, the pieces were in place
to win, win big, and win immediately. On the other hand, his
replacement would *have* to win. If not . . .

On Tuesday, February 10, 1976, news began to trickle out
that the three finalists for the job—on top of Dave Nickel,
who had been Knap's offensive line coach and the preserved
favorite—were Dun Baker, Rich Brooks, and Jim Criner.

Two days later, Criner—who was UCLA's offensive line coach—was hired for the position.

According to then-Boise State president John Barnes, Criner was the unanimous choice among the eight-member search committee. On the day of his introductory press conference, where he was to address the media for the first time as the Broncos' head coach, Criner forced the event to be delayed 30 minutes. There were more important people to speak to first: his players.

"I was very impressed by the personnel we have," Criner said once the press conference began. "It appears you have the best program in the state, and we will work 24 hours per day to make sure it stays that way."[1]

The discourse put out by fans and media alike was that Criner was a bit over his head; internally, he was having none of the talk. Stepping in for Knap was not an easy task, but it was one he was prepared for.

"Pressure is what you make of it," he says now. "If you're not confident, you're going to have a tough time wherever you go.

Boise State was not the lone offer of upward movement for Criner, who was viewed nationally as an up-and-comer with a keen offensive mind. Inquiries for his services poured in from the NFL, as well as various college programs around the country. In the end, the pull of Boise was too much to pass up.

"I talked to Dick Vermeil, because I had a chance to go with him to the Philadelphia Eagles where he had just been hired, but I loved Boise. It was the perfect school for me," he says now.

Criner was born in 1941, in Lurton, Arkansas, a small town in Newton County which boasted just 10,000 residents. Eventually his family would set down roots in California, where Jim would go on to star first at Palo Verde Junior College before finishing his playing career at Cal Poly. Criner's coaching journey began as most: in the high school ranks, before jumping up to lower-level college at Cal-State Hayward. It didn't take long for the next wave to hit: Utah, BYU, and California would all find their way onto Jim's resume before he joined UCLA in 1973.

The following season, Vermeil took over as the head man in Inglewood, leading the Bruins to a Rose Bowl win in 1975 over #1 Ohio State, 23–10.

The following year, Criner would coach his third and final season on the Bruins' sideline. After 13 seasons of being a position or assistant coach, his time had arrived.

When Criner arrived at Boise State—on top of the everyday challenges that awaited—he was also straddled with a recruiting budget that paled in comparison to that of other schools in the conference. The program was operating with an $18,000 budget for the entire recruiting department. That amount had to be spread across various platforms, including travel to visit recruits, video obtainment, food, housing, and entertainment when kids came to campus for their official visits. During his first year, Criner would only see $11,000 of the allotment; the previous regime had already blown through the first seven thousand before jet-setting for UNLV.

Criner was also entering his new job with just four assistant coaches on staff. The "Idaho Rule" at the time, affecting all three of the state's universities, capped the number of coaches allowed. With that, and the minuscule budget, Criner was forced to compromise. His first realization when assessing the roster, and the limited recruiting he would be able to do, was that the offensive philosophy Knap used had to stay. The returning players were built for it, and the staff would need every ounce of their skillset and knowledge of the playbook. The second thing he had to do was hit on every defensive recruit he brought in; as young as the Broncos were, most of the incoming freshmen would have to suit up and play. In that, there was zero room for error.

The third was the need to develop a weight program for the players.

Amazingly, in 1976—even after a nearly 30-year run of dominance—the program did not have a strength and conditioning program.

"The only piece of equipment they had was a small universal machine. It was out in the open, not even under cover where it could stay warm," Criner says now. After taking a walk around campus one afternoon before his first fall camp, the coach spotted two half-completed handball courts sitting idle on campus. It was time to take action.

"We went to the school president and asked if we could have one of the courts. He said yes, and then I got a bunch of boosters who were invested in the program, had them put down a floor, and buy us free weights."

If he was operating without the recruiting budget to help bring Herculean-figures to campus, dammit, Criner would make them himself.

That's what he did—only it didn't happen overnight. The 1976 season, one removed from the Big Sky title and quarterfinal appearance in the playoffs, was a quick fall from grace. His first game as coach, on September 11, 1976, resulted in a loss to Idaho. Wins over Augustana University and Humboldt State, programs even the most knowledgeable fan could not locate on a map, preceded more losses. Victories against Idaho State (36–0) and Weber State (56–31) sent the Broncos into the offseason with momentum, but their overall record of 5–5–1 was the school's worst since a five-win campaign in 1963.

Things would get back on course during Criner's second season, as he claimed his first Big Sky title; the Broncos finished 9–2 overall and a perfect 6–0 in conference play. Their losses, to Nevada and Fresno State, did little to diminish the overall success of the season; Boise State's nine wins came by an average margin of 21 points.

The 1978 season was another move up the ladder, this time as part of a larger movement: the Big Sky Conference was making the jump up from Division II to Division I-AA.

Boise State would win seven games in their I-AA debut—including their second in a row over Idaho—setting the stage for the much-anticipated 1979 season in which, after an opening week loss to Long Beach State, the Broncos went on a roll. They would win their final 10 games of the season, nabbing the best record in the Big Sky at 10–1, and winning the conference title.

Right?

Wrong.

For a moment, flash back to the 1978 season.

Joe Salem, who was the head coach of Northern Arizona, had felt that something was off as his team was preparing to face Boise State leading up to their game on November 11, 1978;

what that feeling was, he could not quite tell. Once he figured it out, Salem pounced.

Criner would be accused of sending a coaching friend to spy on Northern Arizona's practice. The repercussions would be lethal; as punishment—along with a slew of financial restraints—Boise State was forced to miss any postseason action they qualified for during the 1979 season.

In a letter to the Big Sky commissioner Steve Belko, Boise State tight end Webb Spahr said, "Sick is the only word I can come up with for the action taken by the Big Sky Conference. About the so-called 'Crime' . . . football isn't as rosy as everyone must think. The whole game is cheat from the beginning. But I say . . . if the Big Sky wants justice, submit a polygraph to every coach and assistant coach in the conference. The results should make the point."

To this day, Criner is steadfast in his denial of any wrongdoing.

"You have lots of friends in coaching. What happened was one of my friends happened to go by Northern Arizona's practice. The coaches there, in striking up a convo with him, found out that he was a good friend of mine. They immediately assumed he was there to do something for me," he says now.

The media would have a field day with both the accusation and Criner's excuses at the time. Elliott Tannenbaum of the *Philadelphia Inquirer* said, "If Richard Nixon had half of Jim Criner's moxie, he'd be steaming through his third term and heading into his fourth."

Although he would never admit to the actions he was accused of, Criner failed to fully deny the charges, either.

"When this whole thing came down, I stepped up and took full responsibility for anything that was not right," he says now. "I knew no matter what we would never win by fighting the system, which is what we would have had to do. John [Keiser, Boise State's president at the time] basically gave me a slap on the wrist for what had happened. Then we did the best we could under the circumstances."

* * *

The 1980 season was Boise State's most anticipated in two decades. Criner was beginning his fifth season as head coach, and the team and staff he had assembled—on paper, at least—looked to be one of his best. College football was undergoing a massive boom in popularity, and the Broncos—fresh off their 10–1 season—prepared to chase the elusive national title that had been denied to them the year before.

But outside of Boise, and the world of sports in general, all hell was breaking loose.

In the Middle East, tensions were escalating between Iraq and Iran, leading to their eventual war. Terrorist activity was sprouting up all over the United Kingdom. The United States was entering one of its most turbulent eras, too: stemming from the 1979 oil crisis, a recession had hit the country.

Market crashes. The Pennsylvania Lottery scandal. Mount Saint Helens' eruption.

Everything was changing at an accelerated pace.

Things were propelling forward in Boise, too, just in a more nuanced manner. For the group of young men who had spent the summer sweating through workouts in the blistering heat, there was a sense that the program's days of winning boatloads of games, but having nothing to show for it, were coming to an end.

The Broncos entered camp with attainable, realistic championship dreams, unbesmirched by restrictions or talent deficiencies.

Twelve players who earned some form of postseason recognition in 1979 were back; Joe Aliotti returned at quarterback after winning Big Sky Offensive Player of the Year; and the probation from the 1978 scouting violations were in the past.

The formula for a title run was simple: let the players' skills do the talking.

"We don't plan on a whole lot of changes,"[2] Criner said as his team prepared to enter fall camp under the relentless Idaho sun. "We are working to maintain the balance between run and pass. We think it makes it that much harder for teams to defend us."

It wasn't hard to see why. On top of Aliotti, Boise State had all-everything running back Cedric Minter—a visionary blaze who was already the Big Sky's all-time leading rusher—giving them one of the nation's top backfields. If Aliotti was the face of the team, Minter, all 5-foot-10 and 180 pounds, was the heart and soul.

He had reinvented the ground game in his first three seasons. In 1978, as a sophomore, Minter broke the single-season Big Sky rushing record, finishing with 1,526 yards. He held the single-game record, too, amassing 210 yards against Cal Poly his freshman year in 1977.

Now a senior, he and his teammates knew what was taken from them the year prior, and what lay ahead.

"Terry Zauner [another running back for the Broncos] said one day, 'Cedric, I'm going to go in there and tell Criner that you should start every game, and I'll come in when you get tired. We can be a lot more successful, and win every game that way,'" Minter says now.

Zauner's words proved to be prophetic, but it would take a village for the team to reach their ultimate goal.

Bob Rosenthal christened Aliotti and Minter as part of the new-age "Four Horseman," along with Zauner and David Hughes. Rosenthal, who was Boise State's sports information director and de facto publicist, dreamt up visions of Aliotti, Minter, Zauner, and Hughes wreaking havoc over the Big Sky— much in the way the original Four Horsemen of Notre Dame once had. The moniker stuck.

With those men set to control the majority of the Broncos' future, Criner's cry for balance was going to be facing an uphill battle. The year before, Minter had rushed for 1,012 yards; Zauner, splitting time with him, gained 538 more Hughes, a fullback, gained 575. Even Aliotti, despite having thrown for 1,870 yards, managed to also gain 440 on the ground.

It wasn't set up for balance; it was set up for dominance.

By 1980, the program had rattled off 24 consecutive winning or even seasons, won just over 75 percent of their games, and amassed four conference titles since 1970.

"I don't know how to compare teams year to year," Criner said as the first week of the season approached. "It should be our best team in four of five years. If they play the way they are capable of playing, it should be our best."

After the 1979 season—in need of a new secondary coach—Criner reached out to an up-and-comer from US International College in San Diego, California, by the name of John Fox. When he decided to leave the recently defunct USIC for the greener pastures of Boise. Fox brought a masterful defensive eye. He would later use this gift to take both the Carolina Panthers and Denver Broncos to the Super Bowl as head coach. In hindsight, Fox was the last piece of the puzzle.

Despite the hype of the Four Horsemen and the potential the offense possessed, it was the defense—fresh off four consecutive years of dominance—that had the staff salivating. Long before Boise State became known nationally for their innovative offense, they were impenetrable on the opposite side of the ball.

That was Criner's MO; when he took over for Knap in 1976, he had one goal in mind: stop hemorrhaging points.

For all of the winning that Knap had done, most of it came despite the defense's shortcomings. After allowing just 98 total points during the 1969 season—their last before moving up to a full-time four-year school—his teams found themselves locked in weekly shootouts. After making the jump to Division II in 1970, the Broncos could no longer outman their opposition; now, they were facing teams just as big, fast, and, more often than not, strong. Their once ferocious defense was no longer revolutionary.

They gave up only 11.8 points per game in 1970, as opposed to 20.5 in 1971. Finally, the bottom fell out during the 1975 season, when they allowed 22 points per game. Knap's offenses were still potent; his defenses were not.

On September 6, 1980, the fruits of the news staff's labor would begin to show.

After months to stew over the reality of being kept out of the playoffs due to probation the prior season, the Broncos unloaded all of their rage on a stunned—and seemingly overmatched—Utah Utes squad, who was favored to win the Western Athletic Conference.

Criner's crew was relentless from the opening kick. They went 80 yards for a touchdown, then 96 yards for another score. Aliotti threw for 138 yards, Cedric Minter ran for 75 and two scores; Terry Zauner ran for 113 yards and another touchdown. The balance Criner wanted came in the form of the running backs each taking turns dominating the Utes.

When it was over, the crowd at Rice-Eccles Stadium staggered out, their team falling to Boise State 28–7.

"This is a great way to build momentum," Criner said afterward.[3]

Unfortunately, that moment would last exactly one week.

Flying high from their wire-to-wire stomping of Utah, Boise State returned home, ranked, ready to face the Southeastern Louisiana Lions.

The Lions came to Boise as first-year members of Division I-AA, having come up from Division II. They were coming off a pedestrian 6–5 season.

On September 13, 1980, 21,342 fans filled a rain-soaked Bronco Stadium, eager to welcome in the 1980 season, with visions of yet another undefeated year in front of them. The first home game of any season carries a special feeling with it; nine long months of reminiscing, daydreaming, pondering what could be—all of it becomes reality. That Boise State was taking on an inferior opponent was an afterthought; the home fans had a team capable of winning a national title. *Faceless opponent*, they thought. After winning 11 straight going back to the previous season, it appeared the only team that could slow down the Broncos was themselves.

All of that changed in one day.

Not only did the Lions waltz undeterred into Boise and win, they took the Broncos out from the opening kick, sucking the oxygen out of the stadium. When it was all said and done, Southeast Louisiana walked away 17–13 victors, solidifying their place in I-AA, and, perhaps for one game, making the Broncos rethink their ceiling.

Afterward, Criner—never a man to mince words—went off.

"Southeastern Louisiana showed up to play," he said. "We just showed up. I'm very, very unhappy about our emotional approach to this game all week . . . the way you eliminate the peaks and valleys, and get yourself ready to play every week is to not worry about your opponents, but to worry about yourselves.

"We did not do that."[4]

"That's sports," Aliotti would later say. "It wasn't like anyone said 'they had just beaten a major college team on the road and now we get an unranked team at home,' but no doubt it was in the back of guys' minds."[5]

Luckily for Criner—and for his players, who had witnessed the business end of his emotions—the Broncos would hit their stride. After splitting their next two games against Northern Arizona and Montana State, they would win five in a row, including a 44–21 beatdown over archrival Idaho, who was ranked ninth in the country at the time. Not only were the Broncos winning, but the defense was beginning to form a ferocious reputation among opponents.

They surrendered just 45 points during the win streak, shutting out Weber State and holding Nevada to just three points. After the slow start to the season, when they found themselves 1–2 after blowing a late lead at Montana State, Boise State entered the final week of the season at 7–3, with a fresh set of eyes locked on the only goal they had all season: the playoffs.

Going up against the Idaho State Bengals, who was also hoping to secure a playoff bid, the stakes were clear: although the Big Sky crown was already wrapped up, the playoffs were not yet a lock. A loss, and their hopes of postseason redemption would take a hit. Win, and the rankings would do the talking.

Boise State and Idaho State did battle on a rainy and cold November day in a back-and-forth tilt. Before the game, Bengals first-year head coach Dave Kragthorpe said that for his team to have a chance, they had to get to the fourth quarter within striking distance. Idaho State had outscored their opposition 84–17 in the final period during the season; if they were close, he thought, they had a chance. He attributed it to "good conditioning, and the fact that sometimes our offense takes a little longer to get going."

However, good conditioning can only do so much when you're facing a team as streamlined as Boise State was.

Behind three touchdowns from Aliotti—two through the air to Kipp Bedard and Duane Dluohy, and one on the ground— the Broncos pulled away from the Bengals late, winning 22–13.

Even after their win over Idaho State, the Broncos found themselves near-deadlocked with Portland State to make the playoffs. PSU finished off their season with a 75–0 victory over Weber State, sending a message directly to the playoff committee, if not to Boise State as well. The selection committee was not scheduled to release their decision for another nine days, leaving ample time for teams to get healthy—and forcing the Broncos to sit idly by, their postseason fate twisting in the winter wind.

Finally, on Sunday, December 1, the news that was denied them in 1979—and that looked perilously out of reach early in the season—was official: Boise State was back in the playoffs.

First up was the Grambling State Tigers, with their legendary coach Eddie Robinson. Not only did Boise State receive a second life by making the playoffs, they were awarded a home game as well.

Robinson's squad, which had to travel 1,948 miles from Grambling, Louisiana, was out of their element from the start. The temperature in Grambling, in December, can range from the mid-40s to mid-60s. Comfortable.

When the Tigers arrived in Idaho, the gametime temperature was 18 degrees.

Game, set, match.

Despite entering the contest as favorites, with their #2 ranking and future hall of fame coach, Robinson's Tigers were strangled offensively from the opening kickoff. The teams entered halftime tied 7–7, battling both each other and the weather, as a thick fog rolled over the sides of Bronco Stadium. Outside of a 62-yard Flea Flicker touchdown to Bedard and a 31-yard touchdown pass from Aliotti to Minter, Boise State's offense had been pushed around, consistently, by the bigger, more physical Tigers' defense.

However, as had been the case all season, the Broncos' defense was just too much to handle.

Twice in the final seven minutes of the game, Boise State's defense came up with game-changing plays, stuffing Grambling State inside the 10-yard line, preserving their 14–9 victory. It wasn't pretty, as defense never is, but it was effective.

"You win championships on defense, and those two drives proved that," Criner said after. "We played good zone football, and that won the game."[6]

Robinson, who was in his 39th season at Grambling State, was more whimsical in his reflection.

"The game was like the West used to be: Last to draw, first to die," he said afterwards. "We drew last."[7]

If the semifinals were an indicator, Boise State was going to ride their defense, make enough timely plays on offense, and use that formula for as long as it worked. The test heading into the Camellia Bowl—the official name of the I-AA national title game—was going to be an entirely different beast. After disposing of Lehigh in their own semifinal, defending champions Eastern Kentucky Colonels found themselves in a position to repeat.

As was to be expected, the nation did not seem to care.

Division I-AA games drew far less interest nationally than bigger levels of college football. At the time, it was no surprise to see previews, game scores, and recaps get pushed to the back sections of newspapers. College football as a whole had yet to catch fire, despite its up-tick in popularity in recent years. The NFL still dominated the ratings, with teams like the Pittsburgh Steelers and Dallas Cowboys being the apple of children's eyes. Still, the Camellia Bowl was more than an inter-conference mid-October squabble; this was the culmination, for all the glory. It was a title game and, regardless of sport or level, those bouts usually carried more intrigue.

That did not stop the *Democrat and Chronicle* from running an article leading up to the game, noting that local channel 13 in Rochester, New York, would not be carrying the game due to a "lack of interest," according to a station spokesperson.

However, two fan bases *did* have a rooting interest, and neither Boise, nor Richmond, Kentucky, home of the Colonels, would feel slighted.

Boise State entered the December 20 showdown seeking not only redemption from the prior season's shortcomings, but also to climb back up to the mountain top, a place they had not reached since their days as a junior college.

Eastern Kentucky, on the other hand, was fresh off the school's first-ever championship. Like the Broncos, they possessed a lethal ground attack and a stingy defense; and, perhaps just as important, they had tasted the spoils of victory and seemed hellbent on another title.

"We were all thrilled about winning it last year," Gus Parks, an All-State high school player in Kentucky before joining the Colonels, told the *Advocate-Messenger*. "But it would feel just as good, or maybe even better, to do it again."[8]

Parks had good reason for optimism. The Colonels had systematically taken apart Lehigh in their semifinal rematch, winning 23–20, and were led once again by the immortal head coach Roy Kidd, who would finish his career at Eastern with a record of 314–124–8.

They had the experience, they had the confidence, they had the title.

Still, Parks knew it was this team, not the one from the year prior, that mattered.

"We are a better team this year," he said.[9]

Boise State, on the other hand, had more than just on-field concerns. Despite the glory and prestige that comes with making it to—and, potentially, winning—a national championship, it did not bring with it the financial boon that most would expect.

Even with the expected gate receipts and television revenue—*no thanks to Rochester, however*—the Broncos were just hoping to break even from the trip. Between the cost to transport players, coaches, and staff, and the splitting of revenue among their Big Sky brethren, they were hoping to bank a win to compensate for the bill they would pay.

But that problem was for Lyle Smith and the accountants to worry about.

In front of just 8,157 fans in Sacramento, the two teams battled to a near-stalemate for most of the game. When the Broncos took possession of the football on their own 20-yard line, 80 yards from victory, with 55 seconds left in the game and trailing 29–24, Jim Criner sensed all of the work he and his team had put in was about to pay off.

"You saw the players. The team, in unison, said, 'There's plenty of time left,'" Criner said after the game. Whether they had or not is stuff of legend, but the truth played out. When Joe Aliotti hit Duane Dlouhy in the back left corner of the end zone for the go-ahead touchdown with 12 seconds remaining, it was official: Boise State had won the Division I-AA national championship, 31–29.

"That 1980 team had this great, driving motivation that, 'OK, you screwed us a year ago. Now you have to play us for real,'" says Criner now. "We had Cedric Minter and Joe Aliotti, which meant everything. They not only brought a wealth of talent, but they were real leaders in their own right. They were the kind of guys that had the ability to rise to the occasion, no matter what."

The three running backs that had arrived four years earlier—Cedric Minter, David Hughes [who turned down USC to come to Boise State], and Terry Zauner—adhered themselves into the community almost immediately. Early in their freshman year, seeing the talent he had in this trio, Criner sat all three players down and said, "Look, I don't think one of you is more valuable to the team than the other. And I always want a guy on the field who can give me his best effort. 100 percent on every snap of the game."

For the next three and a half seasons, that's exactly what he got. And as they jogged off the field for the final time as seniors, the message and execution had all come together.

The finish to the season—winning 9 of their final 11—was a testament to the leadership that cloaked the roster. Players such as Minter, Aliotti, and Dlouhy kept things tight, despite the rocky start to the season, allowing all of the pieces to fall into place.

"A lot of teams that don't have the character of this team would have folded this year," Criner said at the time. "Our team has a lot of character."[10]

Jeff Pittman, who would go on to play center for the Broncos and eventually become one of the most tenured staff members as the team's strength and conditioning coach, speaks glowingly of the impact that title had on him and a legion of young boys around the state.

"I watched the 1980 I-AA semifinal game against Grambling here as a kid with my granddad, and I was hooked. That was the hook for me, probably the most incredible game I've ever seen here. When Grambling walked out, I was like, 'There's no way these guys are beating Grambling, just on the size.' But that spirit—those guys fought tooth and nail, and they were always one step ahead.

"From the players to the coaches to the administrators to the boosters and those type of people, there was a sense that Boise was going to explode, population-wise, and that this program was gonna launch. Just keep grinding, keep pulling the rope, whatever you want to say, and each class of players that came in, the previous classes before them instilled that in them."[11]

The championship also begged the question of "what could have been."

Because . . .

"We all felt like the 1979 team we had was actually better than the 1980 team," says Minter now, laughing.

In reality, the 1980 season should have been Criner's last. Although the team would make the playoffs the following season in 1981, losing in a semifinal rematch to Eastern Kentucky, nothing would come close to the run of 1980. They would miss the playoffs altogether in 1982.

After that season, Criner was gone, off to Iowa State of the Big Eight.

In his seven seasons as Broncos head coach, Criner coached 44 All-Americans, and finished with an overall record of 59–21–1. Between advanced recruiting and his ability to develop and grow talent, he had—even before the national championship—secured his legacy within the program.

Now he was gone.

4

TURNING BLUE

"I think Jim Criner's title in 1980 was the turning point. I don't care if it's Division I-AA, you win one title and it's still more than a lot of schools have."

—Derrick Fox, Boise State, 1983–1986

LYLE SETENCICH IS a delightful man. He's a gentle man. A kind man. Players who were under his watch, to this day, speak glowingly of him. When he answers his phone from the comforts of his home on a cold December day in 2016, the man who replaced Jim Criner in 1983 as the Boise State Broncos' head coach comes across as reflective, positive, and as someone who truly enjoyed his time at the helm. The circumstances that led to his hiring still baffle him to this day—"I never really understood why [Jim] Criner left," he says—but he was grateful for the opportunity.

Setencich was all of the above and assuredly more. He was what you would desire as a parent when you're sending your child off to college. In that, he was the correct mentor.

Unfortunately, from a strictly on-field point of view, he was not the correct *coach*.

Stencich was taking over a program that won despite the shortcomings they faced. As the arms race of college football began, the days of winning with outdated facilitates and equipment were starting to go by the wayside.

"When I took over, we had one great, big meeting room, where we could get all of the players in. We had no individual meeting rooms; guys had to meet outside or in the hallway," Setencich says now, an audible cringe coming through.

Two years before to Setencich's hiring, Lyle Smith had retired from his role as athletic director. Gene Bleymaier, a young buck who had cut his teeth in the ranks at UCLA, had replaced him.

During the fall of 1980, after a reshuffling in the athletic department at UCLA that saw Robert A. Fischer take control as the athletic director, Bleymaier had found himself moving up the ladder, taking over as assistant AD. It was the biggest moment of his career to date, at his alma mater, and all signs pointed to him eventually taking the step up to the head spot should he have the patience.

Then, as quick as it was surprising, Boise State came calling.

One year later, Criner was out, forcing Bleymaier into biggest hire to date. Setencich, a graduate of Fresno State who had spent the previous four seasons in Boise as the Broncos' defensive coordinator, seemed both the safest and smartest pick. Boise State's defense under Setencich had given up just 15 points per game on average the previous four seasons. He knew the players. He knew the staff. He knew the expectations.

For myriad reasons, none of those positives worked in his favor.

Over the course of four seasons, from 1983–1986, Setencich's teams were never bad; they were, rather, the epitome of mediocre. Back-to-back 6–5 seasons to begin his tenure gave way to a 7–4 season in 1985. At 19–14 under Setencich, just five seasons removed from their lone national championship, the Boise State program was at a crossroads. The excitement and energy was . . . *missing*.

Bleymaier, sensing he needed to make a drastic move, conjured up an idea to jump-start the electricity around the football team. An outlandish, unhinged idea. An idea that would, ultimately, set the school apart from all of its contemporaries.

A move that would save them.

The 1986 season, and every year going forward, would be played on blue turf.

"I was on an airplane and just thinking about the fact that we were going to spend $750,000 and pull up an old green carpet and put down a new green carpet, and nobody was going to notice or care that we had upgraded and spent the money to put in a new field," Bleymaier told the *Coloradoan* in 2016.

"At the time of the blue turf's installation, it was something that . . . you know, as football coaches, we perceive what the color of the field should be," Setencich says now. "That was quite a transition. It was Gene's idea, and I guess it turned out pretty well."

"They kept the blue turf really secret," says Kenneth Phillips, a two-year letterman for the Broncos from 1984–1985. "I left in May of 1985, and I didn't find out until that summer. That gave the school the notoriety it deserved. That's when a lot of people started asking questions about the school."

In its infancy, both Boise State and opponents alike found the color to be more distressing than anything. The Broncos would go 5–6 in its first year, although they finished a respectable 4–2 at home. For Setencich, it was not enough; after the season, he was out. His 24–20 record, at almost any other school, coming off of any other time period, would have been adequate. After the school's previous thirty-five years, and a national championship still in the rearview mirror, timing was not on his side.

"Boise was a really nice, isolated community, nice town. People were good. It was a place that coaches wanted to go to," he says now. He would land on his feet, taking over the head job at Cal Poly the following year, where he would stay for six seasons.

In his place came an assistant coach from the University of Washington, one who was seeking to break free from his mentor, the legendary Don James, and make a name for himself.

When Bleymaier called, Skip Hall answered.

* * *

Merle "Skip" Hall was born in the small, mostly frozen town of Alexandria, Minnesota, one of roughly 5,000 residents. Alexandria is a stereotypical Coen Brothers–style locale, where citizens are destined to become yet another number, one who comes, then goes, their ghost and tombstone the lone reminder of their once banal existence.

Skip was not destined for the same fate.

He was a three-sport standout in football, basketball, and baseball. He worshipped his coaches, namely his football and baseball coach, Charlie Bash, and he went on to play quarterback at Concordia College in Minnesota, leading them to an NAIA championship in 1964. All told, Hall was a local star; an all-American boy doing all-American things.

After his playing days, Hall wanted to coach, and football was his route of choice. After taking over a small high school and guiding them to a 23–1 record over three seasons, he made the move to college football. When he moved to Boulder, Colorado, to earn his masters degree, he joined their football staff as a young, albeit slightly more experienced graduate assistant. It was in Boulder where he would meet a man who would shape his life forever: future University of Washington coach, and college football legend, Don James, who was the team's defensive coordinator.

The two grew close, James's gifted genius eaten up by the eager Hall. They were inseparable, bonding over blitz packages, safety concepts, and their future. They found success, too: in 1969, the Buffaloes went 8–4, beating Alabama 47–33 in the Liberty Bowl. James was a rising star and Hall was his protégé.

The next step for James was to lead his own team; Hall's was to follow along. And, despite the overwhelming controversy and gut-wrenching conditions that they would enter into, that's just what they did.

They both went to Kent State.

On May 4, 1970, after weeks of unrest, protest, escalation, and every indelibly flammable ingredient, four students were shot and killed on the campus of Kent State in Ohio. It was inescapable; the innocent lives taken had captured the nation, ushering in a new era of radical freedoms, of the non-submissive youth. Football, at its core, is escapism from the harsh truths of the real world. At Kent, post-slayings, it was not a blip on the radar.

Nevertheless, on December 12, 1970, just over seven months after the shootings, James was headed to Kent, with Skip in tow. James was a local, born in Massillon, Ohio; Hall was an outsider, thrust into an almost impossible situation.

"We had to go out and recruit after that, which was an enormous challenge, but we did a great job, and ended up with a heck of a class," Hall says now.

After going 3–8 during their first season, James and his staff found a rhythm, going 6–5–1 in 1972. That season is notable—if for no other reason—because Hall, in need of some help, nabbed recently graduated Nick Saban and named him as his personal graduate assistant, ostensibly igniting the coaching career of perhaps the greatest college coach to ever patrol the sidelines.

In 1973, Kent State upped its record to 9–2, opening the door for James's and Hall's move to Seattle, and the Washington Huskies.

Fast forward twelve seasons, multiple Rose Bowl berths, a lifetime's worth of knowledge later, and Skip Hall was ready to jump rank and set out on his own.

"Pro scouts were always in Washington, and they used to tell me, 'If the Boise State job ever opens, you ought to take a look. They've got some real potential over there,'" he says now.

After the 1986 season, that's exactly what happened. Lyle Setencich's tenure at Boise State was over. In need of new flavor, Gene Bleymaier looked 503 miles west to Seattle.

"My wife and I flew over to Boise and interviewed, and they offered us the job while we were there," Hall says now. "They tried to get us to *accept* it while we were there, but we wanted to go home and talk to our kids first.

"Then, we decided to accept."

Leaving the dominant program of the Pac-10 for a school struggling to keep its head above water in the Big Sky would be a culture shock, one which Hall was prepared for.

"It was hard to leave Don James. But I was encouraged by our AD, who thought I should go out and get some head coaching experience, too."

However, the environment in which he entered at Boise State was not what he envisioned.

"Sometimes the grass is greener in the other yard, but it has to be mowed, too," he chuckles.

Alas, one month into his tenure, sure enough, a potential bombshell came across Hall's desk.

"I received our players' grades. Over 30 percent of the them were academically ineligible, and there were lots of player issues," he says now.

Facing an exhaustive rebuild, He regrouped and set forth laying the groundwork of a program that was not going to cut any corners.

"I called the staff together and I said, 'We have to change the culture. We need to have character development, academic integrity.' That was forefront in our recruiting, too," he says now. "Six years later when I left, over 90 percent of our players graduated."

* * *

Hall's first season, in 1987, ended much as Setencich's final one had Boise State went 6–5 as players adjusted to the more detail-oriented schemes they were now running. An 8–4 campaign in 1988 and a first round playoff exit followed. That season also saw the Broncos lose their seventh-straight game to Idaho, the longest streak in the rivalry. However, the playoff berth had been a welcome change, the school's first in six seasons.

It was also a mirage. The following year, 1989, saw a return to the median. Through three seasons, Hall, at 20–14, was heading toward the same fate that had undone his predecessor.

Something, *anything*, needed to turn for Hall, lest his fate end up the same. Therefore, the 1990 season—and the tone it would set—rang through loud and clear as Boise State began its sixth decade of football.

Unfortunately, Boise State was embarking on a journey alongside a handful of perceived favorites in the Big Sky that did not include them; among those was Montana, picked by the coaches in the yearly poll to lead the charge for the conference. Of the nine coaches who submitted their votes, four picked the Grizzlies while two more picked the Nevada Wolfpack.

"Based on what happened last year [Montana beating Boise 48–10 in 1989], I would have to say Montana," Hall said when the coaches picks were revealed. "Then a couple of us return a lot of players and would have to be considered contenders going into the season."[1]

Coaching alongside and being deep-rooted friends with Don James afforded Hall a lot of leeway. His gentle nature buoyed his football acumen, lending himself to be a solid on-and-off-the-field combination for the Broncos, much as Lyle Setencich's had been predicted. After so many years, *decades*, of winning 8, 9, 10-plus games, Boise State—for the better part of the eighties after the title run in 1980—was, plainly, *average*. The blue turf was still viewed by many as a sideshow meant to distract opponents and media more than attract positive attention. Because of their erratic play, the turf was receiving much more attention than the players on the field.

To be brazen enough to play on a blue field, to have the gall to fly in the face of the norm, the Broncos had to bring something different and unique in their play. They had to win games to validate their quirks.

Hall's tenure was not doing it; if success remained a mistress, his time would be short.

And win they did . . . for a brief period, at least. The 1990 season would prove to be the high point of the Hall era. After winning their first two games against Stephen F. Austin and Weber State, then losing two of their next three, the Broncos rattled off five consecutive wins in the middle of the season, including three in a row on the road—against Northern Arizona, Idaho State, and Montana State—before falling at home to Idaho for the ninth consecutive season, the longest streak by either team since they began playing in 1971. There was a theme connecting the Boise State coaches: their inability to defeat the Vandals.

Hall was 0–4 against the team from Moscow; he was saved by the fact that his team had made the playoffs, barely, but he was skating by.

If Hall was looking for positive vibes to keep his critics at bay, he was in luck: once again Boise would be hosting the first round, welcoming in the Northern Iowa Panthers, who were making their second trip to the state after losing to Idaho State earlier in the season. Boise State and Northern Iowa finished ranked 10th and 11th in the country in I-AA, respectively, and the Broncos' bid of $150,000—their estimated income from the game, based on ticket sales, food and drink income, and merchandise—was just enough to secure them a home game.

"We're disappointed, because we thought we had put together a competitive bid," then-Northern Iowa athletic director Bob Bowlsby said.[2]

According to pre-set rules from the NCAA, conference members could not meet in the first round of the playoffs. Therefore, the opponent Northern Iowa was supposed to play, Southwest Missouri State—members of the same conference— was out.

Boise State, on the blue turf in the cold, windy conditions, was now their opponent. The Panthers were headed out on the road.

The Broncos jumped out early, taking a 6–3 lead into halftime. When the teams exited the locker room for the second half, a shift had occurred in the minds of Broncos players. Not only had they knocked the Panthers' leading rusher and receiver, Mike Schultz, out of the game in the second quarter, but they were making a mockery of quarterback Jay Johnson. After the half, the mental and physical beating had taken hold, and the Panthers were done. Johnson started the second half 0-for-7 with three interceptions.

"They did an outstanding job defensively," said Terry Allen, head coach of the Panthers. "Physically, up front, they beat us at the line of scrimmage. It was an example of two outstanding defensive teams. They avoided the turnovers. We didn't. I think the defensive pressure got to him [quarterback Jay Johnson]."[3]

It was an understatement; Johnson would finish the game 13-for-45 with six interceptions. In the course of a week, after giving up nearly 20 points per game during the second half of the season, the Broncos looked like the 1985 Chicago Bears, flying around the field, disrupting and destroying anything the Panthers attempted. On top of forcing numerous interceptions, they also had sacked Schultz five times, each one a bloody welcome to the icy-blue turf.

"The way I can describe our defense is 'awesome,'" Hall said after the game, his first playoff win as a coach. "They had to go out there time after time and put the fire out. They played like champions.

"It was a championship effort, no doubt about it."[4]

Quarterback Mike Virden, who went to high school at West Des Moines Dowling in Iowa, managed the Broncos efficiently enough to get the team a win: 22-for-41, 196 yards, one touchdown, two interceptions. He hardly blew the opposition away, but with the defense he had behind him, that was far from a necessity. The blueprint for Boise State by this point was simple: score more than 10 points, let the defense suffocate the opposition, which they did, winning 20–3. Survive and advance.

The following week, in the quarterfinals, they would face top-ranked Middle Tennessee State. Once again, an aggressive financial bid had awarded the Broncos home-field advantage; once again, feathers were ruffled. "I am disturbed by this, and I think it dilutes the integrity of the championship," said Dan Beebe, who was commissioner of the Ohio Valley Conference where Middle Tennessee State played.

Beebe may have been right, but he had no leg to stand on. The Broncos estimated they would bring in $100,000 from ticket sales. Middle Tennessee State, a smaller fish in a larger pond (where they competed locally against schools like Tennessee and Vanderbilt), put in a bid of $20,000. The rules may have been odd, and out of touch with reality, but they were still the rules.

It didn't matter how much Beebe griped. For the second straight week, the playoffs were coming back to Boise. Perhaps, through attrition of simply outbidding the opposition, the blue turf *was* starting to pay off, its mythical identity rounding into form.

The Blue Raiders brought the higher ranking, the better offense, the more dominant defense, and, after traveling halfway across the country, a 747-sized chip on their shoulder. They were coached by James "Boots" Donnelly, a future member of the college football hall of fame. Boots, understandably, was less than thrilled at the thought of taking his team to Boise; after all, they were ranked number one in the country.

"That's a long way from home for my country boys," James told the *Missoulian* before the game.[5]

"I don't know what all goes into picking these games," Hall said. He did, though. *Everyone did.* "Whatever they were, I'm delighted."[6]

The Blue Raiders' record was impressive, and their dominant play throughout the season had everyone on notice. But the win over Northern Iowa had given the Broncos something they had been lacking: confidence to succeed in the postseason.

"I don't think we're intimidated," said Terry Heffner, a wide receiver for the Broncos, to the *Tennessean.* "I think we can play with anyone. I think [we have] a healthy respect for them.[7]

"Being the No. 1 team, we have to respect the fact that they're 11–1 and they had to play some good football to get where they are," Heffner continued. "We'll have to play our best game to beat them."[8]

He gave a half smile, half smirk, then walked away. His teammates followed suit: into the locker room, through the weight room, straight into their own heads.

The next challenge, the greatest one yet, was right in front of them.

When 15,894 exuberant fans packed into Bronco Stadium on December 1 for the quarterfinal showdown, a sense of satisfaction had already set in. Although fans were eager to watch Boise State attempt to pull off the upset, just having them back in the playoffs—and making some noise after they got there—had energized the town. Whether or not they sent Middle Tennessee State back victors or not was almost an afterthought.

Both teams entered the game riding momentum of defensive shutdowns; Boise State allowed only three points to Northern Iowa a week earlier, and MTSU gave up just 108 points *all season*. Through three quarters, both teams stayed true to the narrative. Neither found running room or an open receiver. When the Blue Raiders crept ahead 13–10, Boise State looked as if they had run out of answers. Their offense was a distant rumor. Then, knotted up at 13 early in the fourth, they found one last sprig of magic.

With the ball on their own 18-yard line and facing a 4th down situation, Hall went with the biggest gamble of his career. Given the proper coverage, he told his punter Mike Black to fake the punt and throw. Black saw what he needed, faked the punt, found Elijah George 18 yards downfield, and hit him with the completion. First down. They got into the endzone twelve plays later and took a 20–13 lead. Ballgame.

"We've had that [fake punt] play all week," an elated Hall said after the game, his eyes set deep, red from emotion. "I asked the coaches upstairs and we watched to see who came out on their coverage team. We left it up to Mike to punt or pass, and he's a gutsy little competitor."[9]

Broncos quarterback Mike Virden was the last one in the stadium to know what was going on. After the offense had faltered, he had made his way to the sideline. With his back to the action, before he could take a seat, the stadium erupted.

"I was surprised we went for it," he said afterwards. "I ran to the sidelines and thought we were punting. Then I turn around and saw Elijah jumping up and catching the ball."[10]

When tailback Sean Sanders dove into the end zone for the game's decisive touchdown, the Broncos had secured their first semifinal playoff appearance since their loss to Eastern Kentucky in 1981. By doing so, they set up a game with Nevada, their

Big Sky rival, for the chance to advance to the title game. The Wolfpack had survived a wild, seesaw game against Furman, which they won 42–35. It was the second match of the season between the schools; Boise had taken care of business back on November 10, defeating Nevada 30–14 in front of the second-largest crowd of the season at Bronco Stadium.

This time, the teams would duel in the desert.

On December 8, 1990, twelve days shy of the ten-year anniversary of the school's last national championship, the Broncos and Wolfpack engaged in an instant, a cat-and-mouse affair from the outset. Nevada would jump out to a three-point lead, then six, then thirteen.

Boise State would race back, cutting the lead to six.

Back to thirteen.

Down to three.

Tied.

Boise State would take the lead. Then fall behind.

The game would go on like this until the end, before the Broncos tied it at 38 apiece. Nevada's touchdown response put them up 45–38; Boise State then tied it up *again*.

Overtime.

After both teams came away empty handed in the first overtime—each missed their respective field goal attempts—Nevada and Boise State would score touchdowns in the second overtime, sending the game into an improbable third extra period, knotted up at 52. Finally, it was over. Nevada, on a Ray Whalen 8-yard touchdown run, ended the Broncos' season. Final score: 59–52.

After the game, Wolfpack coach Chris Ault tried to find the words to describe what he had witnessed. "This is a highlight," he murmured.

It was the type of game that defied all predictions. To wit:

- Nevada and Boise State entered as the Big Sky's top two defenses; they gave up a combined 111 points, with touchdowns on eight of the final ten possessions.
- Nevada owned the 7th-best pass defense in the country. Broncos' quarterback Mike Virden and Duane Halliday combined for 496 yards.
- Boise State had the 6th-best run defense in the country. Ray Whalen broke the Division I-AA playoff rushing record with 245 yards.

After the game, a depleted Hall, half-delusional, also stammered when describing what his team had gone through. "I wouldn't have believed any of this could happen," he said. "This was a great college game. I don't have many emotions left. I can't imagine what it must be like for them."[11]

The season was over. As it turns out, the playoff run was the watershed moment in Hall's tenure.

The Broncos would go 12–10 overall the next two seasons, including an embarrassing and eye-opening home loss to the Portland State Vikings, 51–26, in 1992. The Vikings were led by up-and-coming coaching duo of offensive coordinator Al, and their eccentric head coach, Pokey Allen.

After the loss to PSU, Hall says, he knew his time as the Broncos' coach was over. Off the field, Hall was beloved by his players; that his teams failed to deliver at a consistent rate never tainted their belief in him.

Unfortunately, off-field reputations can only carry so much weight. On the field, Boise State was underperforming; despite the sprinklings of success, and an energetic staff that included future NFL head coach Jim Zorn, the Broncos were stuck in mid-level purgatory.

"The thing I'm most proud of was to change the culture and lay down some stepping stones for the guys that followed," Hall says now. "Being a football coach, you need to know when it's time to go into a place . . . but you also need to know when it's time to leave."

When Pokey Allen's squad waltzed into Boise and made a mockery of the Broncos, the bottom had completely fallen out. Hall was finished

He knew it before almost anyone else.

"Going into that 1992 season, we had lost a lot of seniors, a lot of players. We ended up losing a bunch of games by four points or less, and I just felt, at that time . . . you know, you have half the people for you, half the people against you, and I just felt like it was time to make a change, for everyone, myself included.

"So, I resigned."

5

A MAN NAMED POKEY

"We used to go down into 'The Dungeons' to watch film,
would get berated for missing a block. We'd sit in these cold,
wet, dingy areas below the stadium where we wheeled down
TVs. Times have changed, for sure."
                              —Greg Klum, Boise State, 1996–1999

TO SAY THAT Pokey Allen had an eye on the situation
developing in Boise, after Skip Hall resigned, would be an
understatement. Boise State was where he yearned to be. In his
eyes, the idea of it happening was a long shot.

In reality, it was never in question. From his roots, Pokey and
Boise were destined for each other.

Ernest Duncan "Pokey" Allen was born in on January 29,
1943, in Superior, Montana. The following year, his lone
sibling, Jennie, was born. One year later, the family moved
to Missoula, Montana, about 60 miles down the road, where
Pokey would spend his youth. There, he led a simple life: never
poor, never rich, always loved.

Although Allen excelled at sports in high school, he was a jittery, nervous type, bucking the stereotype of the too-cool-for-school jock. After playing football at the University of Utah, he wound up playing professionally in the CFL for the BC Lions and Edmonton Eskimos.

After his playing career ended in 1968, a slew of coaching jobs precluded his stop at Portland State. He spent almost a decade at Simon Fraser University in British Columbia, followed by three years at Montana, two at Eastern Washington, and one at California Berkeley.

Allen made a pit stop in the USFL (with the Los Angeles Express and Portland Breakers), the defunct NFL-adjacent league known for gargantuan personalities and ridiculous marketing schemes.

Although he had bounced around different professional leagues and assorted colleges, Allen was at heart a small-town soul. The upbringing in Montana filled Pokey with vivid memories of the simplicity and beauty that comes with vast spaces. In Boise State, and the potential it carried, Pokey was reminded of home.

Because of that, wherever he went, one eye remained transfixed on the Broncos. Now that he'd made his mark at Portland State, and with things heading south in Boise, he was ready to pounce.

"I watched the coaching situation at Boise State with great interest," Allen would write in his autobiography, *Pokey: The Good Fight.* "Skip Hall's critics had become more vocal; it wasn't enough that he was an unforgivable 0–5 against archrival Idaho, they griped; now he was losing to Division II teams."[1]

As his 1992 season was coming to a close in Portland, Allen, forty-nine years old at the time, envisioned a life closer to home, closer to his roots.

"We [Portland State] defeated Texas A&I in the Division II quarterfinals; a day or so later I surreptitiously flew into Boise to interview for the Boise State job," Pokey wrote. "Actually, I think my first 'Interview' took place October 24 with Portland State's win over Boise State. When a Division II school comes into Bronco Stadium and moves the ball at will against a BSU defense, people sit up and take notice. Would I have been a candidate for Skip Hall's vacated position had we not embarrassed his team a month earlier? No questions about it, I never would have had a chance."[2]

Once Hall signed his pink slip, with a few other candidates slipping in and out, Allen's dream was inching closer to reality.

Gregg Smith, an assistant coach for the powerhouse University of Miami Hurricanes, was receiving strong consideration. Pokey, the salt-of-the-earth outsider, was the popular choice with the everyman who dotted the populous of Boise. Smith, his resume dripping with big-time success, albeit as an assistant, was the popular choice among boosters. J. R. Simplot and Allen Noble, two prominent local businessmen, were so onboard the Gregg Smith train that the two reportedly flew to Miami on December 2, after the Hurricanes had played San Diego State, to try and lure Smith to Boise.

"Big money won't like the selection of Allen," wrote John Millman of the *Statesman Journal*. "Anti-big money will resent the selection of [Gregg] Smith, and there's power in the people. It's Bleymaier's call, and it's a tough one. No doubt he'll do what's best for the program and the community. It's crucial he makes it clear the choice was his with the blessing of the search committee. No doubt he will, even if his choice is Gregg Smith."[3]

The tug of bigger things was weighing on Allen. Portland State was a good job—a safe job—but Boise State was a new and exciting challenge.

Portland State's season ended when the Vikings lost to Pittsburgh State in the semifinals of the Division II playoffs, 41–38.

"I'm not sure what would have happened if we had won that game, but it became academic when [Pittsburgh State] rallied to beat us," Allen wrote later. "Sometimes I think I became too distracted trying to get the BSU job."[4]

Having visited Boise once, a week before the Vikings' playoff loss, Allen flew back for his second interview on December 8. While there, he met with a 22-member search committee. Gene Bleymaier and Lyle Smith were present; so too were prominent boosters of the school, as well as former players.

While in town, he left Bleymaier dazed. Hurricane Pokey blew through Boise in just two days, cementing his status as just the sixth Broncos coach in the previous fifty years.

The fireworks his Portland State team displayed the previous season in Bronco Stadium was all Bleymaier needed to see. "I never talked with Gene about why he gave me the job over Gregg, but I'm glad he did," said Allen.[5]

The Broncos were taking a risk. Pokey's eccentricities were known and his offenses dazzled, but the jump from Division II to Division I-AA was a whole new venture.

Ken Goe, who covered Allen during his Portland State days, recalls a man who connected with his players better than anyone he had seen—no matter what it took.

"One time, when he was at PSU, coaches and the players who were over the age of twenty-one were at the bar drinking," Goe recalls. "Pokey stood up and said, 'I've had enough of this . . . I'm going to show you how to Gator.' He downs his beer, then slid down the dance floor on his stomach."

* * *

That Gregg Smith had even been considering Boise State, in a time when the shine was somewhat wearing off the program, is a testament to the history they had built. Despite the lack of titles in recent years, with Bleymaier at the helm and an illustrious track record already in the bank, Boise State was viewed as a solid landing spot in the coaching ranks.

"I'm not sure if most people realized what a big deal the Boise State job was, but I don't think Gregg Smith would have applied for too many I-AA head coaching positions," Pokey said later. "I mean, he was the assistant head coach at *Miami*."[6]

Before he could begin to muse about the challenges awaiting him on the field, Allen had to shore up the situation *off* the field. Namely, he had one major task at hand before he and his assistants loaded up the (literal) van and headed east toward Boise: Al Borges.

Borges had been with Pokey since 1985, when both came to Portland State, just a stone's throw from the Willamette River. If Allen was the abberant outsider, Borges had been his behind-the-scenes mad scientist. After working his way up from assistant coach at Salinas High School in California, Borges's offenses at Portland State were consistently at or near the top in every national category. After six years, he and Allen were thick as; although bringing Borges to Boise was not part of the contract, Bleymaier, as well as Allen, believed it was a foregone conclusion.

The problem was, Borges wasn't in on the understanding. And Portland State wanted him to stay and become the Vikings' next head coach. Badly.

Before Pokey and his wife packed up their belongings and headed for Boise, as his friends and family were throwing him a going away party at "Jake's," a restaurant in Portland, Borges approached his longtime friend and confidant. "Would you mind if I went after the Portland State job?" he asked.[7]

"Al, I want what's best for you," Allen told him.[8]

Then, panic set in.

The next morning, the *Oregonian* ran a story with the headline, "Borges to accept PSU job." In less than 24 hours, it appeared that his right-hand man, the one responsible, in large part, for the outlandish offenses Pokey had under his name, was gone.

The first thing to do was to call Bleymaier—"We've lost our offensive coordinator,"[9] Allen told him—and the second was to do some damage control. At the time, Pokey was still using Portland State's football facilities; across the hall was Borges, busy himself attempting to cobble together a staff.

However, in a matter of hours, all the commotion would come to a complete halt. Around 10:30 in the morning, Borges entered Allen's office, sat down, looked his friend in the eye, and ended the cordial standoff.

Just before he entered the room, Borges had told Portland State's athletic director, Randy Nordlof, that after a sleepless night he was no longer accepting the job.

"I'm doing what I think is right for me," Borges would tell the *Oregonian.* "To do this job right, your heart has to be in it. I'm not sure mine was, and that would have been reflected in what happened on the field."[10]

The whirlwind 24 hours had resulted in little more than an extra dose of antacids for Allen and Bleymaier. The package that had been so appealing—Allen, Borges, defensive coordinator Tom Mason, and so on—was intact.

"That staff had Pokey Allen, Al Borges, Tom Osborne, Ron Gould . . . they had a ton of people who are now NFL coaches, Division I coaches, coordinators. It was a very good coaching staff," says Jason Payne, a defensive back under Allen. "They really opened my eyes to how much these guys knew. They had a plan in place."

Now, they just needed to win some games.

That task, simple as it may have sounded, would be an arduous one. Just before his inaugural spring ball season, as he pored over game film, stat sheets, and weight lifting numbers, a sickening realization fell over Allen: with certain exceptions, he was inheriting a *bad* football team.

"I quickly concluded that Skip Hall and his assistants didn't lose because they couldn't coach; it was because they didn't recruit well during their last two or three seasons. It wasn't that Hall and his staff didn't have any blue-chippers; they just didn't have enough of them," Allen later wrote.[11]

"I wish I had looked at the film a little better before I took the position," he continued. "I didn't realize we were going to have a total rebuild job ahead of us. Truth be told, I had a feeling our first season at Boise State was going to be a long one."[12]

To help get the team up to par, talentwise, Allen and his assistants recruited the Junior College route—hard. Bringing in players with previous college experience can be dicey. More often than not, players were there because of their academic struggles or behavioral issues; it can also lead to instant success, with players who have have seasoned themselves as their bodies developed. Allen chose to focus on the latter. One of the players they brought in was Joe O'Brien, a defensive end out of Santa Clara University, a Division II school in the Western Football Conference. O'Brien would go on to have one of the most successful, yet controversial, careers in the history of Boise State football. It was the epitome of a boom-or-bust gamble, and the youngster was sometimes both within weeks. O'Brien came to Boise State after Santa Clara, under the new classification rules put down by the NCAA, chose to no longer fund their football program.

It was Allen, and Boise State's, gain. It was also their biggest headache.

Although he was a standout talent, O'Brien had already battled a life of addiction stemming from a rough and wild childhood.

O'Brien grew up in a predominantly black neighborhood in Pittsburgh, California, and was "forced to grow up quick." By the time he reached high school, his on-field talents had begun to blossom through his rough exterior. Hulking in both size and strength, he possessed all the physical tools necessary to exceed at not just the collegiate level, but in the NFL, as well. He had the two traits that were unteachable and uncoachable: he was bigger and faster than just about everyone he competed against.

O'Brien was named the Most Valuable Player in all three sports he played in high school; he was the class officer, team captain, and received over seventy awards from various academic, athletic, and civic doings.

Externally, he was a parent's dream. Internally, starting at age fifteen, he was flailing, beginning his lifelong struggle with drugs, a masking agent to his home life.

Everything shifted for the worse during his senior year of high school: O'Brien's father passed away of a heroin overdose, a clear tunnel into Joe's future. In hiding his feelings during the aftermath, he became a master at deception, formulating his brooding addiction into what he would later call "The Lie" in his tell-all book, *Busted Bronco*.

Although he had only visited the city of Boise one time, during the summer of 1992 for a football camp, the Boise State campus enthralled O'Brien. The program was an opportunity for a fresh start, much as Santa Clara had been, in theory, three seasons prior. But by the time he arrived in Boise, Joe's methamphetamine use was five years in the making. The laid-back culture of Santa Clara had offered him a window into other vices as well, one which he gladly stepped into.

Despite his rampant drug use off the field, O'Brien had become a star when between the hash marks. During his redshirt freshman year at Santa Clara, he accumulated 71 tackles and 7 sacks; his sophomore year was more of the same. By the time Santa Clara had closed shop on the program, O'Brien had accumulated nearly 140 tackles, 14 sacks, and a lifetime's worth of off-field baggage.

When he arrived in Boise, the drug and alcohol abuse was beginning to take up large chunks of his life. But "The Lie" was strong, allowing him to hide his darkest demons from those closest to him.

The Broncos won O'Brien's services over such schools as Oregon, Arkansas, Nevada, California, and Hawaii. "We were attracted to Joe his freshman year, when we were all still at Portland State," Barry Sacks, who was Boise State's defensive line coach, told the *Daily Ledger-Post Dispatch*. "We had an All-American offensive tackle, and Joe was a freshman, and Joe just chewed him up."

Joe Aliotti, the Broncos' former quarterback who was an assistant coach for O'Brien when he was in high school, had a trustworthy relationship with Pokey Allen. When Allen and his staff contacted Aliotti for his unbiased views on O'Brien, and whether or not he was worth taking a flyer on, Aliotti didn't hesitate.

"I told Pokey and Al Borges that Joe was a great kid," he said. "I might have helped a little by knowing some people and giving him a good recommendation, but Joe was the main reason he got the scholarship to Boise State because he was an outstanding football player."

The Broncos were a second chance for O'Brien, who was the vibrant and fiery leader the team needed. To Mason, past issues were just that—the past.

"When he played for me, he was one of the model, full-team guys. The epitome of an overachiever," he says now. "He was a leader; if there was a drug deal going on while he was in Boise, I was not aware of it. I would have bet money that was not going on at that time."

Along with O'Brien, a handful of other JC players were being ushered in for the 1993 season. With just a few holdovers from the previous team capable of playing competitively at the I-AA level, the Broncos took the field on September 4, 1993, in Allen's inaugural outing. They whooped up on Rhode Island, 31–10, igniting a feel-good story across the community, but the victory was a short reprieve from the losing that had become too much of the norm.

A blowout loss to Nevada followed. A win over Northeastern in Week 3 allowed for some chuckles, but it was clear to anyone watching that Boise State was out of their league. The final two seasons under Hall had been average; they had also been fools gold. The team that took the field under Allen had a severe lack of talent and experience. Four losses in a row during the middle of the season buried their confidence even further. Cognizant of the situation he was in, and mindful that things were not likely to turn during the season, Allen was cheerful and honest in the locker room. Outside of it, he was drab.

"This is not a place where you can take a lot of time to get it going," he told the *Oregonian* after the team's loss to Weber State in Week 7. "They want a winner, and they're used to having good offenses. We'd better get it going by next year."[13]

After a 34–27 win over Idaho State, the Broncos would fall to Montana State and Eastern Washington. With the team sitting at 3–7, Allen's first dance with Idaho was on the horizon. The season had been a train wreck, but a win over Idaho—as unlikely as it seemed—would go far in building something, *anything*, for the following year.

By this point, Boise State had dropped eleven games in a row to Idaho; prior to that, the Vandals had only beaten the Broncos two times *ever*. Knowing they were likely to again go down was one thing; the lack of support the Broncos were getting from the fan base was another. In their loss to Eastern Washington, only 10,238 fans showed up, the lowest attendance in twenty years.

In less than one year, Allen's grace period had all but dried up.

"Teams do not have to beat us; we beat ourselves," Allen told the *Idaho Statesman* before the Vandals game. "I feel incredibly bad for the city of Boise."[14]

For now, his gentle words would have to be enough. Boise State would fall, 49–16, in front of just 15,085 fans. Allen's first season, which he had predicted could be a disaster, was just that. The team finished 3–8, their lowest win total since 1946, when they went 2–4–2 in the first year after World War II.

Brusque by nature, Allen did not let his first season go quietly. Speaking to Phil Smith of the *Idaho Statesman*, he laid his cards out: "Give me one more year and I'll straighten it out, or I'll be gone," he said. "I can't take a year like this again. If we don't straighten it out next year, you won't have to worry about [long-term] contracts or anything else."[15]

"Gene Bleymaier came in and said, 'Hey, you guys . . . we're going to be patient with you. Build it right, go out and get your high school kids,'" Tom Mason says now. "Pokey kicks the door shut with his foot—I thought it was going to hit Bleymaier in the butt—and he says, 'Nah, don't believe this. You gotta go out and recruit the best 25 junior college kids you can find."

Allen had set the tone for 1994 season with his declaration to Smith in the newspaper: there would be no wiggle room for him, nor for anyone on his staff. They had one shot at fixing all that ailed them, or, by his own admission, they would be out on the streets.

* * *

In January of 1994, under the rule of the Idaho State Board of Education, Pokey was denied a two-year extension from Boise State. He was granted a one-year deal, and a raise would take his salary from $69,008, to $70,386. Per his own admission, the one-year deal was more in line with where they were.

After a year of transition, the roster looked ready to take the leap, thanks in large part to yet another influx of players from the junior college ranks. Those players brought a fresh approach and an aura of confidence.

"It was a different mentality with the new transfers Pokey had brought in," says Ron Pound, a tight end under Pokey.

On top of the 15 players transfering in, 27 lettermen returned, 15 of which were starters. Because of that, continuity would be the theme for the Broncos in 1994.

"We'll be a lot more talented, but until we get them on the field, it will be difficult to tell," Allen said at the yearly Big Sky Media Day event.[16] The Broncos, and every other member of the Big Sky, were chasing the Montana Grizzlies and their all-everything quarterback Dave Dickenson. Although Boise State was nowhere near the top of the pecking order, they were no longer viewed as cellar-dwellers. That alone was a giant step forward.

Tony Hilde, after an up-and-down debut in 1993, in which he threw for 1,461 yards and five touchdowns and nine interceptions, looked the part of a franchise quarterback for the Broncos. Ryan Ikebe was a future star at wide receiver. There was a sense of optimism around the team.

On the field, Pokey was accumulating the pieces for a drastic turnaround.

Off it, his life was beginning to crumble.

Although he and his wife, Barb, had welcomed their first daughter, Taylor, during the 1993 season, the marriage was splintered. The traits that made Allen so successful at Portland State—his gargantuan personality, the schmoozing and drinking and partying with boosters and alumni—was the anthesis of what Barb was looking for in a marriage. Allen desired to be around people—he *needed* to be around people. Gatherings on his houseboat, alumni events, bars—if there was a crowd, he was there. Once they moved to Boise and the losses began to mount, the fun side of Pokey fell by the wayside. What was left was a loud, disgruntled, ornery man.

Being married to a college football coach can be hellacious on significant others in the best of times; being married to one who is losing is unbearable.

After just one calendar year together in Boise, Pokey and Barb were done.

* * *

As the 1994 season approached, and with his personal life in a state of ruin, Pokey had painted himself into a corner—both with his words and his performance. He was brought in to spark a match for the program, not to watch over a sinking ship.

Art Lawler of the *Idaho Statesman* wrote in the days leading up to the season that "It may be in his mind more than anywhere else, but the BSU football coach feels he's got a year to rebuild his team . . . most people think the pressure by Allen is largely self-inflicted, but [a booster] adds, 'If he doesn't win this year, I think he'll be out of here. But that's just something Pokey has put on himself. Most people I know realize a coach needs three years to build his program.'"

He didn't have three seasons. By his own admission, he had one.

The 1993 team had set program records of the horrendous variety: worst overall record, fewest points scored in a season, and most points allowed in a season. With a large influx of new talent, and the realization that, in all likelihood, things could not possibly be worse than the year prior, Allen—despite the recent setbacks—was optimistic entering his second season.

"It's going to be the most interesting season I've been involved with," he said at the time. "I don't think there's a chance to have any more new people on the team than we have."[17]

On the offensive line alone, the staff brought in six junior college players in an effort to win the battles most often lost the previous season. "We're going to be a lot bigger and stronger on the offensive line than we were last year."[18]

Once the season began, his optimism would begin to make sense.

Although the Broncos didn't open the season against the stiffest of competition—Northeastern and Cal State Northridge, the latter of which entered with just seventeen players on scholarship—they showed clear signs of improvement. When they took down CSN on September 10, moving to 2–0 on the season, their 40 points was the program's most since October 19, 1991 (when they had trounced Northern Arizona, 57–14)—almost three full years prior. It was exactly the fireworks show Pokey was hired for.

"I'm excited about the [Cal State Northridge] victory, but we've got a long way to go," he said as the team prepared for Nevada in Week 3. "It's panic week for the coaches next week."[19]

Their panic was subset a little by the emergence of K. C. Adams, a do-everything running back and special teams star. After two weeks, Adams had already locked up conference awards for offense and special teams. Against Northridge, he rushed for 129 yards and took a punt back 79 yards for a touchdown. What lacked all throughout the 1993 season—the threat of a dynamic play—returned with Adams.

"People are going to have to start opening their eyes and see this guy's skill," Hilde said after the Northridge win. "At any time, he can go all the way."[20]

Hilde was also providing reason for optimism. Although his freshman campaign in 1993 was brief, he showed flashes of an enhanced skillset. As his sophomore season rolled along, Hilde was showcasing the traits Allen and Al Borges knew he possessed: composure, accuracy, and an intuitive knowledge of what to do with the ball.

As the showdown with Nevada crept closer (the Wolfpack had jumped up from I-AA to Division I and the Big West Conference, something the Broncos were hoping to do). Hilde and Adams represented what Allen was looking for in his team: explosiveness, with control and patience. Both needed to be their best if the team was going to atone for the previous season, when Nevada had cruised, 38–10. That game had been so bad that, afterward, Chris Ault (who was then Nevada's athletic director and now served as their coach) said of the Broncos, "unless they improve the quality of their players, I see no sense in continuing this rivalry."

Foot, meet mouth.

When the Wolfpack and Broncos kicked off on September 17, it was impossible to tell from the naked eye which team was a Big West member and which was still toiling away in Division I-AA. The Broncos, with their silky combination of junior college transfers and fast-rising youngsters, stormed out the gate.

Hilde, in particular, was spectacular. In the first quarter alone, he connected on a 47-yard touchdown pass to Jarrett Haussk and a 45-yard swing pass to Adams to set up another score (a field goal by Greg Erickson). Sandwiched between those was a Rashid Gayle 87-yard interception return. When Adams scampered for a 26-yard touchdown with 2:05 left in the opening quarter, it was already 24–0.

In front of 21,669 fans, the largest to see a game under Pokey at the time, the Broncos claimed their most important victory in nearly a decade, defeating the Wolfpack 37–27.

"There's no excuse to lose this game," a defeated Ault said after. "I don't mean I-AA, I-A. It had nothing to do with that. There was no excuse to lose this game, but we did it to ourselves."[21]

Ault could spin it however he wanted, but the truth was undeniable: Boise State, from the moment they got off the bus, was the better team. He tried to temper the flames a bit later, saying, "They outplayed us. It's just that simple, and they made the big plays when they had to,"[22] but it was too late.

Five days later, on September 22, 1994, the pieces for the reclamation project would continue to move in the right direction. Boise State, thanks to the Idaho Board of Education, was granted approval to move up to I-A and the Big West Conference. Although the final decision from the Big West on whether or not they would officially accept the Broncos was still weeks away, approval from the Board was the big hurdle.

After over fifty seasons of playing football, and dominating their competition for large stretches of that time, the Broncos would be moving up again.

To help ring in their (almost) official status as future I-A members, Boise State would breeze through their next three games before dropping their first contest of the season against Idaho State. Their 6–0 start, the best in school history, prompted Pokey to quip that the team had "magic."

Despite the loss in Week 7, all memories of the disastrous 1993 season had been wiped clean. The decision to bring in such a large amount of junior college players was risky, but it was paying off. The Broncos were 6–1, had shown their mettle against a team from an upper-level, and, perhaps most promising, were armed with an offense that was perplexing to any defense it faced.

Through seven weeks, the Broncos were averaging 33 points per game. In fact, their 231 points scored were more than they had scored the entire previous season. Adding to the good vibes was an eight-year contract extension which allowed the Broncos to keep their infamous blue turf, a victory for Gene Bleymaier, who noted, "we get a lot of publicity over it. Visitors stop all the time just to take a peek. It's unique to Boise State and we'd like to keep it that way."

By 1994, the turf had even warranted a profile from *Sports Illustrated*, a feather in the cap for a small school striving for national publicity.

On October 22, when the Broncos took a trip to Bozeman to take on Montana State, they carried a national ranking (#17), a clear path to the conference title, and a potential trip to the playoffs. When assessing Montana State, Allen saw a lot of his 1993. The Bobcats were trudging through a miserable, and the Broncos' turnaround was a blueprint for what Montana State could become. The relationship between Allen and the Bobcats coach, Cliff Hysell, went way back. The potential for a galvanizing upset was in the mix and Allen, aware that all the momentum built up could shatter with a loss to an inferior opponent, stepped lightly as the game approached.

"I feel really bad for Cliff, he's a good friend of mine," Allen said. "But I hope his team doesn't come out of it this weekend."[23]

Any trepidation he had of a rejuvenated Bobcats squad, or of his own team losing focus facing a 2–5 opponent, were quickly put to rest. Facing their first trap game, the Broncos took a lazy and lifeless crowd out early, coasting to a 38–10 win.

Simple. Efficient. Textbook.

It is hard to glean much from a win over a lesser team in the middle of the season; coming off their worst season in program history and their first loss of the season, it was fair to wonder how the Broncos would react. In one game, they answered any questions that may have popped up during the week. It was no longer in question: they were for real.

"We knew we had to jump on them early and make a statement,"[24] said K. C. Adams, who rushed for 103 yards on just 17 carries.

The Broncos, now 7–1, had three more games on the schedule: a home game against Montana and a trip to Eastern Washington before their next shot at Idaho. After disposing of those first two hurdles, the Vandals—their 12-game win streak in the series intact—were next. The significance of the game had reached a tipping point. The Idaho-Boise State rivalry had long been a family affair of sorts, ripping allegiances right down the living room of Idaho homes. Now, with the Vandals seeking their 13th straight win in the series, the pecking order of the rivalry was set. One more win, it seemed, and talk of a meaningful tryst would end.

"The rivalry meant a lot more to the University of Idaho than it did to Boise State," says Bert Sahlberg, who covered Idaho for the *Lewiston Tribune*. "It seems to me that Idaho fans have two teams—Idaho, and whomever is playing against Boise State. You don't like to use the word 'Hate,' but they really do not like the Broncos."

With everything on the line for both teams—the winner would take the conference title and the automatic playoff berth—the Broncos and Vandals set out on a drizzly November day. As Vandals heads coach John L. Smith noted, "Boise State is Boise State. It doesn't matter what the records are. It comes down to who is going to play the hardest. This is the way it should be."[25]

During their run of dominance, the Vandals had more often than not been quarterbacked by an All-American, someone destined for greatness: Ken Hobart, Scott Linehan, John Freisz, Doug Nussmeier. These stars were also coached by the likes of Dennis Erickson or Keith Gilbertson. This version of Idaho was good, but they lacked the starpower that teams from their past possessed. John L. Smith and quarterback Brian Brennan— who was only a redshirt freshman entering the game—were not of the same ilk.

Because of that, the Broncos defense, which had been on a tear since the loss to Idaho State, was ready to pounce. Although his unit had struggled slightly as the season wore on, Tom Mason had devised a gameplan tailored to his personnel and of the challenge the Vandals posed: He was going to blitz the hell out of them.

"When you blitz, sometimes you get burned and give up a couple long passes," Mason would say after the game, "but we felt comfortable with the players we had out on the field. They knew the system."[26]

From the outset, in front of a new stadium record of 23,701 fans, Boise State and Idaho put on a show. The Broncos jumped out to an early lead after a touchdown pass from Hilde to Ryan Ikebe, and a pair of Greg Erickson field goals, taking a 13–0 lead into halftime.

As he walked to the locker room at the break, Allen, despite the lead, was none-too-happy with his team's play. "We should have a lot more points on the scoreboard," he said. "We're shooting ourselves in the foot, making too many little mistakes. But, we're playing hard."

As rain-filled cloud cover rolled over the stadium, and the temperature fell nearly 10 degrees in the 20 minutes between halves, something else was happening: the Idaho offense was waking up. On the third play of the second half, Brennan took the snap from his center, took seven quick shuffles backward, and found his tight end, Avery Griggs, running undeterred down the middle of the field. Griggs caught the wide-open and ran 74 yards to paydirt without a defender in sight.

After a field goal from Idaho midway through the third quarter, Boise State's lead was cut to 13–9. As had been the case all season, Hilde and the offense responded. His touchdown pass to Ikebe—their second of three on the day—gave the Broncos a 20–9 lead, one they would never relinquish.

The Broncos would hang on for a 27–24 victory, ending their decade-plus losing streak to Idaho; and with the victor came the spoils: the win clinched their first conference title since 1980, a spot in the playoffs, and solidified home-field advantage up until the championship game (should they make it).

Adding insult to injury for Idaho, in the wake of seeing their record-breaking winning streak against Boise State snapped, they were then denied entry into Division I-A Big West due to the attendance of the school being below the required amount.

One week, two vital victories for the Broncos.

Two seasons after his introduction as the school's third head coach in ten years, on top of returning the team to its winning way, Allen had cleared a different hurdle, too: winning over the fanbase. During the seven home games they played during the 1994 season, the Broncos averaged 21,685 fans per game, a new Big Sky record.

"The community has really done a great job of adopting Boise State," says Sahlberg.

Hilde's health was a cause for concern as the team's first playoff game approached. At this juncture of the season, his shoulder was a mess; the wear and tear of 11 full games and the beating he had taken was visible. Although he was never ruled out as the starter, the staff knew that one hit, one bad angle, and their star quarterback could be lost.

Unfortunately, a more severe and daunting illness was brewing.

6

IN SICKNESS AND IN HEALTH

"The coaching staff that Pokey had just brought it all together; there was this culture of, 'We plan on winning.' It just kept building and building. It was all positive."
—Bernie Zimmerman, Boise State, 1994–1995

IT RESTED IN the right arm of Pokey Allen, dull at first. As he stood on the field following the win over Idaho, taking in the scene, watching his friend Al Borges climb the goal post among the throngs of elated Broncos fans, Allen felt ill.

No, not just ill . . . *exhausted.*

Although he would take the night to celebrate with friends and family, deep down, under the jubilation and dreams that laid before him, he couldn't shake the feeling that something was wrong. Despite being fifty-four years old, he often carried himself with the energy of a caffeine-fueled teenager. But as the playoffs rolled in, and with North Texas set to invade Boise in the first round, Allen couldn't ignore the fact that something was off.

"I feel like shit," he told Tom Mason in the postgame celebration. "Maybe I'm just getting old."[1]

The previous month had been eye opening for Allen. At Portland State, the Vikings were, at best, the third-biggest college football show in the state behind the Oregon Ducks and Oregon State Beavers. He was well liked, but never under the microscope. In Boise, all of that had changed. The fans were more passionate; the scrutiny was cranked up. The Broncos media coverage rivaled that of some NFL teams, and with the geographic layout there was little else in the area to cover. It was the Pokey and Bronco show, 24 hours a day. During the final month of the season, the poking and prodding had reached a crescendo. The news of Pokey and Barb's split was well known by this point, and stories had begun to swirl of the coach's nighttime shenanigans.

On top of the continuing pain in his arm, rumors of a DUI involving Pokey made the rounds. They were false, as would later be confirmed, but the damage was done. TV stations, newspapers, barber shop flapping—in the public's eye, Allen was guilty. Despite different outlets reaching out and apologizing to Pokey after the accusations were proven false, it was too late. When he returned to Boise from a recruiting trip on the team's bye week after the Montana State game, Dana Haynes, who worked for KIVI Channel 6 in Boise, cornered Allen. "Pokey, I feel really bad about this," she said.[2]

On top of the DUI talk, anonymous sources were also spreading rumors that Pokey's now ex-wife, Barb, was filing assault charges against her ex-husband. Haynes told Allen that she had spent all day in the prosecutor's office, digging through files to find out if it was true. Topping it off, the final rumor to the trifecta was that Allen not only had charges against him *and* the DUI, but that a prominent booster had paid the fine and given Barb $50,000 to leave town.

All of it—the rumors, the attention, the arm, the divorce, the young child, the stress of the season—was bearing down on Pokey as the school's first playoff game in four years approached. Although the rumors of assault would prove to be untrue, the enormity of his celebrity-trappings had been felt. The Pokey Allen who used to pound beers and tell stories with his players at local bars around Portland could no longer exist.

Still, what bothered him most was the dull pain persisting in his arm. For now, it would have to wait.

Boise State's first round opponent, North Texas, was ranked 3rd in the country and riding a wave of momentum. Boise State would escape with a 24–20 win, but the physical beatings were beginning to take a toll.

"Our offense is really battered," Allen said after the game. "Hilde can barely walk and K. C. [Adams] is battered . . . " He trailed off, but the message was clear: If the Broncos were going to keep the ride going, it was going to be up to their defense.

The following week, in a 17–14 win over the Appalachian State Mountaineers, the Broncos' defense was impenetrable, suffocating the Mountaineers attack and allowing the Bronco offense a week of reprieve.

"We had a great defensive game," Allen said afterward. "We didn't play well on offense; we need to play well on both sides this week. We've been wining games in some weird ways."[3]

The Mountaineers had been the only team to beat Marshall, Boise State's upcoming opponent in round three, during the regular season. If Appalachian State had been a barometer, Boise State looked like the clearest threat to take home the national championship.

* * *

While at Portland State, Pokey had made himself into something of a local celebrity by performing outlandish stunts in order to attract attention to his team. If he wasn't being shot out of a cannon, he was sitting high atop an elephant on a football field, gleefully hamming for the camera, ordering all Oregonians to come out to the stadium. In an attempt to ensure a full house for the team's game against Marshall, Pokey made a subtle bet with the folks of Boise through yet another TV commercial: If 20,000 fans showed, he would ride down the city streets on horseback.

"They're going to be playing here on the blue turf in front of a hostile crowd. They're used to playing in front of a lot of people, but not in front of a lot of *angry* people. A hostile crowd will make a difference," he said.

It was vintage Allen, and as long as they kept winning, it was going to work. More than anything, the previous season's 3–8 mark had robbed the fanbase of one of sports' great characters. He was honest with his players, and he made the game fun, a word foreign to most coaches.

And his players adored him for it.

"Pokey would always say, if you were caught past curfew, 'I used to stay out past curfew, but I wasn't an asshole about it.' Everyone will tell you, he used to say he did everything we did, but he wasn't an asshole about it," says Jason Payne. "He was a very honest guy; very caring, very smart, and every single player who played for him would lay out and leave everything on the field for Pokey."

That attitude was evident on December 10, when the Thundering Herd of Marshall came to Boise. Although he had been beat up to end the season, Tony Hilde was announced as the team's starter, his shredded shoulder aside. His availability was paramount; when Hilde was on the field, the Broncos were a different team. By this point in the season he had thrown for 3,005 yards and was completing 53 percent of his passes.

"He's a good athlete and a good quarterback," Allen said.[4]

Against the Herd, he would need to be better than good. He would need to be special.

* * *

Marshall came into Boise as one of the most dominant teams in Division I-AA over the previous decade. Since Jim Donnan had taken over as head coach five seasons prior, the Herd had made three consecutive title game appearances, winning it all in 1992. The semifinal game against the Broncos would be Marshall's fifteenth playoff game under Donnan.

They were the biggest hurdle the Broncos had faced all season. From the get-go, Marshall—which during the season ran a meticulously varied offense—brought a simple game plan with them: run the ball down Boise State's throat. And they did it, over and over again, each run more emphatic than the previous.

Midway through the second quarter, Marshall led 24–7. Hilde was in the locker room by that point; after more vicious blows, his shoulder was shot. Boise State's defense, which had carried them all season, was worn to a nub. The war of attrition that the coaches had worried about was taking over. Although they scored a touchdown on a pass from backup quarterback Mark Paljetak before the half, the Broncos still trailed by ten. The "magic" run the team had been on was on its last leg.

Hilde, however, would have none of it. Despite being in such excruciating pain that he could barely register movement in his shoulder, the Broncos' sophomore quarterback was not going down without a fight. At halftime, he loaded on his pads, told Pokey he was good to go, and set out to carve his own Willis Reed moment, returning from injury in an improbable moment to make his mark on the game.

"I wasn't even going to let Hilde leave the locker room in the second half," Allen wrote later. "But, after checking with the team doctors, Al Borges told me he could play if necessary."[5]

It *was* necessary. As the third quarter was winding to its end, his team still down ten and time running out, Allen reinserted his hobbled quarterback back into the game, his shoulder—which would need surgery after the season—dangling by a thread.

The results Pokey hoped for were instantaneous. Hilde led the Broncos down the field, setting up a 2-yard scoring touchdown run from K. C. Adams. Later, the Broncos took possession on the Marshall 46-yard line with 8:42 to go in the game. After a run from Adams and a completion from Hilde, Boise State had the ball 34 yards from scoring, and a monumental comeback. When Hilde dropped back to pass, he gave a small pump fake, drawing the Marshall secondary up. Sneaking behind them, with nary a defender to be found, was wide receiver Lee Schrack, who was running an uncovered seam route down the left hash mark.

Pass completed. Touchdown.

With patches of snow shoved up against the bleacher railings on the outline of the playing field, Schrack was mobbed by teammates, dancing and parading in celebration. The Broncos had done the improbable, erasing a 17-point deficit against arguably the best team in the country.

It was the only possible outcome for an unfathomable turnaround story. Their 13th win of the season, 10 more than the previous year, marked the second-largest about-face in Division I-AA history.

"Pokey Allen has done the best coaching job in the history of college football," Marshall head coach Jay Donnan would later say.[6]

There was no arguing.

FOCUS, Boise State's in-house magazine under the helm of Bob Evancho, named the comeback against Marshall as one of the great moments in school history.

"It was the crowning moment of a glorious season," Evancho wrote. "It was an improbable comeback in a season full of comebacks against a formidable foe that looked unstoppable."[7]

Reinstating Hilde proved a prophetic decision, and Pokey's magical leadership was the difference.

"This team truly makes plays when it has to," Allen said after the win, the fourth in a row for the Broncos by four or less points. "It's amazing. I didn't know what to expect, but I knew this team wouldn't quit. Everybody talks about magic and destiny and all that stuff, but let me tell you this: We've got to be an awfully good football team to come back from 24–7 and win against a team like Marshall.[8]

"It's been an amazing season—we find new ways to win. I've given up looking for reasons why this team wins. They win because they win, and I don't know why."

Donnan, who came up short in his attempt to make a fourth-straight title game, said, "When you have a lead like that and lose, you blame the coach. Give them credit for coming back. We just got beat in the clutch."[9]

As time ticked away following the win, Pokey found a different level of candidness, citing his own doubts as a reason the win carried more meaning. "The players thought we were going to reach the national championship [this year]. I had a lot of doubts. We've had a magical season; that we're here is amazing. We don't have many seniors on this team, but the seniors we have went out of their way to make it work."

Allen's decision to bring in an almost entirely new cast of players had two possible outcomes before the season began: disaster, or triumph.

"A lot of times when you bring in a lot of new people, there's a lot of friction. This was not the case," he said after the game. "Matter of fact, after two days of double-days, we were a team, which is amazing with all those new people."[10]

Joe O'Brien, who had finished up his final game on the blue turf, emphasized the team-first aspect they played under as the catalyst in their come-from-behind win.

"I think it has to do with a group of players who believe in each other and believe in the people next to them and don't try to do too much," he said. "We had a goal and we strived to go toward the goal. We did everything it took this year."

K.C. Adams had rushed for 56 hard fought yards, which were instrumental in the comeback effort. After the game, he looked at the nature of the win over Marshall as an omen for what was to come. "Now that we've beat one team, everybody believes we have a chance at the other team."

* * *

Youngstown State, with their option offense run by head coach Jim Tressel, would end the Broncos' season the following week, 28–14, in the national championship game. The season as a whole, with 13 wins and a wild playoff run, was a rousing—if not unbelievable—success.

The anguish of losing was sharp in the moment, but Boise State's accomplishments, as time ticked by, came into focus.

"We prepared all week for the option," said Broncos safety Chris Cook following the loss. "We should have been ready for it, but they took advantage of it."[11]

Allen may not have done the best job in history as Jay Donnan had claimed the week prior, but the Broncos' turnaround was nothing short of masterful. In 1993, their eight losses came by an average on nearly 19 points per game. Their offense—Pokey's specialty, as well as that of his offensive coordinator, Al Borges—had been non-existent.

Allen had now proven to be a sovereign motivator; a man blessed at plunging into the psyche of each and every player and finding out what made them *tick*. The Broncos put up 29 points per game in 1994 and, despite a small reprieve during the playoff run, found a consistency and groove that his teams had been known for.

"When you had guys that wanted to be there, who wanted to be a part of the program, it didn't matter who was in charge; it didn't matter who the coaches were. We had a group of guys who just wanted to play, that wanted to win," says former tight end Ron Pound.

After his first season, when a vapid attitude was rampant throughout the program, everything had changed now . . . and it started when all involved—from the coaches to the players— bought in to the system. "The poor-me syndrome, the 'I don't get to play,' was out. Guys were able to play right away, because they *could* play. They were brought in because they were better than the players before them, and they had a different attitude," continued Pound.

"I loved my coach, and I loved my teammates. We were playing for more that year, because we genuinely loved each other," says Rashid Gayle, who was one of the players remaining from the Skip Hall era who had stuck on and played a role under Allen. "We had guys who may have just been a little bit off—not misfits, but just a little off."

Outside of the state of Idaho, the feelings toward the Broncos were far different. On December 14, George Geiss, who was the sports editor of the *Great Falls Tribune*, wrote a scathing takedown of the program, going as far as calling them out for bending the rules in "the contrived Mormon mission that created another season of play for one of Boise State's best defensive lineman," a claim that would ultimately prove to be untrue.[12]

Geiss was ruthless, stating, "it's painful to watch Boise State carrying the Big Sky banner, since the Broncos have become the ultimate symbol of arrogance and greed in a conference not known for those sins."[13] His comments were the after effects of eating a batch of sour grapes. Boise State was moving up to the Big West Conference; in the minds of those staying behind in the Big Sky, the Broncos were now the outsiders.

"Mostly, our support is less-than-hearty because of Boise State's attitude toward its neighbors," he continued. "The Broncos have been Big-Dogging the other Big Sky schools for years, long before they defected to accept an invitation to join the Big West Conference following the 1985–1986 school year."[14]

Hurt feelings from scorned contemporaries aside, the Broncos were riding high. In Hilde and Ryan Ikebe, they had a quarterback-receiver tandem few in the conference could match. The entire starting offensive line would be back for the following season. The defense was awash in size and speed, the likes of which had not been seen around Boise in a long time. Having found their footing, Allen, Tom Mason, and Borges were the perfect trifecta to keep pushing forward.

Everything, it seemed, was perfect.

Until it wasn't.

* * *

On December 19, two days after the title game loss to Youngstown State, Pokey Allen went to see the team doctor. After fighting through the uncomfortable pain in his right arm, something needed to be done. Initially, Allen thought that he had torn a tendon in the arm—he had taken to doing daily pushups in his spare time to stay in shape—but the pain was now too much to overlook.

Although he had been at his most-Pokey two days prior, yucking it up with Boosters at the Bronco Athletic Association luncheon—going as far as to say, "I would rather lose and get to live in Boise than win and have to live in Youngstown, Ohio, any day"—Allen was done with the pain. He wanted to get help.

This day in particular was supposed to be full of celebration. Allen was set to be named the Big Sky Conference coach of the year; it was the highest honor to date for him, and was more than deserved.

So, when he went into the office of Dr. George Wade at the Idaho Sports Medicine Institute, it felt like a temporary restraint on an otherwise bright day. Examine the arm, diagnose some obtrusive ailment, and move on.

Instead, in the blink of an eye, his career, his life, and legacy came to a hault. A tumor, the size of a baseball, was growing inside his arm, leading to the excrutiating pain. The diagnosis was Rhabdomyosarcoma, a rare and aggressive form of muscle cancer. In two years, Allen had gone from head coach at Portland State to Boise State, from a miserable 3–8 campaign, to separating from his wife, to a national title game appearance, and now to the worst news a human being can receive.

After his separation from Barb, Pokey had moved in with Mike Young, Boise State's wrestling coach at the time, and one of his closest friends. When Pokey sat down and told his friend the news, tears began to form in the corners of Young's eyes.

In that moment, the serious nature of the diagnoses hit Allen like a right cross. Trying his hardest to avoid shedding tears himself, Allen jabbed his friend. The situation had two medicines: the intravenous kind, and the kind brought about by laughing.

"Goddamit, Mike, what are you doing?" Allen asked when he saw Young's tears.

"I don't know, it just sort of hit me."

"Well, knock it off."

On January 13, 1995, just shy of a month after receiving his diagnosis, Allen began his first round of chemotherapy. Cocksure by nature, he had always taken pride in his appearance, and the way he came off to people. So, on January 17, when the last strips of hair fell to the floor from his clippers—a pre-emptive strike against the natural byproduct of the treatments—he said, "I'm surprised people look at me different, because I forgot I look different."[15]

Allen was back in his element. Removed from the radiation, the nurses, and the drip, drip, drip of IVs, he was in front of the media, people he had embraced over the years, wise-cracking.

"My staff makes fun of me, but they would make fun of me even if I had my legs cut off."

By February, the tumor was already reduced to half its original size and was scheduled to be fully removed by March. The calendar had turned, the diagnosis was more promising, and Allen was sure he would be good to go by the start of the season.

"You would never have known he was sick," says Tom Mason now. "He never changed; he always believed in having fun. His big statement was, 'If it's not fun, let's not do it.' The players picked up on that."

His lifestyle, on the other hand, had taken a drastic hit. Allen was revered for both his coffee habits—twenty a day, it was rumored—and his beer-swilling. That was not beholden of a man suffering from cancer, one who needed to change his ways in order to fight and survive. So, as best he could, Allen decided to give up one of his two vices.

Naturally, he decided to give up coffee.

"I had to give up coffee or beer, and I made the right choice," he deadpanned.[16]

With the aggressive nature of Rhabdomyosarcoma, Allen was given a 50 to 60 percent chance of survival. But Dr. Carolyn Collins, the director of medical oncology where Allen was undergoing treatment, was seeing what she needed as his therapy progressed. "Things are going quite well," she told local Boise media. "He's been wanting the tumor to shrink, and he's very happy about that."[17]

With his hair a distant memory, Allen, who had experienced his first serious decrease in white blood cells—"that's a good thing," he said—met with his team for the first time since the national title game. It was the culmination of a tumultuous month. It was also a necessity for Allen, who needed to get back on the field with his players to make sure they could all move ahead and prepare for the upcoming season.

"He looks really good," Ikebe said after the meeting.[18]

That became apparent over the coming months. As February rolled by, armed with a renewed sense of vigor and the ability to sell their future as Division I-A members, Pokey and his staff hit the recruiting trail, hauling in the top class in the Big Sky. His diagnosis had not been a derailment or a deterrent to prospects; in fact, it seemed the Broncos, fresh off their title game appearance, were as hot as ever.

"If anybody in the league thinks they did better than Boise, they have a dream coming,"[19] said Eastern Washington head coach Mike Kramer in assessing the conference's recruiting efforts.

With the jump to the I-A level upcoming, the Broncos were no longer recruiting against other I-AA opposition. They had their eyes on players who were a touch bigger, a bit faster, and slightly more developed.

For the staff, that meant knocking on doors they may have bypassed in previous years.

"We had a great year; we got a lot of great people, and we recruited against the Pac-10, the WAC, the Big West," said Allen once the class was official. "It's the best year I have had at any school."[20]

However, the momentum the Broncos were gaining came to a halt on March 1. After initially flirting with the idea of staying on at Portland State as their head coach, then staying loyal to Pokey for two seasons, Al Borges was officially leaving. The Oregon Ducks had come calling, and Borges was on his was to Eugene to work as offensive coordinator under Mike Bellotti, who had recently taken over for the departed Rich Brooks (who was heading to the NFL as the St. Louis Rams' new head coach).

It was a striking blow for Allen; Borges had been under his tutelage for almost a decade, and the two had a bond that flowed far past where the football field ended. They were brothers—not from blood shared, but from blood spilled. They had been through football wars together, caravanning the ups and downs. They lived together, drank together, cried together.

Now, just three months after Allen's diagnosis, an opportunity had presented itself so great that Borges, thirty-nine at the time, saw no other choice.

"My biggest reservation was Pokey's health," Borges told *The Statesman Journal* after the move was official. "Any other time this would not have been as difficult, but I didn't want to make it look like I was running out on him."[21]

The nine-year ride alongside Borges had been more than Pokey expected. When he joined Allen's staff at Portland State in 1986, Borges possessed an offensive mind that few in the country could replicate. That he had stayed loyal to Allen for so long spoke more about him as a person than his decision to leave.

"I have said from day one that he has to take that job; I don't want him worrying about me and my cancer," Allen said.[22]

Dave Stromswold, who had been coaching the offensive line for the Broncos, take over as offensive coordinator.

* * *

In July of 1995, six months after his diagnosis, Allen underwent a stem cell transplant, leaving him hospitalized in serious condition. Stranded in Seattle, Washington, he had nothing to do but sit back and let the medicine, and his body, do the work. His own blood cells, which had been infused back in Boise, would take up to ten days to take effect in his body.

"His sister lived really close to me up in Seattle, so in the summer I went to see him quite a bit," says Greg Erickson, who played under Allen from 1993–1995. "Pokey and I were really good friends . . . we were really, really close."

Allen's stay in the hospital lasted nearly an entire month. At one point, after a bad reaction to the chemo, it looked as if he may not make it home. But he never lost his fire, telling Dwight Jaynes of the *Oregonian*, "I think this is going to make me more intense, day to day. You just don't have any idea how much time you have left."

He would improve enough to leave the hospital for his sister's house in late July, where he packed up his bags a few days later and headed back to Boise. There, he had eighteen starters set to return, a new recruiting class to welcome in, and a farewell parade for the members of the Big Sky that would be left in the Broncos' dust.

But as players filtered back into town, the sight awaiting them was in stark contrast to the one they had left after the prior season. With the radiation taking over more and more of his body, Pokey entered through the door a shadow of the figure that once walked in its place.

Now nine months into treatment, he had been living without the tumor for nearly six months. Two days after the tumor had been removed, the Missouri Tigers men's basketball team wore shirts adorned with the phrase "Get Well, Pokey." The Tigers' head coach, Norm Stewart, was a survivor himself, having beaten colon cancer six years before.

All around the world of collegiate athletics, Pokey and his health were on the tip of peoples' tongues.

Everyone, that is, except Pokey himself.

"He told us, 'You know, I have a rare type of cancer; it's usually found in kids, but I got it. And I'm going to beat it. I might be gone a bit more for treatments, but it's still business as usual,'" says Jason Payne.

Although the Broncos had lost a lot of talent from the previous season, big things were still expected. "We are a lot more solid this year than last year," Allen said during fall camp. "We have a lot of good players coming back, but we are very thin in some positions."[23]

As the season drew near, it was not uncommon to find Pokey curled up on his office couch, lunch resting in his belly, sound asleep between practices. Two-a-days are hard on healthy eighteen year olds; for a middle-aged man battling cancer, it proved impossible. He would rest when he could, watch film when he could, then stomp around, demanding more attention to detail from his players when he could.

But as the days went by, the tasks Allen was able to perform began to dwindle. Still, compared to the resplendent lighting and the monotony of the hospital, the practice field was pure bliss.

September 9, the season opener at Utah State, put to rest one of the most tumultuous off-seasons in program history. Two weeks later, after the Broncos started the season 2–0, winning both games 38–14, the mojo that had swelled up during the 1994 season began to reappear. Borges was gone, but the offense was still sharp. Tony Hilde was now a junior, and one of the top signal callers in all of I-AA. The 1995 season, the Broncos' swan song before their exodus to the big leagues of Division I-A, looked as if it may be a good one.

Then, in the blink of an eye, it all fell apart.

Loss to Montana (54–28). Then to Northwestern State (22–17). Then Northern Arizona (32–13). After the positive start, the offense, now ceased to exist. The defense, whose success had been instrumental during the playoff run the year prior, was inconsistent.[2] Most of all, the energy was gone. Although nothing was imminent, Pokey's demeanor, spirit, and presence was . . . *off.* That was reflected in his players; they were young, but not immune to the reality of what was happening to their coach.

By this point, doctors had told Pokey that he had a 30 percent chance of living another five years. The tumor was gone, but the cancer was spreading. He was running out of options; his hallmark *never-back-down* attitude had invigorated his players on numerous occasions. Now it was beginning to fade. At one point, as the losses piled up, Allen told reporters, "I don't think they can give me any more chemo. If this last deal didn't get rid of cancer, I guess I'll just have to tuck my head between my legs and kiss it goodbye."[24]

The players had other ideas. By now, after what they had gone through, a hardened shell of resistance had built up inside them. For decades, the Broncos had prided themselves on doing things *their way.* They didn't possess fancy facilities, and they certainly did not let uncomfortable circumstances get the best of them.

"Our team meeting room was literally underground; concrete walls, concrete ceilings, drips coming through the ceiling, old,

---

2 The Broncos defense had given up 108 points in those three losses. Compared to the 1994 season, it took until the sixth week of the season for their defense to give up as many points (112).

incandescent lights; it was a place you can imagine torture being done," says Erickson.

If the translucent 1994 season reinforced anything, it was that the program was capable of handling any type of adversity—on or off the field.

Now, they had something bigger to fight for. They had their coach, all the good and the bad that he brought with him in this moment, needing positive vibes to propel him through.

The players couldn't make him feel better physcially, or stop his body from shutting down, or from the disease spreading inside of it. All they could do was win football games and bring a smile to a sick man's face . . . and that's exactly what they did.

Tapping into their championship DNA, the Broncos would win their next five games of the season. They won close games (27–17 over Idaho State in Week 7); blowouts (40–14 over Weber State in Week 6 and 49–14 over Portland State in Week 8); and shootouts (63–44 over Eastern Washington in Week 9). A season-ending loss to Idaho could do little to squelch the joy that had been brought back into Pokey's face as the season came to a close.

7

THE PASSING AND THE NUTT

"Boise State was the loudest place I've ever played, with the smallest amount of people; it was crazy how loud it got there."
—Hut Allred, North Texas, running back, 1995–1998

BY LATE DECEMBER of 1995, Pokey Allen's health was beginning to make a turn—this time, it seemed, for the better. After another round of scans and examinations, in a statement released by Dr. Collins, it was announced that, "There was no indication of cancer anywhere in Allen." After the bleak diagnosis just months earlier, the about-face sent a shockwave of excitement through the program.[1]

The next eight months were a whirlwind. Allen was tackling the two biggest tasks of his life in one frail body: the continuing cancer treatments to ward off anything that might be lying dormant, and the on-going battle of his football team.

By August of 1996, there was again excitement and tension running through the city of Boise. Finally, the Broncos were going to get their shot as Division I-A members. Although it would take the mandatory three years for them to reach a maximum number of eighty-five scholarship players avilable, it mattered little. Allen's health was improving. Sixty-four years since their inception as a junior college, the Broncos were finally in the big leagues. All seemed harmonious when viewed through the proper prism.

Through it all, Allen had gained a healthy respect for what was important—and, just as much, what was *not*. "When you think you could die, it's kind of hard to worry about whether the *Idaho Statesman* is going to write an ugly article about you," he cracked.[2] His spirit seemed as sanguine as ever.

That was on August 4.

Two days later, on August 6, in a gut-wrenching blow, he took a medical leave of absence.

After returning from the Big West Conference meetings in Dallas, Texas, Allen visited his doctors for a check-up. What they found was the news that all involved knew could pop up, ready to strike at a moment's notice.

The cancer had returned, having now spread to both lungs. Although it was not known at the moment the extent of the cancer, it was ominous.

"I am a little scared. I'd like to act braver than I am, but I'm scared," Allen said at the time.[3]

The day Pokey took his official leave of absence, he, along with Bleymaier, walked into Tom Mason's office at 2 p.m., sat down, and delivered the news long feared, but often thought as unrealistic. "Gene told me, 'The cancer's back, and Pokey's gotta go out of the country to get some alternative treatments up in Canada.' He left, and I became the interim coach in our first Division I-A year."

A week later, he would undergo surgery in an attempt to remove the tumors. When he came out of anesthesia, his doctor, Ernest Conrad, painted a bleak picture. "He still has tumor problems," he said. "The long-term prognosis is guarded."[4]

Guarded. It was a word never before associated with Pokey Allen. It was the opposite of how he had lived his life. But now, in an instant—a long, agonizing instant, spread over the past two years of ups and downs—the best anyone could do was look at Pokey with that type of feeling. As he sought treatment in Vancouver, Canada, living with longtime friend Jerry Bradley, Allen did the only thing he could: he put pen to paper. Working alongside Bob Evancho, Pokey wrote a memoir, aptly titled, *Pokey: The Good Fight.* In recounting his life, his family, his career, he spoke with confidence and intellect.

When it came to write about his current status and how he was feeling, he finally let his guard down.

"I'm here because I'm told I'm running out of time and conventional Western medicine is not going to cure my affliction. I'm here because I think I can beat the cancer that has spread to my chest and lungs.

"But I have to admit, I'm here because I'm running out of options."[5]

With Pokey seeking treatment in Vancouver, Tom Mason had taken over the football team. He was well respected around the country; the players liked him and wanted to play hard for him. But it was not meant to be; he was out of his element, and taking over the team under the most dire of circumstances. From the outset on August 6, when he was named the interim head coach, everything was a mess. For Mason especially, the task of stepping in for his friend was a worst-case scenario. Almost making it worse was the fact that Pokey was still, at times, his spunky self, despite the debilitating treatments. By late August, Allen was consuming almost sixty pills per day.

"He's an amazing person," Mason said. "He has the greatest outlook on life, no matter what he's up against."[6]

As the Broncos ushered in a new era as members of Division I-AA, the man who played a large role in seeing it come to fruition was far removed.

"I'm going crazy up here, while everything happens down there," Allen bemoaned from the couch in Vancouver at the time. "Really, I'd just like to go home."

Unfortunately, so too did those involved with the team. The Broncos started off 1–1, an opening season loss to Central Michigan followed up by a win over Portland State. The win over the Vikings was a nice flicker of promise, but nothing more. From September 14 to November 9, the team lost eight games in a row—many in embarrassing, lopsided fashion. It was everyone's fault, and yet at the same time it was no one's fault. Try as he might, Mason was not Pokey; not in acumen, not in his ability to lead, not in any of it. Mostly, he was handed an impossible deck of cards to play with, and it showed. The team was a shell of its potential.

Their heart and soul was home, sick, ravished with illness.

On the field, Mason's defensive unit was almost non-existent. In one four-game stretch, they gave up 202 points. The offense, despite the return of Hilde for his senior year, resembled nothing of the units that flourished under Allen. During that same stretch, they would manage just 56 points of their own.

Due to the nature of Allen's illness and the harsh realization that Mason was not a long-term answer, Gene Bleymaier had to make some phone calls. Sickening, near-insensitive phone calls. As the athletic director, he had no choice. No matter how they sliced it, Allen was not going to be back as the head coach. Aside from the possibility of him returning for a game or two, he would not be on the sideline again.

With that knowledge, Bleymaier had to begin looking to 1997 and beyond.

* * *

Pokey was the last coach on earth to mince words; he was also the last one to complain to you about his problems. For the Boise State team of 1996, this was both a blessing and a curse. They knew their coach was deathly sick; there were too many signs to think otherwise. Pokey had tried his hardest to keep the depths of his illness from the team, but the writing was on the wall.

"I think he treated us like parents treat their kids; he didn't want us to worry about him," says Greg Erickson. "He was really sick that offseason [before 1996]. He was bald and really, *really* thin; threw up all the time at practice. It was hard."

His efforts to keep the severity of his illness quiet were noble in nature, but futile in practice.

"The program was at an all-time high, and Pokey was very popular," Gene Bleymaier said during the season. For Bleymaier, Pokey represented his crowning moment up to that time as Boise State's athletic director. After two middling hires in Setencich and Hall, his reputation as a talent evaluator rested heavily on Allen's ability to pull the program out from the level of "average." Now, after all that had happened, and with the program finally on track, the scene had turned sour. "He was very vibrant and enthusiastic. It was unfathomable to believe he had terminal cancer."[7]

Deteriorated. Frail. Listless. These were not words used to describe the Pokey who had blown through Portland State and, for a brief time, Boise State. Cancer takes a physical toll on you; what was so striking about Allen was what it was taking from him internally.

"His public persona was a little goofy," says Ken Goe, a reporter for the *Oregonian*. "He loved to drink beer, loved to chase women . . . very folksy sense of humor. Witty; not at all a 'details guy,' really, but a sharp eye for talent."

On November 8, Allen called Boise State officials and told them he was coming home, and would be flying into town two days later. He attended practice on his first day back in town, and on that Saturday helped guide his 1–9 team to a thrilling 33–32 victory at New Mexico State on the strength of a 22-yard touchdown pass with 14 seconds to play. "I was a little emotional when I walked on the field," Allen said after the game. "Then I felt like I was never gone."

If Pokey was emotional, his players—and Mason and Bleymaier—were honored. The season may have been a failure, but getting Allen a win as I-A coach saved it all.

"The month before he passed away, we had the pleasure of him coming out on the field, one last time—he was going to go through one more round of chemotherapy—and I remember him acting no different that day than he did eighteen months before," says Payne. "Same outlook on life; lived it to the fullest. It was just going to be OK . . . there wasn't a fear that we were going to lose him."

But they were. The ability to coach a game at the I-A level had sparked Allen, if only for a moment, to his old self. It was a final dose of his aura that had won over so many people.

"We had a little magic out there today," Hilde said after the game. "We just believed. I don't know if that's Pokey, or what, but he's never given up, and so we couldn't give up, either."[8] Hilde had directed the game-winning drive—Pokey's first and last victory as a I-A coach—with broken ribs, his toughness a direct descendent from the coach who was leading him.

On November 25, 1996, penning an article for *Sports Illustrated*, Christian Stone wrote: "Allen was sorely missed in Boise, where he had been an inspiration, often urging his players to 'stud up.' Dig deep. He kept in touch with his team through daily phone calls to interim coach Tom Mason and by viewing videotapes of the Broncos' games.

"In his absence the players erected a wooden sign that read 'STUD UP, POKEY ALLEN '96' over a door of the Varsity Center. Every day, they would touch the sign on their way to the practice field."[9]

Allen's final recruiting class, completed while he was in the midst of chemo sessions, was, in hindsight, a gift to the university. One of his signees, a young, slightly undersized quarterback by the name of Bart Hendricks, recalls the process of meeting Pokey, gloomy outlook and all.

"During the recruiting process, he was in remission," says Hendricks. "He came to my house, and at the time he was great. He kept saying, 'Yep, I'm good, everything is fine.' It was between that time, from the winter to the start of fall camp, that the cancer came back."

Allen's reputation among his peers when he arrived at Boise State was that of a cut-up, carefree, freewheeling kid trapped in a man's body. During his time in Boise, his players came to see the same thing.

When things turned, it was too hard to ignore.

"I could tell, when I got to campus in the fall of 1996, that he did not look right," recalls Hendricks.

* * *

On Monday, December 30, 1996, just over two years after his initial diagnosis, Pokey Allen passed away back in his hometown of Missoula, Montana. He was fifty-three years old.

"I was back home for Christmas break, in San Diego, and I read in the paper about Pokey being in the hospital, and that he was resting comfortably," says Payne, his voice cracking at the memory. "I didn't think much of it; then two days later I got a call from coach [Ron] Gould that he had passed away. I had a feeling it was coming, but I didn't expect it. He was always upbeat, though. He had a couch in his office, and he would take a few more naps. He would always say, 'Shit, cancer isn't so bad. I can still drink beer.' He always found the positive in something."

Pokey's death, while not a shock, hit his players right in the heart. For them, he was more than a coach; he was a pal, a quirky uncle, and a mentor. He could just as easily pat them on the back as kick them in the rear end. He could be both of those men in mere seconds.

"If you talk to every guy [from Pokey's final recruiting class in 1996], they will tell you the reason they came here was because of him," says Hendricks. "We never really had a chance for him to coach us, so we didn't know what his coaching style was. We just knew based off his personality what he was trying to do."[10]

* * *

When Pokey Allen officially retired from Boise State on Wednesday, December 11, 1996, just three weeks before his passing, the program found itself at the ultimate crossroads. Tom Mason was the popular in-house choice among players; he was an Allen-guy, he knew the school, he knew the players. However, his abysmal showing as interim head coach had dented any chances he had at the head spot.

"I really felt like if I could have taken over that team, two years later we would have been a really good football team. We were in the right direction," Mason says now.

Mason had been Allen's right-hand man, his good friend and confidant. On top of that, he was a defensive mind who would have kept stability and cohesion inside a locker room that was in mourning. The entire stretch from Allen's diagnosis in 1994, until his untimely resignation and passing, had been a drain; Mason could be the help the players needed.

During their time together, Mason says, the Utah Utes inquired about Allen. So did the Calgary Stampeders of the CFL. For Pokey, it was never about where he could go; it fell more to the men around him. "He was more, 'Hey, where do you guys want to go?' I think he would have rode that thing out at Boise for quite a while."

It made sense. From the moment he accepted the position, Allen and Boise shared a kinship as outsiders, against-the-grain figures in their fields.

Where rudimentary behavior and stereotypical coach-speak had roamed before, with the likes of Knap and Setencich and Hall, Pokey had been a breath of bewilderment and innovativeness. While Mason lacked the vivaciousness of Allen, he was still a friendly face. Players knew him, boosters knew him, administrators and ticket sellers and security guards knew him. He was Allen-lite, but there was enough spark from the match that Pokey had lit to justify giving Mason a shot.

The Broncos narrowed their coaching search to seven primary candidates. Aside from Mason was Al Borges, as well as Montana head coach Don Read, who had led Montana to the I-AA title in 1995 and was, in some eyes, the frontrunner.

Nick Aliotti, brother of former Boise State quarterback Joe Aliotti, was also in consideration. Gene Dahlquist and Dirk Koetter would get a look. Based on their history, and the direction the program was hoping to take, Borges seemed to be the no-brain hire. After he left Boise State for the University of Oregon following the 1994 season, his reputation in the football world had only improved. Under first-year head coach Mike Bellotti, Borges's vision, the one that began to take shape during his final year at Boise State, took off. The Ducks roared out of the gate, averaging 36 points through their first six games. Though they hit the skids during the second half of the season, their offense still knocked out just over 27 points per game on the season, good for 39th in the country. Included in there were wins over 12th-ranked UCLA (38–31) and 15th-ranked Washington (24–22).

The following year, Borges was off to Westwood to take the same position for the UCLA Bruins, who had seen all they needed to see. Although UCLA was not as talented as his Oregon team the year prior, Borges once again shone bright; the Bruins scored nearly three points more per game in his offense. Despite the shift in philosophies, and starting a sophomore quarterback in Cade McNown, the Bruins scored just over 30 points per game. Two years removed from his time in Boise, Borges had solidified himself as one of the up-and-coming coaches in the country. He was young. He was eager. And, perhaps most importantly, he wanted the job. *Badly.*

Unfortunately for Borges, Gene Bleymaier was not as easily persuaded. Just under two thousand miles away (1,831 to be exact), in the sleepy town of Murray, Kentucky, a man by the name of Houston Nutt coached the Murray State Racers, a football program existing in the shadows of bigger, more successful ones in the Southeastern Conference. He coached well enough to pop up on radars across the country. After playing college football at both Arkansas and Oklahoma State, Nutt had cut his teeth and made his name as the receivers and quarterbacks coach at Oklahoma State, most notably during the time Barry Sanders was scampering to a Heisman Trophy. He returned to Fayetteville, Arkansas, for the 1990 season, spending three years there before joining the Murray State Racers of the Ohio Valley Conference.

The Racers brought a rich tradition of coaches—Mike Gottfried, Ron Zook, and Frank Beamer had already been though the school—and Nutt, who had visions of returning home someday to coach his beloved Razorbacks, jumped at the chance. During the 1995 season, as his team scored a school-record 421 points, he won the Eddie Robinson Coach of the Year Award for Division I-AA. In 1996, for the second straight season, Nutt's teams swept through their conference schedule; they finished 11–2, won the school's first-ever playoff game, and Nutt once again cleaned up on the postseason award circuit.

Although he was gaining a reputation as a future big-time head coach in the south, Nutt's name barely registered out west. Murray State was buried in both Kentucky and Division I-AA. The Broncos were still distancing themselves from those days; they were looking up move up to the big leagues, not to take a step back. Borges was the future. He was Pac-10, high-octane, and familiar. Nutt, if his name ever rolled off tongues, came off as an outsider, a smallball guru, too far removed to matter.

However, as he had proven time and again, Bleymaier did not much care for the obvious. He was forward thinking and a risk taker. Al Borges was safe.

Houston Nutt was not.

One by one names were checked off the list. Mason? Done. Then Borges. Then Dahlquist and Aliotti and Koetter, the latter of which was passed up for the second time after initally showing interest in 1992. In the eyes of Bleymaier, Nutt was the stimulation the program needed in the wake of tragedy. His energy and recruiting savvy was the ticket to I-A success. In Nutt, with his southern drawl, his "yes ma'am" and "no ma'am" persona, families would swoon under his presence and send their young boys to be men under his watch.

He would sell to them as he had sold to Bleymaier, and as he would sell to the current players on campus.

His goal coming in would be to remind those around the program of what the game is supposed to be: fun. Early on, it worked. Everything he had been advertised was proved valid.

Because Houston Nutt is also a living, breathing tornado.

Pokey Allen was cut from a cloth unseen by the cookie-cutter world of Western college football. Tom Mason was a nice man, a good man, but not ready for the job.

But, Nutt?

"Houston Nutt brought the flair. He did. He brought the showmanship," said Derek Olley, an offenisve lineman for the Broncos who played under Nutt.

Flair and showmanship were traits that Allen had in droves, backed up by toughness, accountability, and a keen sense of when to put an arm around you and tell you it would be all right. He was the perfect blend of splashy side dishes and a substantial dose of meat-and-potatoes.

But, again . . . Nutt?

"When the staff changed, and we got Houston Nutt . . . " says Ron Pound, his voice trailing off.

" . . . man, that guy was as lively and exciting as you get. It didn't matter if you were in the locker room, or standing in front of the cameras, he was a wild man."

Houston Nutt was born in Little Rock, Arkansas, in October of 1957. Followed by three younger brothers, Houston was bred for coaching. His father, Houston Sr., and mother, Emogene, both taught at the Arkansas School for the Deaf in Little Rock for over thirty-five years. His father was the school's athletic director and men's basketball coach.[11] Houston had no choices in the matter; he was going to teach, coach, or do both.

He did, and he was fun, boastful, dramatic, and a showman of the highest regard. However, as the Broncos were soon to find out, Nutt was also the perfect pitch man.

For the school. For the program. But, mostly, for himself.

"He was a good coach as far as X's and O's, but in front of the cameras he would always preach the sermon about how religious he is, and behind the scenes he was totally different," says Jason Payne.

His tenure, already ominous for the circumstances he was entering into following the death of Allen, would prove to be an odd mix from the get-go. Taking over for a popular coach was one thing; taking over after an untimely death, robbing young men of their leading figure, was another. "You could tell there was an imprint there that he left. So I embraced it. I embraced coach Allen. Some of the things he did, you don't want to ever take that away, because players believe. You could tell, especially the seniors. They're the backbone," says Nutt now.

When he was officially hired on December 26, 1997, the players he was inheriting—initially and with assured reasons—met Nutt with an arms-distance approach. For his part, the coach understood. The stamp Allen had left was still felt in the hallways, both figuratively and literally.

"One of the first things they said was how much they loved coach Allen," says Nutt. "There was a sign in the locker room that we kept . . . it said Saddle Up, or Bronco Up. You could just tell the imprint of what he left: hard work, commitment. All of those things we tried to carry forward."

The perception of Houston among players early on was that he checked off every box that a coach should. He was successful and confident, bordering on cocky. He expected to win. He also played fast and loose with the rules. As the old saying goes, rules were meant to be broken; Nutt abided by that. The structure and parental nurturing needed to chaperone college players was an afterthought under Nutt. While Allen had been a jokester, players knew the line; they knew where it landed and what the consequences were should they cross.

It was evident early into Nutt's tenure that no such line existed.

"I started using a lot of creatine; at the time, that was big. Guys were using a lot of creatine in the weight room," says Derek Olley, "but I took it to a whole other level: I started taking it with 40oz of Old English. I would take the creatine, dump it in with the Old E, every day, and drink it. I was gaining between two to four pounds per day. Before I knew it, I had gained 65 pounds."

For Boise State, 1997 edition, nothing was off limits.

Nutt's coaching style was out of left field—especially for a group of kids from the northwest who were not accustomed to their coach's burning southern drawl and the quick eye he could flash when speaking of past successes.

"[Nutt] had a bag of rings. He would bust out this black velvet bag full of rings and he'd say, 'Guys, I think I know a thing or two about football.' Championships from all levels," says Olley.

Coming from Murray State, Nutt felt right at home in the country spaces of Boise. He knew the history of the program; of Lyle Smith and Jim Criner, and of what Pokey had begun to rebuild.

"Going back when it was a I-AA, there was success. I just felt like, 'Man, we can win here.' So we took over the program," Nutt says, looking back. One of the reasons Gene Bleymaier hired Houston was the transition of going from I-AA to Division-IA; he felt like, after his successes at Murray State, Nutt could bring the transition full-circle.

"I tell ya—the players, everyone was excited. Gene was building the add-on of the stadium; that was exciting," Nutt says.

When the season began on August 30, Boise State figured to snatch a victory and get the season off on the right foot—or so they thought.

Instead, they got crushed. Destroyed. *Humiliated.*

Of all the possible opponents, Cal State Northridge waltzed into Bronco Stadium and breezed to a 63–23 win. It was embarrassment wrapped in atrocity. The Broncos were not just bad: they were lifeless.

"The fans booed us. They hit us with taco shells from the seats. And rightly so—we were pretty poor," says Olley. After the loss, in front of a record crowd of 26,824, Nutt had already displaced himself from the locals. His team allowed six touchdown passes from CSN's quarterback Nate Flowers while benching his own quarterback, Nate Sparks, in favor of freshman Bart Hendricks.

In terms of debuts, it was as bad as it could get.

The situation would only get tougher the following week when the Broncos packed their bags for a cross-country trip to Madison, Wisconsin, to take on the Wisconsin Badgers at famous Camp Randall Stadium. Looking back, despite the team's disastrous debut and the daunting task of taking on a

Badgers team that roughly resembled the MonStars from *Space Jam*, Nutt says his team showed zero fear.

"None. None. And as the game went on, I could see the confidence building; the more we hung around, the more I could see these guys getting more and more confident. The stadium got quiet, and that's when we knew, 'Hey, we can beat these guys.'"

They nearly did. The 28–24 loss to the Badgers, although not something the players would openly admit, was a boost for the program. Despite the 0–2 record, going toe-to-toe with a Big 10 power, in their own building, showed the players that they had the talent to do good things the rest of the season.

"Houston showed us that we shouldn't be afraid, no matter who we played. It doesn't matter; we're all going to line up, we're all going to put on helmets, we're all going to play," says Josh Alvarez, an offenisve lineman who was among a handful of players to play under Allen, Mason, and Nutt.

The Broncos' near-win gave Nutt all the ammunition he would need in getting his players to buy into his abilities. This was not a middling team that they went in and lost to; the Badgers would win eight games, five of them in the loaded Big 10. If Boise State could compete for four quarters with them?

It was a sign. It had to be . . . right?

"Wisconsin had all these players. They had Heisman Trophy winner Ron Dayne," Nutt says. "But I kept telling our players, 'Guess what? They can only put eleven guys out there at a time.' We're going in with the mindset that we're going to take care of the ball, we're going to get two or three turnovers, and we're going to be in it come the fourth quarter. And that's basically what happened."

The Broncos would trip up the following week on the road at Central Michigan, then secure their first win of the Nutt-era the following week, a 24–7 win over Weber State. The hope that a victory would push them in the right direction was just that: hope. The following week would be a road game at 15th-ranked Washington State, quarterbacked by the eventual #2 overall pick in the 1998 NFL Draft, Ryan Leaf.

Washington State wasn't the bruising, suffocating, road-grading meatiness of Wisconsin. Instead, it was an aerial castration.

Leaf would throw for 356 yards, the Cougars would rack up another 209 on the ground, and the Broncos would be outclassed, outhit, and out performed in every category. They limped home with a 58–0 loss, which could have been worse had the Cougars not taken their foot off the gas. The Broncos were 1–4 on the season; they had no semblance of identity on either offense or defense, and were now staring down the barrel of yet another losing season.

After the game, Nutt was singing a slightly more bitter tune than he was just three weeks prior in Wisconsin. "We're not overall ready to play this kind of schedule," he told the gathered media.[12]

It wasn't hyperbole. They fielded one defensive end and two linebackers who weighed *less* than Ryan Leaf. Physically, in their second I-A season, the Broncos were still light years behind schedule.

Wins against overmatched New Mexico (52–10) and North Texas (17–14) settled the locals for a moment, but six weeks into the season, the team was in need of something. What the "something" was, no one quite knew.

It would not manifest.

Three losses followed, dropping the Broncos to 3–7, the same record Pokey had accumulated at the same juncture during his first season. But this wasn't Pokey. It wasn't comforting. There was no plan, just Nutt's spouting of clichéd coach speak, golly-gee euphemisms in a locker room that, leery from the get-go, was beginning to see through the unfazed coach. The keys to the offense had been turned over to Hendricks, signaling two thoughts: one being a bright spot for the future; the other a clear punting of the current season. Hendricks was talented and driven, but the task of leading a team—and willing them to victories—was still out of his reach.

The November 8 loss to Nevada, in which the Broncos surrendered 400 passing yards by halftime was the bottoming out for a shattered team. Although Hendricks would shine, throwing for 287 yards putting up 42 points, the defense was non-existent. Mentally, the team was done.

After the game, the freshman quarterback painted a rosy outlook for the gathered media, dealing of better days ahead.

"It's frustrating. You score 42 points, almost half of 100, and come away without a victory," he said. "It shows what the potential is of our offense. We got outscored. We would score a touchdown, and they would score right back. It was, like, man, I've got to get a rest sometime."[13]

Hendricks's comments could have come across as a blow to the gut of his defense, except that he was spot-on.

To close out his freshman season, and with an opportunity to build *any* momentum, the Broncos closed out the 1997 campaign with a trip to Moscow to face Idaho.

The Vandals still had a chokehold on the rivalry; the Broncos had lost 13 of 14 in the series. The game was on the road. Boise State was a mess, internally and externally. Idaho was a win away from clinching a winning season. All signs pointed to a long afternoon, bereft of joy.

Then, seemingly out of nowhere, Gene Bleymaier stepped in.

"It was the first time Gene had come down to our office during the middle of the week," says Nutt, reflecting back. "A Tuesday in the staff room, and he looks at my coaches. He says, 'Y'all do understand how important this game is?' And we kind of nod. He says, 'No . . . do y'all UNDERSTAND?' He then went over some basics. When he left that room, I told the staff, 'Uh, guys . . . it's very, very important.'"

In a year in which seemingly everything had been upside down— the hiring of Nutt over more familiar coaches; the benching of Sparks and insertion of Hendricks; the blowout loss to Washington State and near-upset over Wisconsin; all of it made zero sense.

So, of course the Broncos, massive underdogs in a game they had no business winning, would do just that. An overtime thriller, on the road, a team splintering internally, galvanized for one last hurrah. Boise State 30, Idaho 23.

But if the players thought that the win could somehow be the magic potion to a life of order and structure, reality offered up a different outcome.

Thirteen days after the win over Idaho, one day shy of a calendar year since Pokey was forced to resign, Houston Nutt bolted. He took a red-eye from Boise to Fayetteville on December 10 to become the new head coach of the Arkansas Razorbacks, tucking his tail between his legs, avoiding any semblance of decency, and disbanding his duties as coach in the process.

This is the opinion of a lot of players who were left in Nutt's wake. Ask some, and they will say he rode off on the wings of the devil. Others will say he was barely a blip in their lives, and good riddance. Some remember him fondly.

Most roll their eyes, while others are still dumbfounded by the turn of events.

"One thing I've learned is that coaches will all tell you when they're coming in, 'This is the job I've always wanted.' And then, the minute something better comes along, this ain't that job anymore," said Derek Burrell, a defensive end for the Broncos under Nutt. "The thing with Houston, I don't think it was the best of terms, because he never spoke to anybody. He never talked to the team and told us he was leaving or anything like that."

Burrell's reaction and pause speaks volumes all these years later.

"He just . . . left."

Nutt's fly-by-night experiment had ended before any traction could be made. In the here today, gone tomorrow world of college football, where coaches are bound by contracts that snap like old rubberbands, Nutt had taken the concept of moving up to an absurd level.

From the day he was introduced at Boise State to the day he was on a flight to Arkansas, 348 days had passed.

"Boise State is always going to be a stepping stone for coaches. Even former players who become coaches, because they're going to have to go. We can't keep them here forever, so embrace this place as a tree," says Olley.

But Nutt's lack of communication—not even a team meeting to give his side of the story—soured his players. Stepping stone or not, there is a right way and wrong way to handle things. Nutt had done the latter.

"I found out Nutt was leaving because it was on the news. It's always hard when that happens, because you have a group of guys that works hard for the coach and he takes off in the middle of the night," Burrell continued. "He's already off to Arkansas, and this family back here he's moved on from. Now he has a different family."

Nutt left Arkansas after his 10th season in 2007, surrounded by controversies and turmoil stemming from myriad issues. He spent four years at Ole Miss after that, again leaving a cloud of stench behind. Recently, he and Ole Miss settled a lawsuit after Nutt claimed board members of the school, and the Rebels' then-head coach Hugh Freeze, had made disparaging remarks about him behind the scenes.

As Nutt found out after leaving Boise State, the grass isn't always greener. He claims that the Arkansas job came out of nowhere, blind-siding him and his family.

"We [the staff] loved the place. Loved the community, loved the school. Really, with no Boise State, there's no way I would have gotten the Arkansas job."

The respect he had for Pokey Allen when taking over is apparent. But Arkansas was home—"Dreams do come true, and this is a dream"—he said during his introductory press conference, his hand resting on an Arkansas helmet.

Just like that, as quickly and as blurring as he came, he was gone.

He was 4–7, and then he was gone. He was obnoxious and rude, and then he was gone. He was refreshing and energetic, and then he was gone. He was dismissive and effusive, and then he was gone.

He was just . . . gone.

The Broncos would be looking for their fourth coach in three years, a rate of turnover almost unheard of in collegiate sports. For a school that had two coaches from 1947–1976, the shock was visible.

Luckily, one of the people who had survived the turnover was Joe Kenn, the team's strength and conditioning coach. The strength coach has the most access and the best relationship to players year-round. Never was it more important than now; his mentorship kept the players pushing through during the tumultuous time of Nutt's departure.

"The most influential guy was Joe," says Burrell now. "Joe was the heart and soul of our group; he brought us together. He was even more influential than the coaches."

Kenn, who by this point had served as the program's strength and conditioning coach under Allen and Nutt, had become a sounding board for those who were reeling. Players who had heard all of Nutt's rhetoric, and eaten it up like candy, were now turning on the TV or reading the papers and seeing the exact same message, word-for-word, being told by him to his players at Arkansas.

"That was a tough year for a lot of people," says Kenn. He carefully pauses, even all these years later, mindful of his words.

"I don't want to say anymore."

Nutt had used Boise State as a springboard. It's not uncommon in the sport, but doing so in less than twelve months had been the ultimate slight.

"In terms of who they were as people, Pokey and Houston were total opposites. He and Nutt were night and day from each other.

Pokey would get on you, but there was no grey area; he was very honest, very upfront, and he would tell you like it is," says Payne.

In the green room where he is a member of CBS Sports' college football coverage, Nutt lays his figurative cards on the table. When the topic of leaving Boise State on such abrupt terms is brought up, he lets out an audible sigh. Through the phone you can feel his consternation.

"I got a call from back home. That's the only reason I left Boise State, was because where I grew up. I was born and raised in Arkansas. Coach Broyles called me . . . it was a tough time to leave after that short of time. I hated to do that, but the only reason I did it was because it was where I was born and raised."

Nutt's departure, abrupt and, to most, disrespectful, was yet another blow to a program that had felt too many in too short a time. On the other hand, the suddenness of it left plenty of time for Gene Bleymaier to make the most important hire of his tenure.

Nutt told Bleymaier on the evening of Tuesday, December 9, that he was leaving for Arkansas. It was his dream job, one he had worked his whole life toward. That he was at Boise State for less than one year was of no consequence to him; after the call to Gene, that was it.

Then, in the middle of the night, as oddly and out-of-the-blue as he arrived, he was gone.

8

DIRK KOETTER'S
THIRD TIME IS THE CHARM

"Dirk brought stability and accountability. The biggest thing
he brought, to me, was expectation. The guys there had gone
through Pokey Allen, Tom Mason, Houston Nutt . . . Koetter
was there for what seemed like an eternity to us. One thing he
used to say all of the time, which really stuck, was 'Nobody
has higher expectations of us than us.' He really instilled that
in us and brought us some confidence."
—Jeff Copp, Boise State, 1997–1999

GENE BLEYMAIER was staring down his fourth coaching
search in twelve years, and second in less than one calendar
year. This time, he did not have to look far into his Rolodex to
find his next hire.

Within minutes of Houston Nutt's departure, Bleymaier was
on the phone, making the call he should have made one year ago,
nearly to the day, before he went against his better judgment.

He called Dirk Koetter.

In hindsight, this was the easiest hire Bleymaier had made, and before the clock struck midnight on his whirlwind day, Koetter and the Broncos were united. After passing on Koetter before the 1997 season and after a brief, by-the-book interview back in 1992 before going with Pokey, this was a no-brainer.

"It was like God was telling me, 'You're not going to be the coach at Boise State, son,'" Koetter would later say of being passed up twice before. "I wasn't mad that I didn't get it, but I was mad deep down inside because I knew I was the best man for this job."[1]

Koetter was born just down the road in Pocatello, Idaho, home of the Idaho State Bengals, but that meant nothing in the grand scheme of things. His alumni allegiance was irrelevant in the moment. The chance to return home, to take over the top program in the state, was too good an opportunity to pass up.

So, this time, when Gene called there would be no interview. For him and his family, Boise State was the place they wanted to be. Finally, Bleymaier felt the same way.

"We think the future of Boise State is very bright,"[2] Koetter told the arranged media following the formal announcement of his hiring. He was just thirty-eight years old, but came equipped with thirteen years of coaching experience and a lifetime of understudying. His father, Jim, had been a coach at both the high school and collegiate levels. Dirk grew up around the game, immersing himself in his father's knowledge.

His age belied his experience, which he had in spades.

What Koetter brought most visibly to the job was an outstanding offensive mind; with him came visions of what the Broncos were building under Pokey Allen and Al Borges. Their parallels were so in-line that Koetter had actually succeeded Borges as the offensive coordinator at Oregon following the 1995 season, when Borges left for UCLA.

In an eldritch way, with the hiring of Koetter, the coaching tree from Pokey had come back around to where it belonged, with a Nutt-sized hole in the middle.

Although he was young, Koetter had earned his stripes; his reputation and his track record were crisp. The year prior, while at Oregon, Koetter's offense put up 31 points per game, good for 24th in the country, and he had done so with a team largely devoid of top-end talent. Although he had quarterback Akili Smith, who would become the 3rd overall pick in the 1998 NFL Draft, Oregon was not the *Oregon* that they would morph into years later, when conference titles became the norm. They were a middling team. With them, Koetter was able to take a raw roster, with an even more raw QB, and electrify the Pac-10.

Once that was done, any trepidation Bleymaier had in December of 1996 when he passed on young Dirk was now a distant memory.

"He has prepared himself very well," he said at the press conference. "He is ready."[3]

As Koetter prepared to enter the press conference, butterflies crashing into the walls of his stomach, he received a clear message of what he was walking into. As an offensive coordinator, he was set up for criticism, but did not have to stand on the firing line.

As the head man, he had nowhere to hide.

Walking into the small room, overflowing with local press, a raucous fan sitting some 50 feet from him stood up and bellowed, "Beat Idaho!"

No more hiding. It was time to work.

* * *

Although the Idaho State Board of Education still ruled with an iron fist, allowing only one-year contracts for coaches at the time, Bleymaier was clear that the days of uncertainty and looking out the window to see what was coming next were over. Koetter was *the* guy.

While the ink on the contract said one year, Bleymaier noted, flatly, "We have committed to him for four years."

No questions, no second-guessing.

"I am very aware of the expectations of the community for the football team," Koetter said at his press conference. He had led the Idaho State football team to the Division I-AA title in 1981, the year after Boise State claimed their lone title since moving up from the junior college ranks. That year, in front of 20,000-plus fans, Koetter, alongside his teammates, walked into Bronco Stadium and defeated Boise State, 21–10.

Through osmosis, Koetter had been ingrained with the culture of the school for most of his life. He had seen the very best of Boise State, as well as the worst. In December of 1997, no coach on the market—no coach capable of galvanizing a community, a program, and a team—had what Koetter had: moxie, talent, and, after what had just taken place with Houston Nutt, a deep desire for the job.

When Koetter went back to his office to assess the situation he was taking over, he found a mix of good and bad news. The Broncos were returning all but a couple of starters from the year before—"That's the best thing I've heard all day," he said—but those returning players had been run through the mental and physical ringer the previous 24 months.

Seniors on the team had been recruited by Pokey Allen, coached by Tom Mason, and suffered through the blustery and cockamamie year of Nutt.

Now, they would be going through another coach and another message.

Because of the special circumstances, Koetter was going to be part coach, part psychologist, part friend, and part father figure.

He would retain two assistant coaches from the previous staff, Dan Fidler and Darryl Jackson, hoping to keep the slightest bit of familiarity for the players when they returned for spring ball.

When Mark Helfrich was brought on as the team's quarterback coach later that December, along with Mark Johnson and Brent Myers, the staff rounded into form. Helfrich, in particular, would be a sounding board for Koetter; both were at Oregon together, learning under Mike Bellotti, with Helfrich serving as Koetter's graduate assistant.

As his staff came together, Koetter set about the task of selling the most important recruits on his vision: the current crop of players on the roster.

Backup quarterback Bryan Harsin, who would go on to be the head coach at Boise State starting in 2014, recalls the moment the ice began to melt. The first time he met with his players, they sat around their lockers, eyes fixated on Koetter, a no-nonsense type of guy who did not mince words on where his heart was.

Or, for that matter, where it had been for a while.

"He had interviewed when Houston [Nutt] got the job. So when [he] got that job, I remember he was introduced to the team, and one of the first things out of his mouth was, 'You should have hired me in the first place.' I liked it. I liked the edge, and immediately I was drawn to him," Harsin told *SB Nation* in 2016.[4]

With one clear message of loyalty, Koetter had gotten the players to initially buy in, slightly.

His era officially kicked off on September 5, 1998, when the Broncos ushered in what they hoped was the *final* fresh start. Dan Hawkins, who had come over from Willamette University, a small NAIA school from Salem, Oregon, to be Koetter's offensive coordinator, recalls the hesitation that players had toward the new staff. Players were still eyeing them from a distance; as fall camp was ending, their guards remained up.

"When the staff arrived, there was a real Teflon-feeling; nothing we said to the players seemed to stick," says Hawkins. "Initially, there was no buy-in or ownership from the players."

Boise State's first three games under Koetter—a season-opening 26–13 win over Cal State Northridge; a 33–21 loss to Washington State; and a 44–24 win over Portland State—helped slightly. They were 2–1, but had yet to play particularly well. Plus, all three games had been played in the comfort of Bronco Stadium. What was needed, it seemed, was a sense of bonding; for the players, but most importantly for the players *and* coaches.

A Week 4 trip to Utah would be that chance.

For Koetter, his first road trip was an opportunity for the lessons he had been preaching to come to fruition: work ethic, knowledge, caring for yourself and your teammates, attention to detail.

On September 26, in Utah, Boise State found themselves trailing in the fourth quarter, 29–24. Although Bart Hendricks had already thrown three touchdown passes during the game, Koetter was panged by a nagging feeling. Something about the situation felt . . . *different*. So, when the Broncos took over with 2:08 left in the game and the ball on their own 1-yard line, he sent out backup Nate Sparks at quarterback.

Sparks, who had played sparingly to start the season, had thrown 10 touchdown passes the season prior. He was experienced at this point; Hendricks still was not.

For Koetter, this was a do-or-die moment early in his tenure. If the experiment went up in, well, sparks, any credibility built up over the first three and three-quarter games would dissipate. Pulling Hendricks if he had been struggling would have made sense regardless of the outcome. Pulling him despite his positive play, only to see the team go down, would lose Koetter the locker room.

But Sparks came through; 99 yards and a game-winning touchdown later, his instinct had proven right. Boise State walked out of Utah victorious, 31–28. Koetter had scored the biggest win of his career in the most bizarre of ways. The Broncos, at 3–1, were believers.

In some senses, the win over Utah would go down as one of the most important in Broncos' history. What the victory did for the emotional state of all involved, by allowing the players to fully buy in to the "Koetter Way," and by laying out the tangible proof that the plan in place was set up for the long run—all of it was accomplished in one come-from-behind road win.

"All of a sudden, the players saw concrete results for all the hard work we had put them through. It was like they finally realized, 'OK, these coaches know what they're doing.' I don't think the players were sold on that until Utah," Hawkins says, looking back.

Hendricks was also becoming more in-sync with what Koetter was offering. He was the most analytical of all the quarterbacks, and although he appreciated what both Allen and Nutt had brought in terms of their rah-rah attitudes, the way Koetter visualized the field and laid out game plans for the team was exactly what he needed.

"Dirk was all about preparation. If I had to lean one way, I was more on the Dirk side. The emotions of Nutt could only take you so far. But with Dirk, it was, 'You prepare, you're going to be confident, you're going to be successful,'" Hendricks says now.

With one road win, the season began to take on a different feel. Players were now excited to come to practice, to put in the extra work. It had paid off on the scoreboard. The results were no longer a vision but a reality.

"Coach Koetter is probably my favorite coach I have played for; that guy knew football," says David Lamont Mikell. "He had confidence, he knew what he was going to do, and he knew it was going to work. We weren't cocky about it, but we knew we were going to win every game."

They didn't. Not close. However, the sentiment was evident in the way the Broncos finished the year. Despite four more losses, including two blowouts to Louisiana Tech (63–28) and Nevada (55–24), Boise State was on the correct path. They had found a coach with a clear vision and the sense that, for a while at least, he was theirs. They also had Hendricks. His sophomore campaign gave flashes of pop that had the staff salivating at what could be. Hendricks finished the season completing nearly 54 percent of his passes with 13 touchdowns and 6 interceptions. Most importantly, he commanded the offense in a way that both unnerved and galvanized his teammates.

"Hendricks, to me, was a catalyst to a lot that was going on. The winter program [before Koetter's first season], Bart was the first guy to call out the team and not worry about the repercussions," says Joe Kenn.

Although he had entered the 1998 season locked in a battle with Nate Sparks for the starting spot, it was evident that Hendricks possessed something different. "Everybody talks a good game, but everybody wants to be friendly," says Kenn. "He called out the team, not in an asinine way, but in a way where he wasn't afraid for guys to be pissed off at him."

From the time he arrived on campus before the 1991 season, the final under Skip Hall, through the Nutt fiasco, Kenn had helped guide the program though unimaginable circumstances. When they made the transition to Division I-A, he was the one tasked with getting not only the returning players, but also the influx of JC transfers, up to the proper size and speed. It was Kenn who lent listening ears to players who never felt heard during Nutt's tenure. Now, after helping them through yet another transition, he sensed it was all coming together.

"When Koetter came in, it built a sense of, 'OK, now we're going in a direction with somebody who is going to bring stability to the program,'" he says now.

Along with Dirk, coaches like Dan Hawkins and Mark Helfrich were also getting the approval and respect from players.

"I learned more football in my first fall with Dirk and [Mark Helfrich] than I ever thought I would learn in my life," says BJ Rhode, who backed up Bart Hendricks at quarterback. "We feel like he established a new culture—you would come in, you would stay for four years. Dirk would find guys who didn't really fit the bill of a college football player, and the next thing you know he's doing great things."

* * *

The Broncos' 6–5 finish in 1998 was their 14th season since 1980 in which they won fewer than 10 games.

However, Gene Bleymaier knew that Koetter, a fast-rising star in the football world, would not be long for the cause, despite his initial season's mediocre record. Coaches like him don't last at college football powerhouses; they disappear even faster at a school like Boise State.

For now, though, he was theirs.

On January 15, 1999, just weeks after the season ended, reports began to surface that Green Bay Packers general manager Ray Rhodes was prepared to offer Koetter the job of quarterbacks coach, after the man who previously held the position, Andy Reid, had taken the head coaching position for the Philadelphia Eagles.

The extent that the talks got to is unknown. Still, it was clear that Koetter's name was going to start surfacing for jobs around the country.

So, on Tuesday, January 26, Bleymaier and the Board of Education used the universal equalizer in an attempt to keep Koetter from bolting: they tossed an obscene amount of money at him.

Koetter's shiny new four-year contract worth $625,000 was loaded with incentives and a backslap of gifts: clauses rewarding championships, victories, and academic performance standards for his players sparkled throughout.

For good measure, a country club membership was tossed in, too.

Koetter was going to leave at some point; this they knew. Offering this kind of contract, and ensuring it would be a couple years in the future, was all Bleymaier could do.

"Although we squirmed a little, we realize you have to pay to have a competent coach," said Thomas Dillon, who was the president of the Boise State board. "If there are people who have a problem with the contract, if they want to make that kind of money, my advice to them is to become a successful football coach. That's what the market demands."[5]

There were plenty of reasons for optimism heading into 1999, the school's fourth year as a Division I-A school. First and foremost was the return of Hendricks, who was entering his junior season after guiding the Broncos to the 24th-best offense in the country during his sophomore campaign. He was one year bigger, one year stronger, and equipped with a supporting cast befitting of pre-season accolades. Alongside the veterans, 27 freshmen had redshirted in 1998, infusing the program with fresh legs. Throw in the return of the entire coaching staff, seven starters on offense and nine on defense, and Koetter had every reason to look at the 1999 season as the turning point the program envisioned when it offered him the massive contract.

"I am so much better prepared to be a head coach in my second year," he told gathered media before the season. "I found it's much harder to be the guy who solves everyone's problems."[6]

After seven different stops as an assistant coach, the forty-year-old Koetter's grace period was over. With the talent returning to the blue turf, and the pressure of living up to his lofty contract, year two was pressure-filled from the moment players reconvened for fall camp. The momentum was sleuthed a bit when it was announced on August 11 that four players on the roster—running back Joe Stallworth, defensive tackle Tony Altieri, Shaunard Harts, and Aristotle Thompson—would all be facing disciplinary issues for off-field behavior. Stallworth, a freshman, was kicked off the team, while Altieri and Harts would miss the opener against UCLA. Thompson was suspended for the first three games.

"It's like they are our own children," Koetter said when the punishments were handed out. "There are discipline things you have to take care of, but you love them, and you want them to get better."[7]

Despite the minor setback, the summer was for officially welcoming players back from their homes, ready to take on the season. There were smiles and laughter, and the energy that only youthful exuberance and a new beginning can bring.

Then, in an instant, all of that vanished.

During a practice on Wednesday, August 18, freshman defensive tackle Paul Reyna landed awkwardly on the turf during a drill. The impact caused him to suffer a torn blood vessel between his brain and skull; still, he walked off on his own power, grabbing a seat on the sideline. Shortly after, Reyna began complaining of discomfort, and paramedics administered oxygen and intravenous fluids before rushing him to the hospital, where he underwent emergency surgery just weeks into his collegiate career.

But it was too late. The bleeding had developed into a blood clot, and on August 23—five days after the injury—Reyna passed away at 2:20 p.m. PST in the intensive care unit at Saint Alphonsus Regional Medical Center.

Reyna, who attended La Puente Bishop Atma High School in La Puente, California, was just nineteen years old. The night of his passing, members of the entire Boise State athletic department, including athletes from the football team and various other sports, were scheduled to gather inside Bronco Stadium to kick off the school year.

Instead, shortly after 7 p.m., Koetter, flanked by Dan Hawkins and assistants Tom Nordquist and Dan Fidel, arrived to deliver the news. Awash in tears, Koetter choked through the announcement of Reyna's death.

It wasn't long before the news spread throughout the community. Reyna's teammates were devastated. Although they all knew of the risks football presented, this was something altogether new. For many, this was a wake-up call, perhaps for the first time in their lives, of how quickly a life could be taken.

"We had to accept the fact that Paul could have been us, and it could still have been," says Jason Turner, Reyna's classmate and fellow lineman. Perhaps the age and innocence was a blessing in disguise, cocooning them from the ultimate reality.

"There was nothing wrong with him. It's not like he had a pre-existing condition; it just *happened*," says Turner. "It was eye-opening in the sense that the game we were playing since we were kids . . . turned out to be more than a game. It made us appreciate the game more, and respect it."

For the second time in three years, the university was dealt an unimaginable blow. With Reyna, the suddenness of his passing was perhaps the hardest for teammates and coaches to accept.

Koetter would be facing the biggest challenge of his life; not only did he have an obligation to make his team better . . . now he was doing so in the face of grief and shock, with nearly a hundred young men looking to him for guidance.

"It's been extremely difficult," he told the Associated Press from the Rose Bowl in Pasadena before the opening game against UCLA. "We obviously took last week off to take care of business. It was pretty solemn. That, coupled with the fact that we hadn't practiced for a long time, we were pretty numb."[8]

Somehow, the Broncos would have to lace up their cleats and play a football game. In some ways it was the truest way they could honor Reyna. Running out of the tunnel, every member of the team adorned a #95 sticker on their helmet, the number their fallen teammate would have worn.

And here they were in the Rose Bowl, perhaps the most mystical and famous stadium in all of college football. Only eleven days after Paul's passing, his teammates stepped out into the California sunshine with nothing to lose, yet everything to play for.

"We had already lost a teammate. Even though this is just a game, that game felt like something bigger," says Turner.

Unfortunately, despite missing 12 players themselves due to suspension, UCLA would run circles around Boise State. The Broncos would fall, 38–8; they played tough and with a clear determination, but the Broncos still lacked the up-front talent to hang with a team like UCLA.

"When you go to a school like Boise State, who had just recently gone to D-I . . . as a kid, you're just happy to be a D-I player. But the mentality was, basically, that we could play with anybody," says Derek Burrell. "You really don't know any different. We went to UCLA, and I really thought that we were more physical than them. We hit harder, and I thought that we were stronger."

The scoreboard, and those watching, might have disagreed.

"We all called ourselves 'The Pac-10 rejects.' We knew we could play, we just lacked the tangibles," says David Lamont Mikell. That had certainly been the case against UCLA. The Broncos' physicality was never the issue; they were just missing a piece here and there. The score was lopsided, but Boise State walked out of the Rose Bowl feeling good about what they had done.

A Week 2 win against Southern Utah (35–27) was followed by a loss to Hawaii (34–19). Suddenly, the fire and fury that Koetter had promised was threatening to disperse; that's when the leadership of the team shone through.

The seniors called a players-only meeting. No subject was off-limits.

"It was really awkward at first. There was the core group of upper classmen, and then us freshmen. No one knew us, and then we got off to a bad start. Everyone was beat up, tired, and worn out from everything that had happened," says Turner. "The seniors then had a players-only meeting in this old abandoned room under the stadium. We had a chance to talk about whatever we wanted and get everything off our chests.

"Basically, we came out of the meeting with the attitude of, 'We've lost two games already. We've lost a teammate. The season can't start off any worse than it has.' But the guys in the room left all of the bad stuff there. We realized that we just had to play for each other."

A handful of players led the meeting, prompting swift changes in both attitude and performance. Dismayed by their play to that point in the season, players finally said "Enough." It was terse, it was emotional, and it was necessary.

"We were not happy with the standard; we wanted to create a new one," says Matt Strofhus, a fullback for the Broncos. "Every player needed to put it on their back that what we were doing wasn't OK."

Accountability, be it in the weight room, the film room— whatever the situation—was now the focal point. The coaches only carried so much weight; the Broncos' players were looking inward to find what they were made of.

"After we lost to Hawaii, we all said, 'We don't want that feeling from here on out.' That's really where we started to pick up steam," says Strofhus.

The results were immediate; they would win three straight against New Mexico (20–9), Utah (26–20), and Eastern Washington (41–7).

On top of the emotional impact from the meeting, a new, subtle shift in philosophy from Hawkins and Koetter—opening up the playbook and letting Hendricks throw the ball more—began paying dividends. Before the Broncos faced Nevada on October 23, Koetter—noting that stagnancy that had overtaken the offense—threw caution to the wind. If they were going to win, and win big, they needed to start throwing the ball . . . a lot.

"I was thinking," Koetter told the *Reno Gazette-Journal*, "if we don't improve on offense, we might not win another game."[9]

Before the Nevada game, the Broncos were averaging 22.5 points per game; against the Wolfpack, they scored 52. Hendricks would throw for 241 yards and two touchdowns. The conservative approach that had shackled the team was gone.

The Broncos averaged 47 points per game over their next three, setting up a vital trip to Moscow to end the season against Idaho.

Despite their recent dominance in the rivalry, in one game, it became clear that the Vandals no longer belonged on the same field as Boise State.

"Someone once observed that while Idaho was winning all of those games in the '80s and '90s, Boise State was building facilities," says Bert Sahlberg of the *Lewiston Tribune*. "So, when Boise State caught up, there were no comparisons. They had state-of-art everything; they built up the stadium. When they turned the corner, they *really* turned it."

The "caught up" was now. It was Koetter, and Hawkins, and Hendricks.

"He kind of instilled that cockiness in us," said quarterback Ryan Dinwiddie, who was backing up Hendricks at the time. "We're going to go out and win. We started believing. We started winning."[10]

If the rivalry had become dormant in the eyes of Broncos fans due to their lack of recent success, November 20, 1999, was its awakening. Boise State showed no let-up in their dismantling of the Vandals, skipping away with a 45–14 win, the Big West title, and a clear message: something big was beginning to take place in the western corner of Idaho.

"We didn't know how long Koetter was going to be there, but we knew *we* were all going to be there, and we were going to win some football games. That feeling only snowballed," says Strofhus.

The win also secured a Humanitarian Bowl berth, which would be played in Bronco Stadium. The Broncos had won 11 of their previous 14 games at home, cementing the blue turf as one of the toughest—and most outlandish—home-field advantages in the sport.

"The blue turf is a cultural thing. It started out as a, 'What is going on?' but it's become the symbol for a lot of things: we're different, we're blue-collar, we do a lot more with a lot less," says Hendricks now.

There would be no better time to display that than in a bowl game against the visiting Louisville Cardinals of the Big East.

Before preparations for the bowl game began, Hendricks had to make a quick pit stop to collect a couple awards: the Big

West Conference Offensive Player of the Year and MVP, to be exact. His regular season had been electric, accounting for 30 overall touchdowns: 22 of them through the air, while nabbing another eight with his legs.

"It's not one thing, but its every thing," Hendricks says now when asked about his improved play from year one to two. "You can't pinpoint it, but you focus on the little things, when you're in the moment—on the practice field, in the weight room, in the classroom, you just work as hard as you can in that moment to be the best at it."

The Humanitarian Bowl would be played on December 30, in front of 29,283 fans, bundled from toes to nose in an attempt to escape the blistering Idaho winter. The game would also be a homecoming of sorts for Cardinals' head coach John L. Smith, who had previously coached at Idaho and Utah State. His familiarity with Bronco Stadium gave him pause when assessing the game. "It'll be a hostile crowd," he said as his team prepared to board their Boise-bound jet. "I don't really think the kids will realize until they get there. They're going to get after us. I know it will be packed, but we don't care who people will be cheering for."[11]

Smith, who had gone 5–1 against Boise State as the coach of Idaho and 2–0 when he was at Utah State, had been witness to the mental game the cold and wind could play when combined with the blue turf.

Despite having gone 9–3 on the season, besting Louisville's 7–4 record, the Broncos were two-point underdogs on their own turf. That motivation, and the emotional moment of silence before the game to honor Paul Reyna, was all the Broncos needed.

Before the game, all 99 scholarship players gathered around a plaque honoring Reyna, as did every member of the coaching staff and the Louisville football team.

"I think about Paul's death every day," Koetter said two days before the game. "It was one of the toughest things I'll ever go through, and I'm not just talking about as a football coach, but as a person. It was so hard for everybody involved."[12]

The Humanitarian Bowl was an opportunity for players to close a chapter in their lives, one that would be hard to believe if it came straight out of Hollywood.

"The things we've been through, it's been a crushing change," said Hendricks. "We had the death of a coach, the death of a player. This is destiny."[13]

Willie Van Gorder, a senior offensive lineman at the time, said of Reyna, "He's the reason we're out there playing. Every time we rub his face as we go on the field, it's just a reminder that he's with us. I know he's there."[14]

It was even more evident once the game began.

Behind a breakout game from Brock Forsey, the scrappy freshman running back who gained 152 yards on the ground, the Broncos held off the Cardinals for a 34–31 win, capping off their championship season. Hendricks threw for 335 yards and a touchdown, outplaying Louisville's Chris Redman, who was being hailed at the time as a surefire NFL player.

"I didn't expect to have this good of a game," said Forsey afterward. "I knew I'd do a good job running the ball, but I have to give a lot of credit to the offensive line. They opened a lot of holes for me."[15]

Koetter joked with the media after the game, saying, "At the beginning of the season, Brock had come up to me and said he was mad he wasn't getting to play more. I said he needed to improve in some areas, and he did."[16]

In one of the more emotional postgame moments, Hendricks spoke profoundly of the seniors; of their leadership in helping the team navigate through the shock of Reyna's death, much like they had been guided their freshmen season when Pokey Allen passed away.

"This game was definitely an emotional experience for all of us," he said. "This win is great for the seniors. After all they've been through, it's a great way to finish it up."[17]

On August 23, 1999, a group of brothers lost one of its own in a tragedy. On the second to last day of the year, in a game and season dedicated to his memory, they ended up on top. It wouldn't bring Reyna back, but in an all-out attempt to honor his name, they had done the only thing they could do.

They had gone out as champions.

9

IGNITION

"You can't help but respect what Boise State has done. It really is amazing what they went from, to what they've become. If you really pinned Idaho Vandals fans down, they would say, 'Oh, yeah, I respect it. But I don't like it.'"
—Matt Baney, sports editor, Lewiston Tribune, covering the Idaho Vandals

BEFORE THE 2000 season began, the Big West Conference conducted a poll among local newspaper beat writers, asking them to pick their predicted conference winner. When all was said and done, 26 of 29 reporters picked the Broncos to secure their second-straight Big West title. Five of the six coaches that were polled did as well. New Mexico head coach Rocky Long went so far as to say that the Broncos were "the class of the league, and I would guess they're expecting to be as good as they were last year."[1]

The strong finish to the 1999 season—and the plethora of talent returning—made the Broncos the clear choice to not only win their conference, but potentially make some noise on the national stage, too.

"We went into 2000 thinking, 'We'll just repeat what we did last year.' We just said we'll win the Big West and go back to the Humanitarian Bowl," says Bart Hendricks now. "To us, at that time, that was the only bowl game we were ever going to. Never did it occur to me, or us, to go undefeated. In 2000, we could have. But it wasn't in our mindset."

Before the season had even begun, the Big West—viewed almost unanimously as the weakest conference in the country—decided to pull the plug: the 2000 season would be the final for the conference's football teams. From the outside, it didn't appear to be a big loss; only Boise State carried a shred of respectability, and it was obvious that the Broncos were due for bigger things.

As the offseason drew to a close, the Broncos' potential for dominance was at the forefront of the conversation. However, the praise heaped on his squad did not sit well with Koetter.

"One of our goals for this team is the approach of the hunter," he said when the polls were released. "We can't allow ourselves to listen to the people who tell us we're the hunted."[2]

Once again, the outlying reason for optimism was Hendricks. He had entered Boise State in 1996 as a self-appointed "football player" more than a quarterback. When he left Procter R. Hug High School in Reno, Nevada, the 6-foot, 200-pounder was an improvisational wizard more than a gun-slinging signal-caller. It hadn't stopped then-head coach Pokey Allen from courting, but no one would have pinned Hendricks as a future star. Allen, to his credit, had seen something different. He saw a student of the game, a player with an almost maniacal attention to detail, and a kid who was an old soul, wise beyond his years.

When teammate and roommate Davy Malaythong walked into the dorm he shared with Hendricks for the first time four years prior, it was obvious that he wasn't bunking with an average eighteen-year-old.

Plastered over the wall running alongside his bed in their quaint room were dozens of index cards, the playbook detailed out on them, being absorbed by the studious Hendricks.

"At first, I thought I would be living with a junior college transfer," Malaythong said.[3]

"When I first got to Boise State, I wasn't really a quarterback yet. I just got thrown into the role," Hendricks says now.

So he studied. And studied. And studied some more.

The slow burn of improvement had taken off like rocket fuel during his junior year in 1999 once Koetter pulled the reigns off of the offense. The kid who entered Boise State as an athlete was now officially a quarterback. Hendricks had turned into a full-fledged leader; the team, seeing what they could be with the proper mentality, followed suit.

"Things started changing when summer workouts took off. We never really did that until my senior year, when guys stuck around to train," says Hendricks. "And I think that made a huge difference; not just from getting into shape, but the bonds it built when you're doing your own practices, running your own drills, without your coaches involved."

With nearly every major passing record in sight—both for Boise State and the conference in general—Hendricks was no longer a secret around the country. His name was now sitting side-by-side with the nation's best—be it Chris Weinke of Florida State, Michael Vick of Virginia Tech, or any other top-tier name from a bigger, more established school.

"Any time you come off a season like we did, you expect more from yourself," he said as the season approached. "Once you taste blood, you want more."[4]

He was starting to *sound* like a killer; his play was backing it up. The team was not far behind.

"You could tell things . . . we certainly had our road blocks, but the attitude was different. Going into my senior year [in 2000], it was something that we knew was going to be special," he says now.

Heading into the season, Boise State had all of the pieces to put together a massive run game. Joining Hendricks in the backfield was Davy Malaythong and Brock Forsey. Koetter couldn't help but boast about the other side of the ball, too—specifically his all-everything corner, Dempsey Dees.

"I've been coaching college football a long time," Koetter said, "and Dempsey is probably the best corner I've ever been around."[6]

Dempsey led a secondary unit set to anchor the Broncos' defense. Despite teams avoiding throwing the ball in his direction as much as they could during the 1999 season, Dees still led the team with six interceptions.

When the season kicked off on September 2 against the New Mexico Lobos, Hendricks would put forth a workman-like performance, throwing two touchdowns and rushing for one more, propelling Boise State to a 31–14 win. It was just the second season-opening win for the school since 1995. It was also their seventh straight win dating back to the previous season.

After a Week 2 win over the Northern Iowa Panthers (42–17), it was time, once again, for Houston Nutt to reemerge onto the scene. The Broncos were making the cross-country trip to Fayetteville to take on the Arkansas Razorbacks and Nutt, who were in the midst of a 14-game home win streak. Unlike their season with Houston at the helm, which had been stagnant and, for the most part, boring, the Broncos' offense under Koetter was electric. Against the Panthers, Hendricks had completions of 38, 87, 42, and 32 yards. The team had runs of 46 yards (twice), and Forsey continued his evolution into a reliable everydown back, having racked up 265 yards and three touchdowns through two games.

The Broncos were also developing an attitude off the field. Confidence and swagger had replaced a feeling of unease. But the week of Arkansas brought about a more buttoned-up approach, begging the question: did they still use Houston Nutt as lighter fluid for their drive?

Possibly.

Did they dwell on him, almost three years later?

Hardly.

"The attitude among us was that we were always hungry to prove to people that we could play with them," says Derek Burrell, a defensive end for the Broncos. "We never got respect; we were always disrespected, because the media and people never gave us the respect we deserved. We had points to prove."

In the eyes of many in college football, as members of the fledgling Big West, the Broncos were still well off the radar.

"Nobody is going to respect us; we're always going to be the underdog, so we have something to prove every week," says David Lamont Mikell, a running back for the Broncos. "That's the mentality Boise State has taken for a long time."

The mentality was there. And, for much of the game against Arkansas, they backed it up with their play. In front of 54,286 fans chanting "Whoo! Pig Sooie!" Boise State waltzed into Arkansas and went toe-to-toe—not just with the Razorbacks, but with Nutt, as well.

"We were just rolling on offense. It was fun to be a part of it," says Hendricks.

After Razorbacks QB Robby Hampton hit Bob Williams for a 54-yard touchdown, giving them a 38–31 lead, it was on Hendricks and the offense once again. For a minute, it looked as if they were up to the challenge. After driving to the Arkansas 9-yard line, aided by a long completion to Andre Banks, the Broncos faced a 4th and goal situation. Taking the snap from the right hash mark, Hendricks dropped back and found receiver Jay Swillie open near the goal line, fully across the field. His pass zipped into Swillie's arms perfectly, near the left sideline/coffin corner to the end zone.

That's as far as they would get.

Arkansas cornerback Eddie Jackson reached Swillie just before he crossed the goal line, forcing him out of bounds inches shy of immortality. Replays made visible to the home viewing audience showed Swillie gliding over the white chalk goal line. As it was, in 2000, instant replay was not yet a thing in college football.

Game over. Boise State, after traveling 1,588 miles for one of the biggest games in school history, came away two inches short of victory.

"If we have replay back then, we probably get the touchdown," says Hendricks, still haunted by the potentially missed call. "They had good players, and we were right there with them. We should have beat them. We should have."

Two weeks later, after a 47–10 win over Central Michigan, the Broncos were back on the road in Pullman, Washington, to face the Washington State Cougars.

Unlike 1997, the Cougars did not have Ryan Leaf. But like two weeks prior, the Broncos would come up just short in their upset bid.

"We had no business losing to Washington State. None," says Hendricks now. Although he threw for 355 yards, and the two teams combined for nearly 900 yards of offense, it was the Cougars' Jason Gesser's late rushing touchdown that gave them the better end of the showdown. Hendricks's fumble sealed their fate, a 42–35 loss. Boise State, now 3–2 on the year, with both losses on the road to Bowl Championship Series (BCS) schools, came across as one of the most talented teams in the country. On their best day, they seemingly could hang with anyone. Now, facing a conference schedule featuring precisely zero true threats, it wasn't out of the question for them to run the table . . . and that's just what they would do.

"Then we didn't lose the rest of the year; Washington State was a real wake-up call," says Hendricks.

After four wins following the Washington State loss, on November 11, while cruising to another conference title, Hendricks would break five school passing records by throwing for 381 yards as they beat Utah State, 66–38.

The following week, he would put the final stake in the heart of the Idaho rivalry, throwing for a school-record 401 yards in a 66–24 win.

"The Bronco Experience," led by their all-everything quarterback, had turned into must-see football. Their 9–2 record was half the story; the dominating victories to close out the season (Boise State won their final six games by an average margin of 29.8 points) was a small part. Finding their place in the winner's deck of I-A, a place they had yearned to be for so long, was the cherry on top.

As he entered the Humanitarian Bowl against the University of Texas El-Paso (UTEP), Hendricks had already thrown 35 touchdown passes on the season; he was also a virtual lock to win his second consecutive Big West MVP award. On top of it all, he came in third place for the Johnny Unitas Award, given annually to the nation's top quarterback.

"In the quarterback room, Bart was awesome," says B. J. Rhode. "He knew we were there to win, and he was going to do whatever it took. He never tried to act like he was the man; he was a great teammate . . . he was a very quiet leader; he's not a big talker."

Hendricks had worked his way into the most decorated quarterback to ever come through the university. The coach-quarterback relationship between him and Koetter had been strained at times; other times they were like father and son.

"Coach Koetter and I had some clashes, some personality conflicts, that had to work themselves out," Hendricks says now. "They really didn't start smoothing out until midway through the 1999 season, when, what do ya know: we started winning more."

That would be an understatement. From the Nevada game in 1999 on, after the decision was made to open up the offense, the Broncos went 16–2 during the rest of Hendricks's time under center.

Unfortunately for the Broncos, along with Bart's graduation, the long-awaited reality of the Dirk Koetter era was also coming to an end.

After nearly two years of rumors, there was finally too much smoke in the *Koetter-going-somewhere* rumor mill for there not to be fire. The most widely reported landing spots seemed to center on the Arizona schools, with Arizona State leading the charge.

On Monday, November 27, reports began to surface that Koetter and the Arizona State Sun Devils had met to discuss their opening, which came after the firing of Bruce Snyder.

The following day, multiple outlets reported that the Oklahoma State Cowboys were hot on Koetter's tail, eschewing Les Miles and former player Mike Gundy.

Three days after that, on November 31, Koetter was going to Oklahoma State, per broadcast reports.

The day after that, he offically became an Arizona State Sun Devil—"The biggest mistake I ever made," he would later say.[7]

At forty-one years of age, and just two years removed from signing his four-year contract extension—the largest in school history—Koetter was moving on. His 26–10 record, admirable on the outside, paled in comparison to the impact he had made inside the program. The culture shift, the coaches he had brought in, and the offensive philosophy, all of it altered the course of the program. It was palpable.

Boise State knew what they had and what they were losing in both Koetter and Hendricks. The only thing left to do was ensure that the program would remain on course.

So, unlike three years prior, when Gene Bleymaier had to go outside the program to inject life, now all he had to do was walk a bit further down the hall to find his guy.

That's exactly what he did.

On December 4, Gene promoted Dan Hawkins to head coach.

10

END OF THE BEGINNING, BIRTH OF THE HAWK

"Jim Sochor [the legendary UC Davis coach] had a lot of assistants that went on to be very successful, including Chris Petersen, Gary Patterson, Dan Hawkins. All of these guys led to the school as being the cradle of coaching. I see Sochor's philosophical qualities in Hawkins, too."

—Greg Rodgers, UC Davis Alum

DIRK KOETTER'S SWAN song was going to be awash in nostalgia. Not only were the Broncos playing in the Humanitarian Bowl, taking place, again, on their home field, but their opponent, the UTEP Miners, carried a special place in his heart as well. He had coached at UTEP from 1986–1988, and was the offensive coordinator for the Miners during their bowl game in 1988.

The transition period between losing a coach, finding a new one, all the while keeping both your current players and the ones you are recruiting, can be a nightmarish juggling act for schools. For Boise State, this was bordering on silly. To begin with, Koetter's decision to stay on and coach the bowl game, despite his successor being on staff, could have created an ugly power struggle with Hawkins. Secondly, Koetter spent the better part of a week between the season finale against Idaho and the bowl game recruiting—for Arizona State.

"It's hectic; it's not something I would want to do too often," Koetter said of the bowl prep, which he returned for on December 15, just thirteen days before the game. "But if you compare if to a normal football game, we've had eleven days to prepare, instead of five or six. There's no reason to think we won't be ready."[1]

Except that, in hindsight, it was *not* a normal game. Not for the Broncos who, unbeknownst to them, were about to catapult themselves from successful mid-major into an era of unprecedented success.

They had their coach lined up. Hawkins, for all that was still unknown about him, came armed with the repute of an offensive wizard—one who would set the blue turf ablaze.

They had the successor to Hendricks in Ryan Dinwiddie, the would-be sophomore who already carried himself like the big man on campus. Essentially, the Humanitarian Bowl was going to be both the end of an era and the birth of a new one.

* * *

Long before Dan Hawkins ever coached his first game for the Broncos, he faced an uphill battle, one that could have altered his life forever. In reality, Hawkins should never have been the head coach of Boise State. He never should have coached anywhere.

The truth is, Dan Hawkins should never have seen his first birthday. By all accounts, and by all pre-existing notions on how the human body works, he should have died at a very young age, in his parents' arms, a baby taken far too soon. When he was just a few months old, Hawkins was struck with a severe case of pneumonia; the ailment was so significant that his family doctor, carrying the burden of reality, told his parents that it would take a miracle to keep the young boy alive. The only option, should they choose to allow it, was to prescribe a larger dose of medicine—the amount normally given to a grown adult.

His parents, desperate, said "go for it."

So the doctor did. Little Dan, small enough to be held in one hand, was flushed with large quantities of medicine, enough to take down a grown man, in an effort to save his fragile body.

The gamble paid off.

Within days, his condition stabilized.

From there, he would thrive. Hawkins would go on to play college football—first at the College of the Siskiyous, then later for UC Davis, where his craft would be honed. His coaching career began at UC Davis under the legendary coach Jim Sochor. Dan spent three seasons under Sochor, from 1983–1985, before accepting the head position at Christian Brothers High School in Sacramento for the 1986 and 1987 seasons. He bounced around after that until finally landing at Willamette University in Salem, Oregon for the 1993 season.

In five seasons, Hawkins led Willamette to a 40–11–1 record. In his final season of 1997 his team went 13–1, with their only loss coming in the NAIA title game.

He then made the leap, joining Koetter's staff in the spring of 1998.

Now, just four weeks shy of taking over at Boise State, it was time to do something that was very unnatural to him . . . he had to be patient.

As the bowl game against UTEP crept closer, one prevailing theme kept running through the Bronco locker room. It was, again, based on disrespect. The belief from some media members covering the game was that UTEP, a team loaded with players who doubled as stars on the school's track team, was going to gas the Broncos off the field. Boise State was "just the Idaho team with a bunch of walk-ons, the unwanted players," says B. J. Rhode, by this point entrenched as the team's backup quarterback.

However, the Broncos had an ace up their sleeve; if there was a way to counter the speed of the Miners, it was nature— Mother Nature, to be more specific.

With the temperature dipping into the freezing zone, the offensive aerial show between the two schools looked like it could be put on hiatus. Just before his final kickoff as the head coach of the Broncos, Koetter spoke to the importance of focus in the face of yet another array of distractions. "I told [our players] to stay focused, just as they have the past two years. If they do that, they'll be fine."

The blue turf, slick from the Boise winter climate, looked as if it would play a major factor in the gameplan of both teams. When Jim Barber of ESPN asked Koetter how the surface would affect his players, he replied, simply, "We're going to go downtown as often as we can. Our players are used to this weather."

He was spot on. Once they took the opening kick, Bart Hendricks tossed the ball all over the yard, eventually finding Jay Swillie for a wide open touchdown.

No resistance. No worries.

"And then we put it to them. We just *put it to them*," says Rhode.

His prediction was accurate, and the point differential did not reflect the level of the Broncos' dominance.

The scoreboard did not indicate it, but Rhode's assessment was spot on. When Andre Banks hit Hendricks for a late touchdown on a wide receiver pass, giving the Broncos the 38–23 win, Koetter was off to the desert a winner. After the game, in celebration of their tumultuous tenure, all nine fifth-year seniors took a victory lap around the turf one last time, honoring those who could not be with them.

Hendricks was one of the nine to have witnessed all a college football player could handle. His 316 yards and four touchdowns in the bowl game earned him the Humanitarian Bowl MVP. He had two touchdowns through the air, one on the ground, and one more receiving.

With the 2000 season complete, the first year of the new millennium, was in the books with a 10–2 record.

The next chapter, under Dan Hawkins, was now officially underway. His staff was nearly complete. Ryan Dinwiddie looked the part of the next great quarterback. Hawkins's top two running backs, five of his top six receivers, and seven offensive linemen from 2000 were set to return.

All there was left to do was to find an offensive coordinator.

* * *

To be declared a genius, it is often thought that an individual must possess an IQ higher than 140. As a whole, "genius" is a term thrown around far too often. Albert Einstein was, undoubtedly, a genius. Charles Dickens and Michelangelo were indisputable. But what exactly *makes* a genius? It's a rhetorical question with wide-ranging answers.

But you know one when you see it.

Chris Petersen's IQ score is not public knowledge. For all we know, he himself is not aware. However, from the time he graduated from UC Davis after the 1986 season and slid into the head coaching position for the freshmen team at the school, there was something about the slight kid with the toothy smile and sun-kissed skin that stood out to those around him.

Petersen's success, like that of Hawkins, can be traced back directly to his college coach, Jim Sochor, whose run of success at UC Davis is almost unfathomable upon first reading. He took over the Aggies program in 1970 and retired in 1988. In between, Sochor—whose coaching tree includes Paul Hackett, Mike Bellotti, Dan Hawkins, and Petersen—won 18 consecutive league championships, a Division II record. Under his mentor's wing and gentle nudge, Petersen decided to give coaching a try, bypassing his dream of being a school psychologist.

The philosophies implemented on Petersen would have a profound impact. In fact, it was after Petersen's first game as the starting quarterback at UC Davis where he would learn a life lesson that he has carried with him ever since.

After that game, a loss, which was tied back directly to the team's kicker missing a game-winning field goal, Petersen witnessed first hand how to handle adversity—and people—in the tough moments.

As Pete Thamel wrote for *Sports Illustrated* in 2014, "Davis coach Jim Sochor spent the next practice testing his field goal kicker by gathering the whole team to scream at him during field goal attempts, a common tactic to manufacture game pressure. When Petersen loudly mocked the kicker for his mistakes in the previous game he suddenly felt a hand on his shoulder. 'That's not the purpose of the drill,' Sochor told Petersen, 'We never tear guys down here, we're not going to make them feel bad about themselves.'"[2]

The blended version of high-pressure, yet comforting support that Sochor was trying to get across to his players, struck a chord.

Two years later, after leading UC Davis to two conference titles and compiling a 19–3 record as quarterback, Petersen's coaching career officially began. He was named the head coach of the Aggies' freshman team, tasked with molding the minds of young men who were just a few years his junior.

At first, it was a disaster.

"Of course, I thought I had all the answers, too, because I'd just gotten done playing. I couldn't even get our guys in stretch lines. It was unbelievable. It was like herding cats," Petersen said.[3]

He would figure it out quickly, moving up to coach the wide receivers for the varsity team starting in 1989, before heading east to coach quarterbacks at Pittsburgh in 1992. His first job as a major college assistant coach came with an added bonus—a home for him and his wife, Barb.

As Adam Jude wrote in the *Seattle Times*, "Paul Hackett, then the head coach of the Pittsburgh Panthers, had offered the twenty-seven-year-old Petersen the job as quarterbacks coach, with a couple of conditions: First, Chris and Barb's wedding date that spring conflicted with a football camp, so Hackett asked if they would be willing to move it. Barb agreed, and they wed instead on June 13, 1992, in their native northern California. Second, Chris and Barb were invited to live at Hackett's home—in the loft above the garage—but they would have to share a wall with Hackett's twelve-year-old son, Nathaniel. More than twenty-two years later, as Petersen sat on a leather couch in his office at Husky Stadium on a recent summer afternoon, he chuckled at the memories of his one season with Barb in Pittsburgh."

Petersen was a West Coast guy, though; the wicked winters in Pittsburgh could drive out even the most devout coach. And it did after just one season. When Hackett was fired after posting a 3–8 record, Petersen was back in the Northwest for the 1993 season, working under the legendary Tim Walsh at Portland State for the next two years.

After the 1994 season, in arguably the biggest move of his young career, Petersen joined Mike Bellotti's staff at the University of Oregon. The Eugene lifestyle, and the ability to work under Bellotti—a man he had known and respected for years—was too good to pass up. The Petersens packed their bags for Oregon. Chris, at thirty-one years of age, was joining the Pac-10 as Oregon's receivers' coach.

Off the field, he was a loving husband and father to two kids, Sam and Jack. Just before the start of the 1999 season—Chris's fifth in Eugene—Sam was playing in the bleachers alongside

Jack while the football team slugged through another fall camp practice; on the field below, Chris was running his receivers through a set of drills. A split second later, his life changed forever: Sam toppled off the railing to the ground below, his head bouncing off the turf.

One of Oregon's team trainers, after rushing to Sam's aid, told Chris and Barbara that he might have a concussion. Moments later, after Sam threw up in the parking lot, he was rushed to the hospital, where doctors kept him overnight for further tests.

The next day, a parent's worst nightmare was realized: discovered in the tests performed was that Sam had a cancerous brain tumor. He would require immediate transportation up to the city of Portland, two hours north, where he would have surgery.

There, the tumor was removed, but the cancer had spread to Sam's spine. He would require years of treatments and physical rehabilitation. While the distance from Eugene to Portland was not ideal, it allowed Sam to get the proper care, and Chris to continue his rise up the ranks in Eugene. It was, as far as unfortunate circumstances allow, the best-case scenario.

"It was a long time ago, but in some ways it was just yesterday," Petersen told the *Seattle Times* years later. "It completely changed our outlook on so many things. And I think it's why we've stayed in certain places for long periods of time rather than chasing things around. I think it put a renewed focus on priorities and what's important."[4]

With his life outside of football a constant reminder of how fragile it can all be, Petersen did not feel encumbered by the typical coaching lifestyle that accompanies many. He put in the long hours just like the rest; he devoured film and recruited as hard as any. However, he had perspective and he took pride in knowing there was more outside the enclosed hallways. There was a sense of reality that accompanied his work ethic and his connection with players. "I love his sense of humor," says his wife, Barb, who Chris married in 1992. "I love his spontaneousness. He just kind of goes after things that he's interested in. He has a real sense of fun. A lot of times that's not really seen in his job."[5]

With Sam's disease priority one, Oregon became a safe haven for the Petersen's. During his time there, big names in the coaching ranks filtered through: Al Borges. Dirk Koetter. Mark Helfrich. Jeff Tedford. The brains that Petersen was picking on a daily basis would make any defensive coordinator cringe in agony, and here he was, in the same offices, on the same planes, digesting information in the same meetings.

"He's got a very strong vision about what [the offense] is supposed to look like," said Dan Hawkins. "And he makes sure that picture gets completed."[6]

When Hawkins took over before the 2001 season, step one was putting together a staff that knew their roles; specifically, guys who were *really, really good* at their roles. On top of that, Hawkins knew that what had been accomplished under Koetter could not be squandered. One bad season, one dry stretch, and all of the goodwill and momentum the school was starting to accrue could slip away.

"When you have people that row in opposite directions or poke holes in the boat or don't care if it sinks, it's problematic. To me, that was what was special about Boise State," Hawkins says now.

The Godfather of Boise State," Lyle Smith (right, bottom) followed his 20-year run a ead coach with an equally successful run as the school's athletic director. *(Boise State)*

on Hutt (#81) battles three Louisiana Tech defenders in the 1973 Pioneer Bowl in ichita Falls, Texas. *(AP Images)*

Jim Criner's time at Boise State is often overlooked, but his impact is undeniable.

The 1980 Boise State Broncos, led by Jim Criner (holding trophy), captured the school's lone national championship as a four-year university.

(Photos courtesy of Boise State University)

A rare low moment in Boise State history, a 37–0 loss to rival Idaho in 1984.

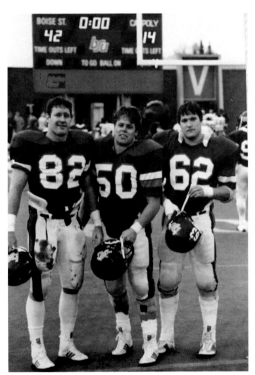

The Alumni Game, an annual rite of passage for former Broncos players to come back and have one more shot at glory.

(Photos courtesy of John Kilgo)

The enigmatic and beloved Pokey Allen's tenure at Boise State became the ultimat "What if?"

Earnest "Pokey" Allen eventually succumbed to his cancer, passing away on Decembe 30, 1996.

(Photos courtesy of Boise State University)

Houston Nutt's time at Boise State (1997) will go down as one of the most bizarre in the school's history.

Dirk Koetter inherited a fractured and disorganized roster in 1998, and promptly turned the program into a consistent winner.

(Photos courtesy of Boise State University)

Boise State's win in the 2000 Humanitarian Bowl was the perfect send off for Koetter, who had accepted the head job at Arizona State just weeks prior. *(AP Images)*

Ryan Dinwiddie battled through injuries and off-field issues to become one of Boise State's all-time great quarterbacks.

Dan Hawkins is both a hero and a mystery in Boise, where he guided the Broncos to heights never seen, but also alienated players and locals with his bizarre tactics.

(Photos courtesy of AP Images)

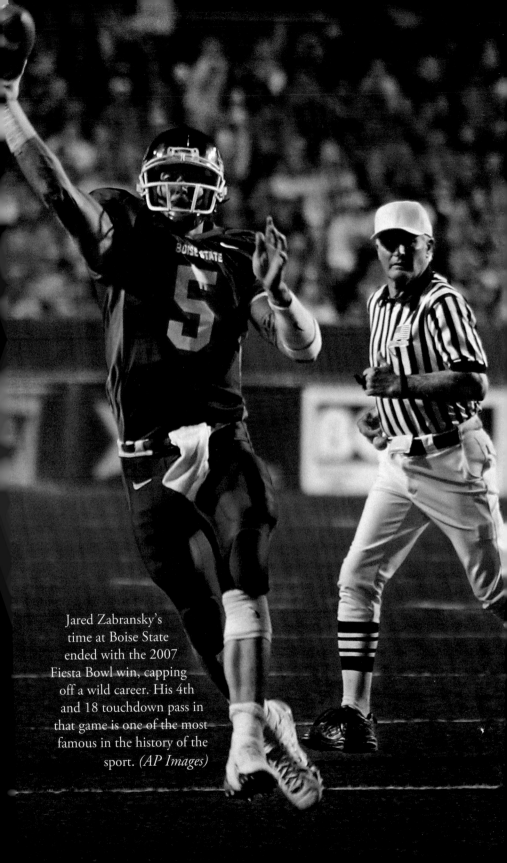

Jared Zabransky's time at Boise State ended with the 2007 Fiesta Bowl win, capping off a wild career. His 4th and 18 touchdown pass in that game is one of the most famous in the history of the sport. *(AP Images)*

The "Statue of Liberty" two-point conversion during the Fiesta Bowl, run in by Ian Johnson, set off a decade of dominance from Boise State.

The on-field celebration of the 2007 Fiesta Bowl.

(Photos courtesy of AP Images)

The 2007 Fiesta Bowl, the moment Boise State announced its presence to the country.

he scene that captured a nation. Ian Johnson (right) proposed to his girlfriend, Chrissy
opadics, moments after securing the Broncos' Fiesta Bowl win over Oklahoma.

(Photos courtesy of AP Images)

Kellen Moore would quarterback the Broncos from 2008–2011, accumulating a stag
gering 50–3 record as a starter, shattering school and national records along the wa
(AP Images)

yle Smith takes in a practice on the blue turf. He would pass away on July 26, 2017,
101 years of age. *(Boise State)*

The Broncos' defensive line—so often lost in the shuffle due to their high-octane offense—carried the team in 2010. *(Boise State)*

Facing a decidedly pro-Virginia Tech crowd to open the season in 2010, Boise State's victory on Labor Day backed up their preseason #3 ranking as Doug Martin (#22) finds an open lane. *(Boise State)*

Doug Martin's touchdown leap helped propel Boise State to its second Fiesta Bowl title, this time over the TCU Horned Frogs in 2010. *(AP Images)*

Chris Petersen took over for longtime friend and mentor Dan Hawkins and blew all preconceived notions of the program away. His time in Boise is one of the most successful in the history of college football. *(AP Images)*

The blue turf, installed in 1986 at the behest of then-athletic director Gene Bleymaier could have backfired if the program failed to produce. Instead, it became arguably the best marketing tool any school has produced. *(AP Images)*

Albertson's Stadium, home to the Boise State Broncos. *(John Kilgo)*

Getting Petersen from Oregon was step one. It was also the biggest challenge. Sam was still spending time up in Portland for treatments; however, by this time, the visits were becoming less frequent. They were happy in Eugene with the care their son was getting, and they were living the life they had envisioned when Chris took that first position fourteen years prior.

Still, Hawkins knew what a guy like Petersen could do for a program, and he knew what offering the position of offensive coordinator—a significant step up both in stature and financial security—could do for his friend. By the time the season rolled around, Sam had reached the point of recovery where the family could make the proper jump if it came.

It did. Hawkins called Petersen, offering him the job.

After mulling it over, Chris and Barb knew the opportunity was too good to pass up.

Just like that, they were headed to Boise.

11

TAKING FLIGHT

"Fresno State in 2001 meant so much to us, psychologically, more than anything else. It gave us the idea that we can beat anybody. I mean it gave us the confidence that we can step up and beat anybody."

—Rusty Colburn, Boise State, 2001–2003

DAN HAWKINS AND Chris Petersen would become synonymous with success. But before that could happen, they had to figure out just what in the hell they were doing and how they were going to go about getting it—whatever "it" was—done.

"Our expectation is to win," said Hawkins as his inaugural season approached. "But we have a lot of question marks."[1]

After putting up a national-best 44.9 points per game in 2000, Boise State was making the leap to the Western Athletic Conference, joining the likes of Fresno State, Hawaii, Rice, SMU, and Nevada, among others. The Broncos would have a rematch of the previous season's bowl game against the UTEP Miners, another member of the conference.

The WAC was an uptick in the level of competition on a weekly basis; combined with a new coach and quarterback, many questions lingered over the program as the season crept closer. While Ryan Dinwiddie had a world of talent in his right arm, how he would perform as "the guy" was still unknown. Defensively, Bob Gregory, who had previously been the secondary coach for the Oregon Ducks, was brought on as the Broncos' coordinator, taking over a unit that had surrendered almost 23 points per game in 2000. Gregory had served in the same role for Hawkins while they were at Willamette.

From the outside looking in, the Broncos and the Western Athletic Conference were the perfect match for each other; both had been searching for an identity to claim as their own. The Broncos had begun to develop theirs; the WAC was still searching. One reason Boise State was welcomed in had to do with the departure of Texas Christian University [TCU], which was jet-setting to the Mountain West Conference. Besides Boise State, Louisiana Tech was also coming aboard, and conference commissioner Karl Benson, who had seen more turnover in recent years than he cared to recount, announced that, for the first time in five seasons, they were free of "lame duck" members.

"I hope this is it," Fresno State's quarterback David Carr said. "It's time to start developing some rivalries."[2]

The questions that remained as the season descended were plentiful, but so too were the solutions, and Hawkins viewed them as optimistically as anyone. And, as it related to Dinwiddie—who Hawkins had seen every day in practice during his first two seasons—the coach was ready to see the youngster get his chance.

"Ryan is a very accurate passer and very football smart," he told the *Reno-Gazette Journal* before the season began. "I think he is a tough kid who has the advantage of being in our system for three years now. For Ryan, he just has to get his feet under him in game situations."[3]

What he lacked in college experience, Dinwiddie made up with his secondary schooling pedigree. At Elk Grove High School in Sacramento, California, he had compiled a 27–1 record as the team's starter. His freshman year at Boise State, when he completed 11-of-19 passes for 137 yards, was not enough to prepare him for the rigors of being a full-time starter. It did, however, enhance a trait he already carried in spades: confidence.

"Dinwiddie was a leader by fire, but a lot of people—younger people our age, and people on campus—did not like him at all," says Jeff Cheek, an offensive lineman under Hawkins, chuckling at the recollection. "He was very arrogant, very cocky, and he was unabashed about it. That is just how he was. He has calmed down tremendously since, but we were in college, and he was the quarterback. It comes with the territory."

The act Dinwiddie had to follow in Bart Hendricks—10,039 yards and 78 touchdown passes for his career—would be nearly impossible to duplicate. Still, belief remained that the Broncos could carry on without skipping a beat. Hawkins's shiny record as head coach of Willamette led players and media to believe that he at least *knew* what he was doing; however, the opponents in the WAC were seismically different from what he last coached against in the NAIA, but so too were the Broncos.

There was one problem that Hawkins could not get out of with simple X's and O's: as had been the case when Dirk

Koetter had taken over three years prior, Hawkins would have to win over the locker room. However, unlike Koetter—who entered the program from the outside—Hawkins was facing a different, perhaps more difficult, scenario: he was doing so with a built-in reputation.

To many of the players in the locker room, Hawkins was too eccentric for the job. Which made sense, because at the end of the day, that thought was 100 percent correct. Hawkins was *weird*. He was a nice man, but, just . . .

"As players, he was the last guy we wanted to get the job. As a team, we just didn't have the respect for him, for whatever reason. He was just different," says Cheek.

He wasn't weird in the "if you see him coming, head the other way" manner; but the way he communicated with those around him was a complete 180 from the previous regime.

His offensive brain was evident . . . the rest of it, though?

Those who had been coached under Hawkins on the offensive side of the ball the previous three years had experienced his grandiose stylings and philosophy preachings. In meetings, on the practice field, even in huddles during games, he would speak the words of famous philosophers or drop Buddhist quotes. Those thoughts in theory are fine, and work for a time; with eighteen- to twenty-two-year-old football players, that time is limited.

Transitioning from Koetter (straight-lace, no bullshit) to Hawkins was viewed by some as too drastic a change.

"Koetter will tell you exactly how it is. He'll let you know; he'll be up front and honest with you," says Cheek, "but he'll also go out of his way to protect his players. He was, and is, very loyal.

Earning the respect of his players was challenge one for Hawkins, one that would have to be earned day-by-day; the next was the team's schedule. After opening the season against Lou Holtz's South Carolina Gamecocks, they then had to follow up with Pac-12 powerhouse Washington State.

Going up against Holtz brought another side story: Hawkins, a vivacious consumer of knowledge, had idolized Holtz—the former Notre Dame coach, who was entering his 30th season as a head man—as he came up through the ranks.

"I've spent a lot of money buying his books and reading them over the years," Hawkins said. "I have a tremendous amount of respect for what he's done."[4]

Unfortunately, idolization can only get you so far. As it came to the actual players on the field, Holtz held a significant advantage. South Carolina was a quality team filled with NFL-ready players. Boise State, needless to say, was not. On paper, it was a collossal mismatch.

Holtz, who had a reputation as the game's biggest fluffer, was buying none of that gibberish.

"Boise State presents more anxiety than I have ever had," he said before the game. "I'm scared to death of them."[5]

Holtz's MO, one that continued into his tenure at ESPN as an analyst, was to build up every opponent his team faced—regardless of competition level or talent disparity—as the second coming of the Messiah. His comments on Boise State, outlandish and unrealistic as they may have been, were right up his alley.

For his part, Hawkins tried his best to downplay the matchup and what it meant for him on a personal level. When asked if he would be intimidated by going up against Holtz, he was blunt.

"No. When you start trying to get ready for an opponent, you try to get ready the same way every week," he said. "It's not so much whether you're playing coach Holtz, or Bo Schembechler, or Woody Hayes. I think we're trying to get down to the nuts and bolts of it and trying to figure out a way to get a first down."[6]

As his first game as a starter approached, Dinwiddie was not shying away from the task at hand, either. South Carolina was not a top-end team in the Southeastern Conference, but they *were* in the SEC, and that meant a dramatic increase in talent over what Boise State was used to.

"It will take all of us to have a perfect game," he said. "But I've been saying all year long: I picture us beating them."[7]

Dinwiddie was the perfect representation of the Boise State temperament. His temerity and the cloud of confidence that billowed from him were in stark contrast to the soft-spoken, almost public invisibility of Hendricks, who was the last person to make outlandish claims or predictions to the media. Dinwiddie was now the flag-waver for the program, one that expected, without hyperbole or lies, to walk into South Carolina and win. And although they had yet to embrace it at the time, the confident demeanor of the players matched perfectly with their new coach who—although a bit more translucent in showing it—came with a swagger that belied his quirks.

One of the ways Hawkins would earn his players' trust was simple: every spot on the roster, regardless of starpower, was up for grabs. "We played a lot of guys. I promised them, 'If you can do something well, consistently, we'll find a place for you.' I don't believe in starters," he says now. As his first game neared, Dinwiddie had earned the trust of his coaches, and his obsessive work ethic was wearing off on his teammates, too.

"As players, we worked on the weekends all summer long, even though it was outside our requirements. [Before the 2001 season] We were trying to work out, but everything is locked. Someone then broke into the coaches office so we could get out onto the field and work out," says Dinwiddie. That dedication from the team was helmed from senior leadership, but the new quarterback was in the center of it all.

"He demanded the work from himself, and he demanded it from us," says Cheek.

"I think we knew something special was building," Dinwiddie says now. "The thing with Boise is that we have guys with Pac-12 talent, that didn't have Pac-12 bodies. They don't look the part, but they can play it."

In the four seasons prior, Boise State had faced Wisconsin, Washington State three times, UCLA, and Arkansas. Their lack of success in those games had diminished the gallant slightly; until they actually *won* these games, and did it consistently, not much would be made of their efforts, but their confidence heading into South Carolina was palpable.

"We won 20 games the past two years; we've won two bowls; our kids know how to win," Hawkins told reporters before the South Carolina game. "They have played up in schedule before."

South Carolina was coming off a vibrant turnaround during the 2000 season. In 1999, the first year under Holtz, when they went 0–11, they scored just eight points per game; they scored nearly 24 per game in 2000, clawing their way to eight wins and a bowl berth.

* * *

After receiving the opening kickoff, with 80,000 fans towering over the field like extras in the movie *Gladiator*, Ryan Dinwiddie trotted onto the field, his first snap as a starter in front of him. Then, reality set in.

False Start.

Incomplete pass.

Short run by Brock Forsey.

Scramble from Dinwiddie.

Punt.

The speed at which South Carolina flew to the ball in comparison to Boise State was akin to a high-level college team playing a powerhouse from the National Football League. The Broncos were good, but not great. Boise State was fast; South Carolina was faster. The Broncos were big; the Gamecocks were bigger.

Every measureable was working against them, as had been feared.

After falling behind 13–0 in the first quarter, the Broncos finally threatened; lining up for a field goal late in the second quarter, which would have cut the lead to 13–10 going into the half and perhaps propelled a second half shootout, the game flipped. Langston Moore, a defender for South Carolina, blocked the attempt. His teammate, Rashad Faison, returned it 82 yards for a touchdown.

There may have been a half to play, but that gut-wrenching turn of events, giving South Carolina a 20–7 halftime lead, broke the Broncos' spirit. Boise State would succumb to the relentless pressure as the game progressed, eventually losing 32–13.

The loss was an awakening of sorts. Although the Broncos were returning back home with an 0–1 record, they had shown enough grit and toughness in the face of a superior opponent to leave with a belief that, once they returned to their normal schedule, against teams more befitting of their talent level, the pieces were in place to do something good.

Dinwiddie held his own, completing 18-of-31 passes for 162 yards and a touchdown. He took viscious bodyblows, continuously pulling himself up off the baked South Carolina turf. Despite the outcome, players reflected back on the experience in a positive manner. The cross-country trip, and the refusal to let the conditions and superior opponent break them, was a message to the rest of the country (those who were paying attention, at least) that Boise State was not going to be bullied.

"We're a big-game team," says Rashaad Richards, who played safety for the Broncos. "We don't play a lot of them, but we'll play you at the beginning of the season, at the end of the season, and you better expect a game."

The "big game" theme would continue in Week 2, when they faced Washington State, led by their dynamic quarterback Jason Gesser. The matchup was a paradox of prophets:

Boise State entered the game 0–7 all time against the Pac-10.

Washington State was just a 10–24 record since losing Ryan Leaf in 1997.

Boise State had won 14 in a row at home.

Washington State had throttled Idaho in their season opener. Something had to give in Hawkins's home debut. Unfortunately, the thing that gave was the Broncos' defense. Gesser spearheaded the Cougars' offensive attack, completing 18-of-27 passes for 252 yards and three touchdowns; Dinwiddie, on the other end of the spectrum, was dreadful. Making his first home start, the sophomore looked overwhelmed, flustered, out of sorts, and generally overmatched for the majority of the game. He completed just 49 percent of his passes; although he wound up with 314 yards and three touchdowns, it was all window dressing.

Dinwiddie's three interceptions, including one that was returned 54 yards for a Cougars touchdown, all added up to a 41–20 loss, one in which the Broncos at one point trailed 34–6.

That they had lost their opening two games was not the most pressing issue; it was the team's inability to keep their quarterback upright. Dinwiddie had been sacked eight times in two games with most of them, according to Hawkins, the result of his own doing.

"I think the biggest thing is [Dinwiddie] needs to start throwing the ball on time," Hawkins said during the Broncos' bye week, which came perfectly after the loss to Washington State. "We can't hold it for too long and that certainly has been an issue."[8]

Not only was Dinwiddie hitting the turf with alarming regularity, but even when he remained standing he was under duress. The Broncos' offensive line had turned into a liability, albeit to better-than-average defenses; both South Carolina and Washington State would finish the season in the Top 40 nationally in overall defense. The Gamecocks finished 18th overall.

Boise State had yet to play a conference game in the WAC; however, the first two weeks were a sign that the season was not going to be a cakewalk as it had been in the final days of their Big Sky tenure, when they won their final 10 games. Not only was the conference deeper and more talented, but a juggernaut was forming down in the state of California. It included a head coach by the name of Pat Hill, a quarterback named David Carr, and a nasty, viral defense.

It was the Fresno State Bulldogs.

Carr, who just weeks into the season was already gaining steam as a Heisman trophy candidate, was on the cover of *Sports Illustrated*, buoyed by early season wins at Colorado, against Oregon State, and at Wisconsin. The Bulldogs were steadily climbing the ranks, threatening to become the first team from outside the BCS conference to make it to a BCS game.

But Fresno State was down the road; first, the Broncos needed to get Dan Hawkins a win.

On September 22, against the UTEP Miners in their conference opener, the Broncos did just that. With Brock Forsey scampering for 132 yards and Dinwiddie throwing three second-quarter touchdown passes, the Broncos secured their first win as WAC members, and the first for Hawkins, with a 42–17 victory. Following that, a win over Idaho, a loss at Rice, and another win at Tulsa left the Broncos at 3–3 overall, 1–1 in the conference, and smack dab in the middle of an identity crisis.

The loss to Rice showcased a number of problems, the most significant being the health of junior defensive tackle David Altieri. After making a tackle, the 274-pounder's neck snapped back awkwardly; he lay motionless on the ground as teammates and members of the Rice Owls knelt in unison. After what seemed like an eternity, Altieri was placed on a board and stretcher and ambulanced to a nearby hospital. After nearly 36 hours in Hermann Hospital in Houston, Altieri returned to Boise.

"He's very scared, and glad he dodged a bullet," said Hawkins the Monday following the injury. "He's disappointed he can't play, but he's doing OK."[9]

Altieri's injury was the most significant, but not the only one to hit the Broncos. Both running backs, Brock Forsey and David Mickell, went down as well, although their injuries were not nearly as severe.

The loss highlighted the fragility of the team; it also posed the question: Who were they, exactly?

Were they the team that had been outclassed by Power 5 opponents to start the season, and in the one-sided loss to Rice? Were they the team that had scored more than 40 points in their three easy wins? Or, most likely, were they a combination of the two?

Soon, they would have a chance to answer that question.

* * *

Before there was Boise State and Dan Hawkins and Chris Petersen, before there was BCS-busting and Power 5 upsets, there was Fresno State.

And *"Anybody, anytime, anywhere."*

The 2001 college football season had been turned on its head early on, as the trifling, scrappy squad from Fresno, California, burst onto the scene. By October, Fresno State had morphed into the darlings of the country. Tucked away in a city residing almost directly at the halfway point between Sacramento and Los Angeles, the Bulldogs had it all: the top quarterback in the country, and the gruff, mustachioed coach with the ever-present scowl.

Fresno State was everything Boise State aspired to be. They were violent hitters on defense. They were efficient, almost military-like on offense.

But what teams most yearned for was the Bulldogs' mentality. In the new-age world of college football, Fresno State was a pure throwback. It came from the top down: Hill, who looked like he walked straight off the set of *Sons of Anarchy*, was as uncompromising as they came.

The Bulldogs were the perfect reflection of their coach; they dripped the same blood. They carried the same torch for pain.

Fresno State had made their way into the Top 10 nationally across all polls. In some, they were ranked as high as 8th, the highest ranking for an opponent that the Broncos had ever faced.

The game was a significant occasion for a litany of reasons, the least of which was that Boise State would be making their national television debut on ESPN. There, they would have the opportunity to stand toe-to-toe with the darlings of the misunderstood. "All we heard going in was 'David Carr, David Carr.' He was going to be the number-one pick in the NFL Draft," says David Lamont Mikell. "But a lot of our guys were from California, so that game was bigger than just him. It didn't matter who we were playing against, it mattered where we were playing. Lots of family and friends were there."

Although the Bulldogs were Top 10 both on paper and in the eyes of voters, in their minds, the Broncos were not far behind. They were in the same league, both figuratively and literally. Fresno State recruited the same players as Boise State. They operated under the same budget. They faced the same stereotypes from pundits. That they were ranked so high was testament to the work they had put in during years prior, and to a generational talent at quarterback.

Outside of that, Fresno State was Boise State, just in different colors.

"Going into Fresno, with them being so highly ranked, it was the first chance we had to say, 'We have a chance to get somebody who has built something great. We can really show that we can play with these guys,'" says Matt Strofhus.

Two days before the game kicked off, Hawkins found himself in a precarious situation. Six weeks into his tenure, some thawing had begun between him and his players. After winning four of their previous five, the team had found cohesion with their new coach. Dinwiddie had settled into a rhythm, completing 69 percent of his passes in conference play. The defense was rounding into form.

And yet, being on ESPN was a double-edged sword: show well, and the brand goes up; perform poorly, and all of the prevailing fears come to light. For Hawkins, he was choosing the former. A nationally televised tilt, in the opposition's backyard, was the perfect setting.

"Any time you have an opportunity to get on TV, it is great for your program," Hawkins said before the game. "The last two Humanitarian Bowls we have had really helped with recruiting. The more you can do to get your name out helps your institution, your city, and your football team."[10]

Locally, Fresno State was dealing with backlash as the game approached. Their high-ranking and primetime matchup was met with some consternation with local high schools, which felt that attention was being pulled away from their games. The WAC, wisely, had adopted Fresno State's "anytime" belief. Because of that, if ESPN, or FOX, or any of the big brands were willing to put their teams on, no one was going to argue.

"A lot of people understand, but they don't agree with it," said Hill of the decision to schedule Friday night games. "ESPN has been very good to us . . . they wanted to fill a Friday slot with us and we weren't in a position to say no."

When the Bulldogs and Broncos kicked off arguably the biggest game in Boise State's history, it took less than two quarters for a tone to be set. All of Fresno State's reputations were coming to light: they were more physical, more dynamic, more versatile. With two minutes remaining in the first half, Boise State trailed 20–7; Fresno State had built the lead despite being their own worst enemy: a Kendall Edwards penalty after smashing into return-man Tim Gilligan on a punt; a missed field goal by Asen Asparuhov.

When Dinwiddie found Jeb Putzier in the end zone for an 18-yard touchdown pass just before the half, cutting the lead to 20–14, the Broncos, miraculously—despite their porous play— had a chance.

It set up a wild, back-and-forth second half.

When Dinwiddie hit Jay Swillie for a 54-yard touchdown with 7:12 to go in the game, the Broncos had their first lead, 35–28, capping off a 21–0 run. After a safety on their next offensive possession brought Fresno State to within five, 35–30, it was time for Bob Gregory's defense to make one final stand.

After Carr drove the Bulldogs downfield, they faced a 4th and 4 from the Broncos' 5-yard line. With one play remaining, the balance of power in the conference was up for grabs, sending two programs on near polar-opposite trajectories.

Score the touchdown, and Fresno State's dreams stay afloat. Fail, and Boise State takes the crown of the Underdog King. That's when it happened.

Sack. Fumble. Ballgame.

Boise State's defense had stifled the Bulldogs one final time, securing the victory. It was, unequivocally, the biggest win for the Broncos since moving up to the I-A level.

It was also the most deflating loss for Fresno State. Ever.

"Our dream of a BCS is over," Hill said after the game. "But we can still have a helluva season." His words were hollow; everything the Bulldogs had worked for in the months prior were over in an instant, slipping from Carr's fingers.

As he sat near his locker after the game, the Bulldogs' disheveled quarterback was lost. His body was a canvas, the blue, black, and purple bruises a symbol of the hell Boise State had put him through. Although Carr had performed well in defeat, completing 30-of-49 passes for 345 yards and three touchdowns, the Broncos' ability to get him to the ground when it mattered most had been their death knell.

"You kind of get in a euphoric state when you're 6–0," Carr said, his voice barely rising above a whisper. "Even when you're going down, you can't believe it. You look at the clock, and you think, 'There's still some time left. We should be able to win this.'"[11]

But they couldn't. Not against Boise State's opportunistic and stingy defense; and most assuredly not against Dinwiddie and their ever-improving offense. For Fresno State, their 17-game win streak, their BCS hopes, all of it was now a myth . . . while Boise State's was just beginning.

To the players in the Broncos' locker room, and to their first-year coach, taking down the 8th-ranked team in the country—in their own building and in front of a national television audience—was simply the next step in the process. Making too much of it would belittle what was already happening.

"I told our guys throughout my career, I've been involved in a lot of so-called upsets," Hawkins says now. "Upsets really happen when guys don't consider it an upset."

Still, it was hard not to look at the victory as anything less than a major upswing for the school. Entering the game, Boise State had been outscored 184–27 against Top 25 opponents all time. So, when the Broncos scored 21 straight points after trailing 28–14—and holding the Bulldogs to just two points in the final 27 minutes—it's as if the tectonic plate of the program had shifted. Lower-level bowl games and moral victories against behemoths were things of the past.

"Beating Fresno, that was a big, 'Hey, we can play.' That was big," says Hawkins now.

"Fresno State was probably the most important game for our program," says Wes Nurse, a safety for the Broncos. "Going against a team who had all these big names, and we knew, 'They have this guy, they have that guy,' they had David Carr, and it was one of those deals where we thought, 'Hey, let's see what they got against us.'"

The rest of the 2001 season was a blur, riding the wave of their night in Fresno. A 3–1 finish gave every member of the program—from the head coach on down—a slingshot of emotion.

* * *

One of the many advantages to having Bronco Stadium as the host for the annual Humanitarian Bowl was the birds-eye view it gave Boise State when the participants descended upon the town. Such was the case for the 2001 game, one which the Broncos came perilously close to making. A mistake here, a close loss there, had cost them their bid. The Louisiana Tech Bulldogs, one of those mistakes from the season—the Broncos fell to the Bulldogs, 48–42—would be taking on the Clemson Tigers of the Atlantic Coast Conference at Bronco Stadium.

Louisiana Tech head coach Jack Bicknell, one of Dan Hawkins's closest friends, made sure the Broncos' head man would be in attendance.

After the game, which Clemson won handily, 49–24, Hawkins was making his way from the one of the elevators to meet with Bicknell. As he was passing through an open corridor, he was met by a throng of Boise State boosters who were also taking in the action. After exchanging pleasantries, Hawkins was off again, the handshakes and smiles all part of the gig. When the elevator door closed behind him, one member of the group turned to his comrades and said, "Someone should ask him how he lost to Louisiana Tech."[12]

Hawkins's four-loss debut may not have been the firework display locals were hoping for. However, what the Broncos had done was navigate a successful turnaround from one coach to another, aligned themselves for a more successful 2002 season, and provided a blueprint of what needed to be fixed.

The first area to address was the off-field behavior of Ryan Dinwiddie, who had been suspended for the final game of the 2001 season, a melancholy 26–10 win over Central Michigan, after he was found unconscious in an idling car under the influence of GHB, a street drug commonly known as liquid ecstasy. Police later confirmed that the paramedics took Dinwiddie to Saint Alphonsus Regional Medical Center where he was treated and released. He was not arrested or charged with a crime.

"He's been suspended because he broke team rules and we're going to leave it at that," Hawkins said at the time.[13]

His actions—not his words—would go a long way in determining both his future and the fate of the Broncos. Despite his poor off-field decision making, Dinwiddie still provided the Broncos the best chance to win. And with Hawkins's "Three strikes and you're out" rule, he had a second chance at redemption.

So, with nearly seven months to go before the season started, the embattled quarterback set about correcting course. In March, he began speaking to local youth about the dangers of GHB and what it can take away from you. Now a redshirt junior and the clear leader of the team, Dinwiddie had gotten off with one year's probation, the one-game suspension, and public ridicule. But he was still in uniform.

As their quarterback was going about internal changes, other parts of the program were receiving external ones. For starters, the famed blue turf was moving into the new age. Out was the disastrous, non-forgiving AstroTurf; in was a new rubber-granular surface, designed to better absorb players.

"There was a time when that old AstroTurf had an allure," Hawkins said at the time. "Not anymore. You get banged up on it a lot. You don't want to be 300 pounds running around on that stuff."[14]

With the momentum coming off the 2001 season, the program was ready to capitalize however it could. A little makeup to the already famous playing surface was step one; they had won 21 of their past 22 games on their home field. What had started out twenty years prior as a marketing scheme had morphed into a bonafide home-field advantage. The blue hue brought an alluring presence; once the action began, it turned lethal for the opposition. Over the previous two seasons, the Broncos had taken to degrading opponents who dared challenge them:

San Jose State: 56–6

North Texas: 59–0

Idaho: 66–24

Nevada: 49–7

"Its sort if our identity. We have a saying here that, 'We don't lose on The Blue.' Our crowd gets after it and that adds to everything here," said Hawkins.[15]

Though he had only completed one season as head coach, Hawkins was already a lot of things to a lot of people around the city of Boise. To some, he was an odd figure sitting high atop mind-mountain, festering up metaphors, swimming in his own self-fulfilling thoughts. To others, he was just a quirky dude who had yet to fully prove himself. As Jeff Pittman, who was the strength and conditioning coach for the program, told Bill Connelly of *SB Nation*, Hawkins was also adept at reading the state of his program, and what was necessary to go to the next level:

> Hawk went around to everybody and said, "Hey, in your area, what do you need in order to succeed?" I was like, "This is just another thing Hawk's having us do." So I [wrote down requests, starting with an improved weight room]. And when Fresno came up here the next year, we beat them 67–21, Hawk tells me I need to listen to the press conference or the booster luncheon or something that Monday after the game.
>
> I'm thinking, "I don't know why I need to listen to this, but whatever." I heard him doing something with a piece of paper, and he goes, "You guys like that win?" Of course everybody goes nuts. He goes, "If you want that to continue, this is what you're gonna do." He named off a new weight room and all these other things. You could hear a pin drop. But he said, "If you want us to stay here, we need all these things." I thought that was really ballsy of Hawk, and it needed to be done. That was to me the moment that everybody was kinda like, well okay, we're taking the next step.[16]

With a weight room on the way, and the new, softer surface of the playing field, the familiarity of the program was drifting . . . but the majority of players who had propelled the Broncos to their eight wins the season prior remained. In addition to Dinwiddie, all-everything running back Brock Forsey and five other offensive starters were back. The defense returned the same amount, giving the staff an experienced group to unleash.

Dinwiddie, who had finished fourth nationally in pass efficiency in his debut season, was expected to take an even bigger leap, assuming he could stay off the police blotter. Forsey was teaming with David Lamont Mikell to ease his burden in the backfield. After putting up 34 points per game in 2001, much was expected of the Broncos' offense. Now in his fifth overall season with the school, the players knew Hawkins's system; Chris Petersen had also slid in perfectly as offensive coordinator.

* * *

On August 31, 2002, in front of 30,870 fans in Bronco Stadium, Boise State kicked off their bid for the WAC championship against Idaho. It wasn't an onslaught as many predicted, but Boise State did what it set out to do: take care of their rivals. Entering the contest, the toughest opponent appeared to be apathy, and looking ahead to the following week when they would face former coach Houston Nutt's Arkansas Razorbacks.

Boise State's 38–21 win over Idaho marked just their third opening-game victory since 1995, and their third in a row over Idaho.

Although four full seasons had removed Nutt from his Boise State tenure, watering down the bitter feelings, the Razorbacks still represented a chance to do something the Broncos had yet to do: defeat a Power 5 school on the road.

"We've yet to beat a Pac-10 team since I've been here, and we're yet to beat a formidable opponent in an upper-tier conference," Hawkins said during the week leading up to the Razorbacks. "That's a big step to take."[17]

In Fayetteville, Nutt was facing his own problems: the lack of discipline involving his team was turning into a black eye on the program. Two of his best players, Ken Hamlin and Cedric Cobbs, were seemingly gifted autonomy leading up to the game against the Broncos, skirting disciplinary action for their off-field behavior (Hamlin would be suspended indefintely the following season for a separate incident). Those two were just the latest examples of the blind eyes being turned by the football program; by the end of the 2003 season, twenty-six players would be arrested under the coach's watch.

Never one to miss an opportunity, as the game approached and the subject of Nutt's non-discipline came up, Hawkins said, "I'll just say this: I've got three guys missing a month of camp and one game, and what they did wasn't as serious."[18]

Four years into his tenure, Nutt's return to Arkansas had been a mixed bag. His record—30–18—was respectable, especially for a fanbase that was not accustomed to winning big. He had saved himself by performing well in big games; to this point his teams had knocked off the 9th-ranked Gamecocks of South Carolina; Mississippi State, twice, when they were ranked 12th and 13th; and 3rd-ranked Tennessee. While they had yet to gain traction in the conference, Nutt's Razorbacks were the worst kind of pain-in-the-ass for the opposition: never truly threatening conference superiority, but a consistently tough opponent.

For Hawkins, this would be the first true opportunity to set his program free for the world to see. The Broncos needed another shape-shifting victory over a formidable opponent; the win over Fresno State in 2001 served its purpose, but a road win in the deep south, over a school from the big, bad SEC would be something altogether different.

Regrettably for the Broncos, Arkansas would not be that opportunity.

With as many spark plugs as they brought to the table, the Razorbacks offered more; for every country-strong lineman Boise State threw out on the field, Arkansas threw two. Combine those deficiencies with Ryan Dinwiddie breaking his ankle, as he did early in the game, and it all became too much to overcome. Arkansas rolled to an easy 41–14 victory. Boise State's season, once again, began with a thud.

"I don't think we have seen too many games where you have seven turnovers and then lose your starting quarterback," said Hawkins after the game. "It was more than a double dose of adversity."[19]

Dinwiddie's ankle injury was expected to keep him out for six to eight weeks. After an entire offseason rehabbing his image, and then himself, internally, this healing would take place on the most-watched right ankle in all of Idaho. Senior B. J. Rhode would run the show in his absence. Rhode had an army of weapons around him, making his task a simple one: don't mess it up.

Rhode had kept himself prepared through four years on the bench. Now it was going to pay off.

"The summer before, we were running the upper decks, as we did once a week in the summer; I was coming down, and [Jeff Pittman, strength and conditioning coach] said, 'What are you still doing here?' I was a senior, I wasn't going to play, so why stick it out? I laughed, and said, 'I don't want to screw this up in case I have to go in,'" Rhode says now.

One snap of the ankle, and that is exactly what was happening.

"I told Pittman after the Arkansas game, 'Weren't you the guy on the upper deck who told me I shouldn't be here?' He shrugged it off and didn't know how to react."

He *was* here, and he was ready, confident, and completely in charge of the playbook.

"B. J. has been in our system for five years, so he knows the system," Hawkins said after the Arkansas game. "He is very capable."[20]

Hawkins's words would prove prophetic. Over the next four games, Rhode and the Broncos' offense exploded. Because he knew the playbook inside and out, the staff was free to run the same offense and exploit defenses from every imaginable angle. Even without Dinwiddie, the Broncos were setting the scoreboard ablaze:

Week 4: 63 points against Utah State.

Week 5: 58 points against Hawaii.

Week 6: 52 points against Tulsa.

If the loss to Arkansas had been a blow, every subsequent week was shattering that result.

Rhode, for one, was loving every minute of it. During the four-game stretch following his insertion into the starting lineup, he would complete 65 percent of his passes for 969 yards while tossing eight touchdowns (with five of those against Utah State). After years of clipboard and extra-point holding, Rhode had rocketed onto the main stage. In a sense, he was the poster boy for what the Broncos were becoming: unheralded, unrecruited, and, out of nowhere, unstoppable.

"The guys we had in the locker room, that's what allowed us to go on that run," Rhode says now. "Guys like Jerry Smith, for example—a little guy that nobody gave a chance. But he made plays. Tim Gilligan, T. J. Acree. We just had *football players*. Other than Dinwiddie, we also stayed healthy. Our defense was good, and we had this mentality of 'Here's what we have. We're going to give you what we have. After that, we'll see what happens.'"

Rhode's preparation had not only saved himself, but also the team from certain doom. He avoided the dreaded backup quarterback nightmare scenario, too.

"It was right after the Billy Joe Hobart situation, where he went in and didn't know any of the plays because he wasn't prepared. I wasn't going to be that guy."

After having thrown just 60 career passes entering the season, Rhode was now the captain of the country's most dynamic and diverse offense. For fans and pundits who viewed the Broncos' season in peril after Rhode took over, those fears were quickly put to rest.

"Everyone's got a role, and if you believe in your role, you can do it any time," he says.

As is the nature of the game, that role would soon change; Ryan Dinwiddie would return, reclaiming his spot as the team's starting quarterback.

Although Rhode had performed as well as could be expected, Dinwiddie was the starter for a reason; his physical gifts and moxy gave him an edge that no other quarterback on the roster could muster.

Adding another layer to Dinwiddie's return was the Broncos' opponent, Fresno State, a team seeking revenge from the preceding season. But before the quarterback could mark his comeback complete, and the Broncos could continue on their bowl quest, another wrench was thrown into the mix.

"The first day back in practice that week, I was cutting off my ankle tape and one of the blades pops out of the tape cutter and sliced my leg wide open," says Dinwiddie now. "I had to get 40 stitches . . . on my broken ankle."

After all he had been through, Dinwiddie was far past the point of playing it safe.

"So, they stitched it up and I played."

"I played" would be a massive understatement. Just six weeks removed from the nightmare in Fayetteville, Dinwiddie would throw five touchdown passes in less than three quarters of work, igniting a statement win over Fresno State, 67–21. In doing so, he squashed any and all talks of a "quarterback controversy" that were threatening to creep up due to Rhode's fill-in performances.

"He was laser-like," Hawkins said after the game.[21]

It wasn't just his numbers that were other-worldly (although they were; he finished the game 19-for-22 for 406 yards).

Dinwiddie's presence alone electrified a Broncos team already in the midst of their best season to date. If they hadn't missed a beat under Rhode, this version was another ethos in itself. Although Rhode had started the game, spotting Dinwiddie a 13–0 lead, the Broncos hit another gear when he emerged from the shadows.

It was the Broncos' fourth-straight game scoring more than 50 points; their fifth-straight conference win; and the team's 668 yards topped the previous school record of 664, set back in 1995.

"That whole emphasis is on preparation, not about trying to prove people wrong," Dinwiddie said after the game. "Last year we left a couple stones unturned."[22]

In other words, there would be no let up from the players. Not this time.

The following week they took down the San Jose State Spartans, 45–8, compiling 650 yards in the process. After the game, the defense, which held the Spartans scoreless for the first three quarters, was all Hawkins could talk about.

"I'm very proud of our defense," he said. "To shut those guys out for three and three-quarters of that game was impressive."[23]

The uptick in offense and smothering defense was differentiating the season from years past. One of the factors was the continuity of the staff, but just as much credit was due to the buy-in of the players, who were beginning to see Hawkins as a mastermind—*an idiosyncratic mastermind*—but one nevertheless.

"Coach Hawkins would bring in guys to chat, and half the time it wasn't even about football," says Derek Olley, an offensive lineman for the Broncos. "It would be philosophers. But at the same time it was about football." Hawkins was a master in the tactful art of showing how Zenful, Eastern philosophies could pay dividends on 3rd and 11 in a rainstorm on a football field.

The Broncos were running over a hapless and overmatched Western Athletic Conference, but with four games left in the season, the rest of the country had yet to take notice. It was mid-November, and they were not ranked. But it hardly seemed to matter; Boise State would topple UTEP (58–3), Rice (49–7), and Louisiana Tech (36–10).

Finally, after the win over Louisiana Tech and a 10–1 record, the Broncos had made the splash they were looking for, snatching a 23rd ranking, the first in school history. All that stood in their way of a perfect conference record was Nevada. Entering the game, even the Wolfpack knew what they were up against, and weren't shy about expressing it.

"They appear to have no weaknesses," said Nevada's head coach Chris Tomey. "They are solid at every single position."[24]

The Broncos would cruise, taking down the Wolfpack, 44–7, locking in another Humanitarian Bowl appearance—this time against Big 12 upstart Iowa State. As they had all season since the loss to Arkansas, the Broncos cruised to an easy victory.

The 34–16 bowl win, which capped off a 12–1 season, was the final arrow. In just two seasons, Hawkins had clinched the school's first-ever ranking, first 12-win season, and the first offseason where pundits across the country would have to take notice.

"It was dream season," said Bobby Hammer, a defensive tackle and Humanitarian Bowl MVP. "We set goals high. But we wanted to do more than set them; we wanted to achieve them."

* * *

Boise State's #15 ranking to end the season was a high mark for the program. The reward for Hawkins was a shiny new contract, one that would ostensibly keep him in Boise through the 2008 season. A "total package to $300,000 annually" was the provision.

As had been the case when working with Dirk Koetter, the Boise State Board of Directors were cognizant of their place: Hawkins was quickly becoming the hottest name in all of college football, and he was unlikely to be a lifer on the blue. As such, squeezing every year out of him was a necessity.

After a bumpy start, the coach had washed away any doubts that his personality cast. His record through two seasons (20–5) spoke less than where the program as a whole was headed. The bump in pay and increase in years was more for what Hawkins *could* do than what he had done.

Winning has a cure-all effect when it comes to understanding people. What may come across as odd and peculiar initially, when put through practice, and the ensuing results, can become endearing. The 2002 season had shown players that while his "Hawkisms," as they were known throughout the complex, were out of touch with what normal eighteen- to twenty-two-year-old kids would relate to, he was well adept at correlating his preachings and making them work for his audience.

Over the previous decade, when he was not in the film room, on the practice field, or out recruiting, Hawkins had been accumulating random quotes, plays, diagrams, flow charts, etc., compiling them into what he called his "thesis philosophy." By the end of the 2002 season, his collection pushed out to nearly 154 pages. "It's a piece of art; it's something that's always in process," he told the *Statesman Journal.*

"When it comes down to it, all of those sayings and perspectives, they're all true," said safety Chris Carr. "You sit there and think that they're corny and they don't make sense, but when you think about it, they make perfect sense. If you really take it to heart, it can make a difference."[25]

Although Hawkins's favorite quote—"Success is the ability to control the quality and balance of your life"—was something his players had heard ad nauseam, and had, for the most part, taken to it, one individual was struggling to follow suit: Ryan Dinwiddie.

After having served out his punishment following his 2001 arrest, the star quarterback had become a model citizen inside the locker room. His teammates flocked to his personality; it was a blend of supreme swagger, confidence, and brutish work ethic and drive. Although he missed out being named the nation's pass efficiency leader in 2002 due to the fact that he did not play in enough games to qualify, his on-field performance had earned him every bit of praise he was receiving.

Then, strike two.

Along with two teammates, Jason Turner and Travis Burgher, he would be forced to miss the team's spring practice due to a violation of an "unspecified team rule." Although it lacked the seriousness of his arrest at the end of the 2001 season, the incident showed that Dinwiddie's leadership role was becoming perilous. Staying out of trouble and on the field was vital; the Broncos were losing eight players from the previous season, in which they finished first overall in the country, scoring 45.6 points per game. Among those lost was Brock Forsey, who ended his career by leading the nation in total touchdowns (32) as a senior. Three offensive linemen needed to be replaced as well, and the team's receivers were thin on experience.

All of it added up to a hold-your-breath take with Dinwiddie. One more strike, and he—and, likely, the entire upcoming 2003 season—would be gone.

That was out of their hands, a fate yet to be determined. What was in their control was the influx of talent that was beginning to transcend the Broncos' program.

Or, perhaps more accurately, the *correct* talent that was coming in.

Robert Tucker, an assistant coach under Hawkins, says, "I don't know if the talent necessarily got better, but I know there were a select few guys that did have bigger offers, and they still ended up at Boise State. Those guys couldn't stand losing in anything they did. I think modeling that . . . I certainly know for sure this was Hawk's motto: Great people who truly value education, and are highly competitive. If you have those three things, man . . . you're going to have a championship program."

The staff was showcasing a pristine eye for talent, plucking kids from innocuous places, fitting them into their scheme, and letting them shine.

"We had so many great players. But the nice thing was, too, we had a huge walk-on program, and I think guys realized if they came there and worked hard, they did the right things and busted their butts, they would be rewarded," says Hawkins now. "If you play and work hard, you're going to rise."

* * *

By the time the 2003 season rolled around, the Broncos were no longer searching for an identity. They were the most willing and dangerous underdog in the country, and the flag-waver of their conference.

"It was always fun being the underdog, but knowing at the same time what we could do," says Rashaad Richards, a defensive back for the Broncos.

What they were doing was setting a new standard.

The 2003 season would be the biggest example to date. After a Week 3 loss at Oregon State, 26–24, Boise State would cruise through one of the most dominant stretches of football seen west of Tuscaloosa. Their 13–1 record, which included a PlainsCapital Fort Worth Bowl win over TCU (34–31), was almost unfair in hindsight. The Broncos once again led the nation in scoring (43 points per game), including a 77-point outburst against San Jose State. Their defense ranked 12th overall, allowing 17 points per game; they finished 28th in "Simple Rating System," an algorithm that takes into account average point differential and strength of schedule, shredding the notion that the Broncos were getting by on soft competition.

On top of that, Dinwiddie had kept his off-field shenanigans to a minimum. On the field, he was a despot. He completed 62 percent of his passes, set a then-school record against Louisiana Tech by throwing for 532 yards, finished the season with

4,356 passing yards and 31 touchdowns, and threw just seven interceptions. His preseason WAC Offensive Player of the Year prediction rang true with ease; he won the award, exiting as arguably the greatest quarterback in Boise State history. For his career, Dinwiddie finished 14 games with 300 yards or more passing; four games with more than 400; and two with more than 500. His 4,356 yards in 2003 are more than five hundred yards ahead of the next highest in school history.

As the awards season wrapped up, talk immediately went to the 2004 season; or, as it would be known, Year One A. D. (After Dinwiddie).

Waiting in the wings, after receiving few precious snaps during the season, was a redshirt sophomore, full of spitfire and brimstone. He was just as cocky, just as talented, and just as much a wild card as Dinwiddie had been coming up through the ranks.

It was time for Jared Zabranksy.

12

THE EXPLOSION

"One offseason, we were in the coaches' conference, and I was
talking to June Jones, head coach of Hawaii. Dan Hawkins
walked in, and Jones said, 'I better not talk too loud. I don't
want him mad at me.' That was the feeling the other coaches
in the conference had."
—Paul Schneider, former Boise State play-by-play announcer

JARED ZABRANSKY GREW up with just three television channels in Hermiston, Oregon. One of those channels
was NBC, allowing the bright-eyed boy to watch his favorite
team, the illustrious Notre Dame Fighting Irish. Yearly battles
between the Irish and Michigan, or USC, or Navy drew him in.
The lights bouncing off the deep gold helmets under Indiana
nights were his childhood.

Zabransky was the typical kid—"I could always throw a ball,
no matter what the sport; no matter what season it was in, I was
playing," he says.

All through elementary school, middle school, though his senior year in high school, Jared was "in-season." Football. Basketball. Baseball. Not a sport came by where he was not involved. He played shortstop and pitched during the spring, and spun the ball for the football team in the fall. During his senior year, Jared's school won their first-ever conference title in football.

Although he was not a heavily recruited player early on, by his junior year letters began showing up in the Zabransky mailbox, inquiring about the services of the kid with a big arm. One day, while sitting in class, a stack of letters fell into his lap, twenty deep. Introductory notes from interested schools.

His talents were slowly moving away from secretive. Hermiston, Oregon, in a subtle understatement, is not a hotbed for recruiting. Tucked away in the northeast corner of the state, 249 miles from Boise, the Hermiston Bulldogs possess a typical working-class vibe: work hard, play disciplined football, no individual rises above the team. Their mantras rise straight from the movies; it was also the perfect setting for a young man who would someday helm the quarterback spot at a school like Boise State.

The summer before Jared's senior year, Hermiston attended the "Boise State Team Camp," an annual event put on by the school for regional high school teams. Although he was still off the Broncos' radar at the time—"they were one of the schools that didn't send me a letter," he says now—Zabransky's performance at the camp changed that. He played well, displaying a wide array of throws and an unexpected athleticism, earning overall Camp MVP honors.

His senior season back in Hermiston only further cemented belief from the Broncos' coaching staff. On top of his performance as the team's starting quarterback, he would play defense "when needed . . . or when I chose to," he says now, highlighting his versatility.

"The class I came to Boise State with, there were six or seven of us that played both sides of the ball [in high school], which I think says a lot about the quality of the athlete we had in that class."

As his senior season rolled on, the offers continued to pour in; only now they had a different feel. Schools that had never sniffed the Hermiston air were descending into town, and offers followed suit. Where the Big Sky once came, bigger, more prominent schools like Oregon, Washington State, and Purdue were taking notice.

They wanted Zabransky. They just didn't want to pay for him to be there. "I was offered walk-on spots."

Finally, an offer came that provided the bigger school feel, and the comforts of home: the Idaho Vandals. After initially giving a verbal, non-binding commitment, as the only school to have officially offered a full ride, things again changed: Boise State got on board and offered a full scholarship.

He accepted. Jared Zabransky was finally, and forever, a Bronco.

Joining him in the recruiting class, in an effort to one day replace Ryan Dinwiddie, was a young man by the name of Legedu Naanee, a wiry, 6-foot-2 speedster out of Franklin High School in Portland, Oregon. Naanee offered everything the Broncos were looking for: he had the freakish athleticism and the potential to someday have a quarterback's arm. He also came from a program in a big city. Where Zabransky's high school competition was more akin to the undersized pipsqueaks in the film *Little Giants*, those questions ceased to exist with Naanee. Zabransky knew it, too. "Legedu was probably thought of as the frontrunner, as far as he and I were concerned, to have a chance at being the starting quarterback," he says now, "but the coaches kept their word in regards to giving us a fair and competitive opportunity."

Despite scholarship offers from schools in the Big 12 and Pac-10, Naanee chose Boise State. They were the only school to offer him an opportunity to play quarterback instead of a wide receiver or running back.

During Zabransky and Naanee's freshman year in 2002, while both were redshirting, Dinwiddie would succumb to his broken ankle, moving every other quarterback up a spot on the depth chart. Because of where he was at in his progression at the time of the injury, Zabransky jumped ahead of Naanee into the backup spot behind B. J. Rhode. His role in practice and with the gameplan increased; on top of that, he now traveled with the team on road trips.

Zabransky was forced to learn at warped speed. He handled it perfectly, altering the careers of two young men; Naanee would soon slide over to play wide receiver, where he would eventually be taken in the 2007 NFL Draft. Zabransky became the heir apparent at quarterback.

Entering his redshirt freshman season in 2003, with B. J. Rhode graduated, the battle between Zabransky and Mike Samford, another quarterback on scholarship, for the primary backup role fizzled long before the season began. Samford, a junior, was solid and unspectacular. Zabransky was on a different level.

"I played quite a bit my redshirt freshman year in 2003; I got a lot of carries. Every game that we went into, there was a gameplan with a wildcat package that I was the quarterback for," he says now. "I got pretty significant experience doing that."

Zabransky would end his first year as backup with 16 carries for 78 yards and one touchdown. He also threw the ball 23 times, completing just 11 passes for 180 yards with one touchdown and one interception, even after breaking his collarbone during the team's 51–21 win over UTEP on November 15. It was not particularly impressive, but his feet were wet. Now, when he entered his sophomore year in 2004, all trepidations would be gone.

* * *

In 2004, Boise State looked poised to break through the Bowl Championship Series barrier, one that no team from outside the Power 5 had gone through. Despite the loss of Dinwiddie, leading rusher David Mikell, and receiver Tim Gilligan, the Broncos had accumulated such a solid reputation nationally that it hardly mattered. The Broncos were restocking rather than rebuilding.

Adding to the optimism was a revamped BCS system, which now allowed for a more streamlined path to a major bowl game for teams in conferences like the WAC, Mountain West, or Mid-American Conference.

"It seemed a little bit un-American, kind of a closed system," Hawkins said during the WAC Media Days that July. "Now it's great for everybody to have an opportunity to get in there and slug it out."[1]

During the previous two seasons, when they had gone 25–2, that is exactly what Boise State had done. However, despite their successes, they had not lost the edge that got them there: an overwhelming, borderline sophomoric, sense of disrespect.

"We're always kind of the second guy, the underdog, and they like that. They like having that chip on their shoulder and that someone doesn't know who they are," says Max Corbet, who was the school's sports information director for over thirty years. "Come Saturdays, we're going to show you."[2]

This time out, it would be Zabranksy showing the country. Against Idaho to open the 2004 season, the sophomore was surgical, throwing for 234 yards while scoring three touchdowns on the ground. Boise State won, 65–7.

"We don't have the Dinwiddies and such anymore, but we still have guys who can step up for us," Hawkins said after the game. "Playing in a packed stadium and going against our rivals, I think Zabransky did a good job, and when he settles in, he's going to be just fine."[3]

In his next outing, Zabransky would have an opportunity to prove his coach correct. Oregon State, the only team that had gotten the best of Boise State the year prior, entered Bronco Stadium coming off of an 8–5 season, and were led by Derek Anderson, the latest in the line of burly, strong-armed Pac-10 quarterbacks to face the Broncos.

Early on, a pitiful nostalgia ran through the blood of Broncos fans as Oregon State jumped out to a quick 14–0 lead, stealing electricity from the stadium in an instant.

Then Kory Hall, Boise State's star linebacker, decided he was done with the push around. Over the final 45 minutes of the game, the Broncos would outscore the Beavers 53–20, led by Hall's three interceptions, including a 46-yarder for a touchdown in the second quarter that flipped the momentum.

"All three interceptions were tipped by a teammate," Hall said afterward, smiling. "I was lucky."

Boise State wasn't lucky; they were really, *really* good. And talented. And ferocious. It was the program's first win over a Pac-10 team and their 13th in a row overall, at the time the longest in the nation. It was also the 20th win in a row on the blue turf, known around the country by this point as the "Smurf Turf."

Zabranksy threw for 225 yards and three touchdown passes, rushed for 73 yards and another touchdown; with the win, he solidified his position as the next great Broncos quarterback.

"Jared was our infallible leader. He was, just . . . he was amazing," said defensive end Michael G. Williams.[4] The win over Oregon State also pushed them to #23 in the country, the earliest they had been ranked in-season.

After the throttling of Oregon State, it was smooth sailing through conference play. Boise State would win their remaining nine games—eight of them against WAC opponents—by an average of 23 points per game, setting up their Liberty Bowl matchup against Louisville. Their #10 ranking at the end of the regular season was the highest in program history. Zabranksy had been hit-and-miss throughout the season, but ultimately proved to be the right choice for the job. He finished the season with 16 touchdowns to 12 interceptions; he ran for 13 more touchdowns; and, most importantly, had guided the Broncos to their first-ever undefeated regular season as Division I-A members.

For the Broncos, it was all they could have asked for.

For the committee deciding their fate, it wasn't enough.

Despite their ranking, Boise State was left out of the BCS conversation. Utah, playing in the Mountain West Conference— one of higher stature—was not. Led by quarterback Alex Smith and head coach Urban Meyer, the Utes finished the season 12–0. Buoyed by a preseason ranking of 20, they were in the driver's seat for a BCS berth from day one.

Like the Broncos, the Utes failed to play against a ranked opponent all season; unlike the Broncos, it failed to matter.

"Unfortunately, there is a lot of politics. I'm not a great politician but our play speaks for itself," Hawkins said after the team's regular-season finale, a 58–21 win over Nevada.

It was not much, but a small reprieve came when it was announced that Utah would be playing Pittsburgh in the Fiesta Bowl. Pittsburgh played in the Big East, widely considered the weakest of the automatic BCS conferences, and a team that had gone just 8–3 on the season. It took nothing away from Utah's accomplishment, but the matchup felt more secondary than a BCS berth is supposed to. It did not allow the small school, Utah, the opportunity to test their mettle against one of the true giants of the sport.

Boise State, meanwhile, had their own challenge. Their Liberty Bowl matchup against Louisville—who came into the game ranked #6 in the country—looked on paper to be a nightmare. The Cardinals' lone loss on the season had been to #3 Miami, on the road, in a thrilling nip-and-tuck game. The Cardinals didn't have an offense as much as they had a flaming hot torch used to brand their opposition. They were scoring nearly 50 points per game, had a gallant defense, and their quarterback, Stephon Lefors, was the definition of efficent, completing nearly 74 percent of his passes.

If the Broncos had an edge coming into the game, it was the ongoing fiasco surrounding Louisville head coach Bobby Petrino.

Petrino, who had cut his teeth at Idaho in 1989, was—to put it delicately—an ass. His players saw it. Administrators saw it. Boosters assuredly saw it. Petrino was also the first guy to bail for an opportunity that better suited him, to hell with those left behind.

So it was no surprise, then, when the week leading up to the game was more about his obsessive flirting with the opening at Louisiana State University than the actual matchup.

"I want our players to think right now that this is the biggest game they've been able to play in, so they get used to that, preparing for the biggest games," Petrino said mid-week before kickoff. He may have been spinning the proper yarns, but inside the Louisville program, all eyes were aimed south toward the LSU campus. If they wanted Petrino, who, much like Hawkins had done at Boise State, had taken Louisville to unprecedented heights, all they had to do was offer. It may have the been the biggest game in Louisville's history, but their focus was elsewhere.

Across the country, Boise State was in a similar position . . . minus the turmoil. They, too, were aiming to end their most successful season in school history on a positive note. Unlike Louisville, though, the Broncos were not yet facing the looming coaching change.

As his fourth season was coming to an end, Hawkins had accumulated a 44–6 record. His team was on a 22-game win streak and had locked up their highest ranking ever. They had won 23 in a row at home. The previous four months' successes were written in pen, never to be taken away. The undefeated note, if they got there, would be the feather.

"You try and sustain your way of life and standards," Hawkins said before the game when asked about his team's pursuit of perfection. "Those are the kinds of things you try to keep alive. I've been on a few undefeated teams before; you're just trying to do things right."[5]

It may have been the quintessential Hawkins-esque answer, but it belied a bigger point: the Broncos were aiming to win this one game, not their entire schedule.

So, with one coach seemingly out the door and the other whose head seemed to be floating among the clouds, the Broncos and Cardinals would engage in the highest scoring Liberty Bowl of all time. In their final game as members of Conference USA before heading off to the Big East, Louisville outlasted Boise State, 44–40.

"We wanted to come out here and prove to everybody that we're not a team in the WAC that's not very good, and we just beat up on little teams," Chris Carr after the game.

Despite the loss, that's exactly what they had done. The Broncos' showing, keeping the Louisville offense six points under their season average, earned more respect than all 11 of their victories during the regular season combined. After leading 31–21 at the half, Boise State ran out of steam late, being outscored 24–9 in the second half.

An emotional Hawkins stood in front of his team in the locker room after the game, his blue BSU pullover a stark contrast to the bleach-white walls behind him. As he spoke, his voice began to crack as he looked back on the season.

"Hey, I'm proud of you. I love you—you guys battled, you scraped, you didn't give up," he said. "You did everything we asked, and most of the time, that's going to result in a win."

For the third consecutive season the Broncos had come up short of the elusive white whale, the undefeated season. Still, Hawkins sensed the need to not harp on the shortcomings, but acknowledge what the team *had* accomplished. The undefeated regular season. The toe-to-toe battle with Louisville, the 6th-ranked team in the country. The growth and maturity of his team as they survived regular season thrillers against BYU (28–27) and San Jose State (56–49).

"You started fast and finished strong. Tonight, we just weren't able to score more points than Louisville," he continued. "You should be proud of the way you played. Don't hang your heads."

The loss carried one positive caveat for Hawkins: his ear lobes would remain untouched. Before the season began, in joking with some of his players, the coach mentioned that if the team finished the season undefeated, "I would agree to pierce one of my ears and wear an earring." Defensive tackle Alex Guerrero had selected a diamond perfect for Hawkins, should the occasion arise.

Unfortunately for the team, the dream failed to materialize. His focus remained on the team and the triumphant season they had just completed.

"You need to pay attention to a lot of subtle things that happen in this program," Hawkins said. "Number one is having high goals, and high aspirations, and not being afraid to think big."[6]

Come September 2005, they would get that shot.

13

GEORGIA ON MY MIND

"When I got to there, the attitude was still a little more on the
fun side. They wanted to win, but it was a little less professional.
Our class brought the seriousness and being the best you can be.
We started to get a more serious type of attitude."

—Brett Denton, Boise State, 2002–2007

THE STAIRS.
Ask any member of the 2005 Boise State football team
about the stairs, and the color drains from their face. Hands
become flush with sweat, breathing shortens to a choke, and the
tongue swells.

"The Stairs" is in reference to the upper deck of Bronco Stadium,
which in September is a contented, relaxing view for fans; a clear
sight line to the peaceful mountainscape of outer-Boise.

However, in June, July, and August of 2005, those stairs became
hell's breeding ground; a myopic, concrete touchstone between
past successes and the opportunity that stood before them.

Boise State was once again headed south to SEC country, this time to open the season against the Georgia Bulldogs.

"We'd come out to practice, and they would be playing 'Georgia' chants over the speakers," said backup quarterback Bush Hamdan.

"We had so much time. Whether people want to admit it or not, we had that whole offseason looming out there, like, 'This is our chance.' We trained a little differently. It felt like the coaches put more into that one, which may have resulted in some of the early jitters. They built it up," says Ian Smart, a defensive lineman for the Broncos. "People ask, 'Do players read the papers and the press clippings?' Absolutely."

As the game neared, national pundits weighed in. Naturally, Boise State was predicted to fall, succumbing to the brute size of the Bulldogs and the scorching Georgia heat.

"I can't see Boise upsetting the Dawgs," said broadcaster Brent Musberger during the summer. "No team from Idaho stands a chance in the September humidity."[1]

Said ESPN analyst Trev Albert: "Georgia should be able to line the ball up, run 45 times, and win 55–17. But you just don't know. If they get behind, you don't know what's going to happen. Boise State will be ready to play when they come to Athens."[2]

Jim Donnan, ESPN analyst: "I've seen Boise State in person, and while their offense is talented, their defense is very small. I think they will have a tough time against Georgia's size. That, and the heat, is going to be a real problem for them."[3,4]

The Georgia Bulldogs were coming off a 10–2 season in 2004 in which they finished #7 in the country in the Associated Press poll. Their head coach, Mark Richt, had just finished his fourth year and their quarterback, D. J. Shockley, a towering, hulk of a man, was ready to emerge from the shadows of David Greene, who had graduated as the winningest quarterback in college football history. After throwing just 26 attempts as a junior, Shockley was expected to keep the Bulldogs' offense in its explosive state, alongside a stable core of running backs.

Georgia's two losses in 2004 came at the hands of Tennessee, ranked #17, and Auburn, #3. They were viscous defensively, even by SEC standards, giving up just 16.5 points per game. They had a deep receiving core, led by tight end Leonard Pope.

Above all else, though, they had the hedges.

Sanford Stadium, in Athens, Georgia, is one of the toughest and most iconic stadiums in the country. Part of it is Georgia's tradition-rich program that includes Heisman trophy winners and national championships. The 92,746 fans that pack it on a weekly basis, surrounding the world-famous hedges, create a funnel of noise.

In the early 1900s, then-university president Steadman V. Sanford lived with the dream of having the "best football stadium in Dixie." Charles Martin, who through his time in Athens held almost every position possible in the athletic department, believed rose hedges would enhance the spectacle of the new structure and distinguish it from others around the country. This was the pre-stock market crash; everything was bigger and better. Martin wanted to be *different.*

There was one problem: the roses he desired would not grow in Athens. Therefore, they pivoted.

As John Lukacs of ESPN wrote, "The date was October 12, 1929, a momentous occasion on which the most famous flora in football, if not all of sports—the distinctive privet hedges ringing the field at Georgia's Sanford Stadium—was first planted, in a matter of speaking, into America's sports consciousness.[5]

Seventy-six years later, the Bulldogs had crafted a football program worthy of their infamous hedges. Boise State was a unique but challenging test.

"It's a big game for us, I can guarantee you that," Mark Richt said before the game. "They have done a wonderful job of stopping the run game, and that's our strength."[6]

Richt was still seeking his breakout moment. Although he was 42–10 as the Bulldogs' coach, there was a sense that all his cards were already played; that he was a solid 10-win coach, but lacked a certain . . . something . . . to get his teams to the next level.

"The whole summer, we were like, 'Man, we're gonna show these guys something special,'" says Michael G. Williams, a lineman for the Broncos.

On September 3, 2005, the Broncos—who were familiar with a unique home setting themselves—put nine months of single-minded focus into the biggest non-conference game in school history. At this point they now had the roster, the experience, and the opportunity to crash the BCS party and solidify themselves as the preeminent Group of 5 program in the country.

On the sideline before the game, Hawkins, black shades wrapped tight around his face, was asked why the previous night he had shown his players excerpts of the film *Star Wars: The Empire Strikes Back*. With a smile creeping across his face, Hawkins replied, "Well, you know my man Yoda, 'Size matters not.' So, if he can get it done, we can, too."

Getting off to a fast start and silencing the crowd was the Broncos' only hope of pulling off an upset. Despite his sophomore year successes, Zabransky was still prone to mental errors and costly turnovers. If that side of him arose in this setting, the Bulldogs were the exact type of team to capitalize.

On the first play of the game, with the crowd and humidity beating down on him in an unsufferable manner, Zabransky took the ball, dropped back, and let fly his first pass of the season.

Interception.

Three more interceptions—and two fumbles—would follow in one of the most lopsided, numbing losses in program history. Georgia outgunned Boise State by almost 300 yards, defeating them 48–13.

Things went so poorly for the Broncos that they practically waved the white flag, pulling Zabransky from the game in the second quarter. As Hawkins ran off the field at halftime, he was asked why he took Zabransky from the game.

"Did you watch the first half?"

As Zabranksy headed toward the sidelines following the pulling, sensing his quarterback was in for relenetless ridicule from fans and media alike—on top of the mental damage he would inflict internally—Hawkins knew his young signal caller could use a laugh.

"Hey, Z," Hawkins said to Zabransky, "the good thing is that you're never going to play this bad the rest of your life."

Reflecting back on the memory, Hawkins recalls both the frustration he felt as a coach and the sympathy he had as a person who helped mold Zabransky.

"Sure, I was frustrated, but what good would it have done to berate him?" he says now. "He was pressing, and he felt bad enough without me getting in his face."

Unfortunately, no one on the Broncos' roster played any better. For the game Boise State accumulated just 292 yards of offense, surrendering 574. Most concerning was the fact that they did not look like a team that belonged on the same field as Georgia. A win may have been too much to expect, but some competitive fire and a semblance of competition was the expectation. Neither happened.

"We got spanked," Hawkins said after the game, his face a deep, sun-soaked red. "Georgia is a good football team. They had a lot to do with it."[7]

Going into the game, a massacre was a possibility; what transpired was worse than anyone could have predicted.

It took D. J. Shockley less than three quarters for the Georgia faithful to wonder if the team would skip a beat. The Bulldogs entered 2005 coming off a mass exodus of players to the NFL—including three star defensive players in David Pollack, Thomas Davis, and Odell Thurman.

None of that mattered on this day. Boise State was overmatched and overwhelmed from the opening kickoff. The outcome was an embarrassment for a program that was looking to take the next step, on the biggest stage available.

Shockley threw for 289 yards on just 16 completions with five passing touchdown passes and an additional one on the ground. Like Zabransky, his day ended early, too. He did all of that in less than three quarters, spending the fourth dancing and whooping it up with his teammates on the sideline.

"It really hasn't hit me, yet," he said after the game. "There's no way I ever could have imagined something like this in my head. It's too big."[8]

Across the locker room, buried in a sea of smiles, one of his teammates yelled, enthusiastically, "Shockley for Heisman!"

The visitors' locker room was the complete inverse. Shock and confusion spread through the team like wildfire; an entire offseason devoted to this one game had eroded in a matter of minutes. Now a junior, this was supposed to be Zabransky's grand introduction to the nation, igniting an organic Heisman campaign built through his on-field performance.

Instead, the reset button needed to be hit: on expectations, internally and externally, on their place in college football as a whole—and, perhaps, on Hawkins as well. It was one game, but everything that he had prided himself and his program on— the Zen-like approach, the innovative nature, the physicality, the sense that they could stand toe-to-toe with anybody—was shredded in one day.

"After the game, I remember listening to a national radio show, and the host said, basically, 'Boise State, that was your chance. Don't expect a call any time soon,'" says Ian Smart.

The Georgia debacle did more than just drop the Broncos to 0–1; it represented the first real downtrodden moment for the Hawkins regime.

Throughout his first four years, Hawkins's coaching had transfixed the community. Before Georgia, he had gone an incredible 44–7; four of those losses were from the transitional 2001 team, when he was taking over for Koetter. Other than that year, the Broncos had blown through their schedule with such unabashed ease that wins were expected. Losses would come here and there, but even then the team would be competitive and put up a positive showing in the process.

The loss to Georgia was something different. Something . . . *bigger*. Inside the walls of the football complex, Hawkins's behavior had always come across as a bit quirky, yet effective. His outside-the-box comportments were eyebrow raising, but they worked. When you win nearly 90 percent of your games, it is hard to question how you get there.

But when a crack appears—especially in a foundation that had been so stable—it is even more visible. Before the Georgia game, Broncos' wide receiver Vinny Perretta told the *Idaho Statesman* that he planned to "sprint down the field full speed, knock some heads, and crush some skulls."[9] Confidence had never been an issue under Hawkins-led teams—he was indeed brash, in a more tongue-in-cheek way—but outright boasts of headhunting and an attitude of disrespect? This smelled of something else. It was beginning to feel that, especially after the brutal beatdown the Bulldogs administered, Hawkins's preachings were falling by the wayside.

The following week would be a good litmus test for the team's overall psyche. Oregon State, who Boise State overwhelmed the season before, 53–34, was waiting in Corvallis. The Beavers were not a good team—they would finish the season with just four wins, but were motivated.

The season before, much like Boise State was doing now, Oregon State entered the contest after a loss to an SEC foe. However, when the Beavers lost to LSU in 2004, it was in the most heartbreaking of ways: three missed extra points had doomed their upset bid, and the team was emotionally shattered; all Boise State had to do was pick apart the pieces that remained. The Broncos came into this September 10 matchup a stunned group. The entire eight-month span leading up to the season had been about the Georgia Bulldogs. Losing in the fashion they did had left them a shell of the team that entered Sanford Stadium the week prior.

"They're either looking for blood, or down," said Oregon State defensive end Jeff Van Orsow as the game approached. "Most likely looking for blood."[11]

Oregon State's head coach, Mike Riley, was a little more sure-footed in his assessment of the Broncos' state: "I could not imagine them not bouncing back and being ready to go. And, really, we can't worry about that. That's their problem to deal with."[12]

When the game got under way, Riley's prediction was spot on: Boise State was ready to battle. From a talent standpoint, despite being in the Pac-10, Oregon State was on-par with Boise State. When the Broncos jumped out to a quick 14–0 lead, it looked like the misgivings that took place a week before were put behind them, and all of the talk of a season slipping away may have been premature.

Then the skies opened, and everything changed. Rain charged. Hail torpedoed the turf. And, in one quarter, Boise State's season went from perilous to disasterous. Oregon State's quarterback Matt Moore led two first-half scoring drives, keeping Oregon State in the game when Boise State had threatened to blow it open.

"The hail, the rain, and the whole game," Moore said, "it was unbelievable."[13]

With a chance to extend their lead heading into halftime, Boise State's drive stalled out on the Beavers' 6-yard line, culminating in an incomplete pass on fourth down; with a second shot of life, the Beavers capitalized. Moore threw a touchdown pass to Mike Haas and Alexis Serna, the latter of which was a national punchline the previous season after his nightmare at LSU, kicked three second-half field goals, including the game winner, with 1:06 left.

Boise State was 0–2, with their first two-game losing streak since the start of the 2001 season, Hawkins's first with the school.

"I was proud of our guys," Hawkins said after the game. "They played much better than last week. Not good enough to win, but some things to build."[14]

If whispers were permeating though Boise after the Georgia loss, loud, bemoaning groans were now in its place . . . but Hawkins never flinched from his glass-half-full outlook. "We've taken a couple of knocks in the head, but I fully expect us to rally," he said after Oregon State. But it could not stop the questions from popping up.

Had he lost the team? Was his heart still in Boise? After four seasons of unprecedented success, was it time for both parties to move on?

Nevertheless, despite having lost three in a row dating back to the Liberty Bowl, one beacon of hope remained: Boise State still had yet to play a conference game; a conference in which they had gone undefeated since 2001.

All of the chatter, all of the distraction, all of the questions could be answered by simply doing the one thing they had not done since November 27, 2004: win.

Luckily, for all involved, the roster was made up of guys who carried more pride than shame.

"Most of our team was from California; for us, not being recruited by the USCs of the world kind of gave us a chip on our shoulder. The school kind of had a chip as well, from not being looked at as a national power, so I felt like we had something in common, trying to prove something," says Smart.

The lone way for Boise State to prove anything was to win games, which they did starting against Bowling Green State, 48–20, knocking the monkey off their back. Once conference play began the following week, with a 44–41 win at Hawaii, all seemed right with the team. The 2005 Broncos were a little closer to the pack, but still the class of the conference.

Over the course of conference play, San Jose State, Utah State, Nevada, and New Mexico State would all be wins; only the 56–6 win over the Lobos would stand out as a quantifiable blowout. But wins were wins, and when the team loaded the bus on November 8 and headed to the airport for their flight to Fresno State, they carried a 31-game conference winning streak, a 7-game win streak for the season, and another conference title within reach.

"The level of execution that our guys expected from themselves, and demanded of themselves . . . it was really special," says Hawkins, looking back. "We had a lot of stars, a lot of really good guys who played in the National Football League, and then we had a bunch of tough, hardworking, team-oriented guys."

That concoction headed to Fresno seeking their 32nd-straight conference win.

What they encountered was a nightmare.

In the eight games since his 70-yard, six-turnover game against Georgia to start the season, Zabransky had been electric. He was completing 65.2 percent of his passes for the season, had thrown 15 touchdowns to just 6 interceptions and, most importantly, had kept his head and emotions in check.

Now facing another Bulldogs team, this one from Fresno State, Zabransky—and the entire offense—completely dropped the ball (both literally and figuratively). They scored just seven points, totaled 294 yards, and had three turnovers. After running back Jeff Carpenter went 67 yards for a touchdown in the first minutes of the game, Boise State was a ghost; they were there in spirit and uniform but, outside of that, nothing about their performance looked normal. Fresno State held onto the ball for over 40 minutes, racked up 513 yards of offense, and used every previous whipping as fuel in their 27–7 win.

"They came in and took something form us, and we've never got it back,"[15] said Fresno State head coach Pat Hill, still discomposed from the Broncos' win in 2001, which knocked the Bulldogs from BCS consideration.

For Boise State, the ending of their conference winning streak was not the biggest disappointment of the night; the way it happened, and by whom, is what stung. Fresno State was the school that Boise State had ripped the crown from early in the 2000s. Back then, Fresno State were the little dogs taking down bigger, badder dogs. They were David Carr and Bernard

Berrian; Lorenzo Neal and Trent Dilfer and Logan Mankins. Boise State had beaten up on star-studded Bulldogs teams before . . .

But now?

Paul Pinegar—*Paul Pinegar!*—had thrown for 307 yards against them.

Fresno State was good, sure. But this was not the Fresno State of old, the group that dismembered their opponents. Because of that, the loss felt unique.

"I really didn't know it would feel this emotional," said Fresno State's Paul Williams, whose 98-yard touchdown broke the seal. "Everyone was excited, especially those seniors. They went four years without beating those guys, but we made up for everything."[16]

Boise State had become every opponent's championship game. Despite their early season struggles, their reputation still stood strong.

Now, bigger issues were lurking.

The conference title was out; so, too, it seemed, was their coach.

Following the loss to Fresno State, the Broncos finished up their regular season with convincing wins over Idaho (70–35) and Louisiana Tech (30–13), but rumors were swirling about Hawkins. They were swirling through the athletic complex, down the sidelines at practices, through the ever-growing media, and across the national airwaves. Hawkins and his success were no longer a secret. What he had accomplished at Boise State to this point—53–10 heading into the bowl game against Boston College—was not an anomaly. With his beautifully coiffed hair, his personality, and his penchant for dominating stretches of success, it seemed he had become bigger than the program.

"The thing about Hawkins—I love Hawkins because he was real. He didn't know how to sugarcoat, for the most part. We would read the papers and see that he was getting offers from this school, and that school, and he always came to us first and told us what would happen," says Rashaad Richards.

And the offers were pouring in. The Colorado Buffaloes seemed to be the most persistent in their pursuit. The fit was a good one: Hawkins was a western guy; the Buffaloes played in the Big 12 yet held a territorial advantage over many of the schools, owning the Rocky Mountain states for recruiting. The school had a great tradition, including a national title in 1990, without the barrier of unrealistic expectations and a cutthroat alumni base.

As the Broncos prepared for their bowl game, less and less focus was placed on Boston College; just two weeks out, the MPC Computers Bowl, played in Boise, was an afterthought. With each passing day, the likelihood of Hawkins being the head coach in 2006 dwindled. Unlike Koetter's exit, which was expected and came after three rebuilding years, Hawkins's was going to sting.

"What I understood was he's going to do what's best for his family, and what he thinks is best for him. Personally, I didn't really care; you know, the guy leaves? Good. We'll win without him," said Zabransky.[17]

No one had to opine long. Just shy of three weeks after his fifth season came to a close and twelve days before the bowl game, Hawkins made it all but known what his next move was.

"Officially, nothing has been decided," he said, before adding he would be the next head coach at Colorado "if certain things happen."

By this point, "certain things" were just a formality.

"You can go 99 yards on a football field," he continued, "but you have to go that last yard, otherwise you don't get a touchdown."[18]

Zabransky's sentiments—dismissive and perturbed— were common among his teammates, with a few exceptions. However, one overwhelming fear ran though the locker room: if Hawkins were gone, the team would move on and be fine . . .

. . . but if he took Chris Petersen with him?

"When the Colorado situation came, he was forward with it," says Richards. "We were just thinking, 'Dang, he better not leave and take Petersen.' Being inside the program, we knew how it went. It was because of Petersen's offense. And sure enough, it proved—Boise State kept climbing, and Hawkins went to Colorado and kind of fell off the map. I really feel like Petersen was our engine."

The answers would not take long to reveal themselves. Hawkins officially interviewed for the Colorado job on Saturday, December 10, 2005. On Friday, December 16, his cryptic, nonsensical comments about finalizing the deal were official.

Later that day, he was introduced as the newest head coach at Colorado.

His deal was for five years, making $900,000 annually. His press conference was boastful, engaging, energetic; a 45-minute whirlwind with a gold-blazered Hawkins directly in the middle.

"I think if you look around the landscape of college football, I don't care if it's BSU or UCLA, you look at how much turnover there has been in college football, it's increasingly difficult to stay somewhere for 15 years because of the scrutiny, pressure, and the dynamics of it," Hawkins said during his press conference.[19]

His feelings were mutual from many of the players he was leaving behind in the locker room.

"For me, and a lot of guys on the team . . . we needed a change," says Brett Denton, who arrived at Boise State in 2002. "The 2005 season was rough for a lot of reasons. Five losses isn't a lot, but for Boise State it is. Those losses came due to people not necessarily buying in to the coaching philosophy or methods anymore.

"Guys were getting a little bit tired of it, so the motivation wasn't there," he continued. "Coach Hawk did a good job until his magic ran out. Once we started hearing the same things over and over again, it just was not having the same effect. The team wasn't working like it could, and how it had in the past. Most people were excited for the transition."

Jeff Cheek, an offensive lineman who played under both Dirk Koetter and Hawkins, when comparing Hawkins to his predecessor, saw the personal relationships as the shining difference. Koetter, despite his tunnel vision of the game, cultivated relationships with players. He stood up for them and understood that they were prone to missteps. "If we got in trouble in the community, Koetter would talk to people and say, 'Hey, I'll take care of it. If it happens again, he's all yours.'

If it happened under Hawkins, he would go out of his way to hand us over to the authorities."

The day after Hawkins was officially introduced in Colorado, the transition Denton speaks of would be official. In a quiet and reverential manner, Boise State named Chris Petersen as their new head coach.

14

ALL ABOARD!

"Things under Petersen got a lot more personable. Going into
the Fiesta Bowl year, we knew we had as much talent as any
team the school has seen. When it came to the actual game,
we were taught pretty well not to pay attention to the media.
Because of that, we didn't realize how big of underdogs we
were. We were too busy watching film."
— Marty Tadman, Boise State, 2004–2007

ON JANUARY 1, 2006, three days after Dan Hawkins's
tenure ended in an uninspiring and awkward bowl game
for Boise State, Chris Petersen officially took over the program.
After five years under the tutelage of his mentor and friend, the
forty-one-year-old was now in the driver's seat.

"When the transition was happening, guys who were still
there would ask me, 'Who do you think would take over and do
good?' And, honestly, I hoped they'd get Petersen. I just didn't
know if he'd take it. That just wasn't his deal; he was an X's
and O's guy," says Andy Weldon, a tight end for the Broncos.

It was true: Petersen's mantra was not to hop in front of the camera and sell; his was to work in the shadows, formulating a gameplan to rip out opponents' hearts.

Despite their similar paths and long relationship, Petersen was in many ways the antithesis of Dan Hawkins—quiet, unassuming, film junkie, tough, open-minded.

"Hawkins always said that one of the reasons he got things done here [in Boise] is the chemistry is just unbelievable," Petersen said when he took over. "And that will be my goal: to get the same mojo and chemistry going on with my staff."[1]

To ease the transition, Petersen's first year would be buoyed by the returning star power on his team. They were bringing back, arguably, the best team in school history. Ian Johnson had emerged as a potential star at running back after finishing with 663 yards as a freshman the year before. Orlando Scandrick, Kyle Wilson, and a host of stalwarts on defense were also back. If the Broncos were going to improve upon their 9–4 season of 2005—a blasphemous record in Boise—turnovers were going to be the biggest key. The season prior, Boise State ranked 94th in the country, losing the ball a staggering 34 times in 13 games.

"For us to have a 9–4 record with that turnover margin is truly amazing," Petersen said a week before the 2006 season began. "We've got to get that thing corrected. Our defense did a good job of getting us the ball, but on offense we need to hang on to it more—especially at that quarterback position."[3]

Ah, yes, the quarterback position. Petersen may not have been aiming his words directly at Jared Zabransky; they were more likely to all the quarterbacks on the roster. However,

Zabransky alone had committed 24 of those turnovers in 2005, after throwing 16 interceptions and losing 8 more on fumbles.

A criticism and flaw of the 2005 team was that the locker room had begun to tune Hawkins out and take a more laissez faire attitude into games. Zabransky, based on his play, may have been the biggest culprit. He was too talented, too competitive, and too vital to put up such median numbers.

One of his interceptions, in the waning seconds of the MPC Computers Bowl—which played a role in the loss—drove the senior quarterback into his most dedicated and focused offseason yet.

"Since my last interception [in the bowl game], all I can think about is the season," he told reporters after a fall camp practice. "I feel that the quarterback can change the game at any given time. I think what operates the teams is turnovers; the guy who doesn't turn the ball over gives his team a better chance to win."

Internally, the hope was that Petersen and his meticulous, detail-oriented nature would have more of an effect on Zabransky now that he was the head man. Mostly, though, the development would have to come from himself. If the offense could slash their obscene turnover numbers in half from 2005, things figured to go much smoother.

Zabransky knew the stakes. After the ups-and-downs in his career, he knew what his senior season meant; not just to the team, but to his entire legacy.

The path to redemption was simple.

"When I don't turn the ball over, our team usually does pretty well."[4]

* * *

Identifying the talent of Chris Petersen was a testament to one of Hawkins's strengths, one that often went unnoticed due to his outgoing personality: he let his coaches coach, without an overbearing, helicopter-like approach.

Because of that, the players had seen Petersen work his magic.

"When you have a guy like Petersen . . . I think Hawkins did a great job by just letting him do his thing," says Donny Heck. "He obviously knew what Petersen was capable of. I think they [Petersen and Hawkins] had a great thing going, because we were able to spend more time with Petersen, and he made us a lot better. And then Hawkins would do his thing."

Petersen's greatest strength—his affection for devouring game tape and knowing his opponents inside and out—were going to take a hit as the head coach. Now that he was at the helm, he would be pulled in a thousand different directions, most of which were outside the one thing Petersen loved to do most: study.

His days of locking the door and gorging himself on hours of film were over. Media obligations, boosters, chancellors—everyone would want a piece of him. How he handled that would go a long way in determining the Broncos' success.

"The head coach is kind of a figurehead, and doesn't get time to dive as much into the X's and O's as much as he wants, and that's the kind of guy coach Petersen is; he likes working with the guys, he likes setting up the drills," says offensive lineman Pete Cavender. "But obviously he took the job, because I think he felt loyalty to us. He made a promise that he would see things through, and he wanted to make sure we were going to have the best coaches possible, and he wanted to step up to the plate and do that for us."

In doing so, Petersen was now the guy taking all the criticism. As the offensive coordinator, his play calling ability was rarely questioned (Boise State averaged over 40 points per game in the five years he held that title), and he was able to hide in the shadows during times of recession. That was no longer the case.

If his capacity to handle the additional pressure was a concern for people on the outside looking in, Petersen was one step ahead of them. He had been doing that, internally, for years.

"When we lost a game in the past, I basically thought it was my fault anyway because we didn't score enough points."[5]

Scoring enough points didn't figure to be a problem in his first season; with 10 starters returning on defense, allowing too many on the other side was not a big concern, either.

"We take pride in stopping the run," said Korey Hall, who led the team in tackles for the 2005 season. "If you stop the run, it makes a team one-dimensional. After that, it's not too hard to stop the pass."[6]

* * *

On paper, the 2006 Boise State Broncos appeared to be a rocket ready to explode. In actuality, the team was in the midst of yet another coaching change, coming off a four-loss season. Although Petersen provided a foundation of normalcy, he was still a first-time coach who had not been shy with his players in the past about his desire *not* to be a head coach.

It begged the question: When the chips were down, how would Petersen handle himself?

One way of ensuring that the chips would stay stacked was opening up with a Division I-AA patsy.

The Broncos did just that on August 31, 2006, when they ushered in the Petersen era by welcoming the Sacramento State Hornets into Bronco Stadium.

Before the season began, Petersen had said, "It's kind of what I expected. I've been around for a long time, and around a lot of coaches. I've seen a lot of things."[7] Still, he had never been on the sidelines at kickoff as a college football team's head coach.

The opportunity to make a lasting impression had finally arrived. A statement win would send the locals home singing an optimistic tune. A bad performance would raise a bounty of questions.

The Broncos wasted little time in making that impression one to remember.

Touchdown. Touchdown. Touchdown. Touchdown.

The Broncos performed as if they were playing against air; with all due respect to the Hornets, they may as well have been. The offense scored touchdowns on four of their first five possessions, took a 28–0 lead into halftime, got Jared Zabransky off to a fantastic start with three total touchdowns, and sent a clear message to Boulder, Colorado: *We'll be just fine, Dan. Thanks.*

The defense also sent an emphatic blow to offenses all over the WAC. There was a belief heading into the season that they could be a special unit; giving up one first down, and 33 yards of offense in the first half, cemented those thoughts. Sure, it was Sacramento State, but the performance was nonetheless eye-opening.

The 45–0 win did not open eyes around the rest of the country, but that was not the goal. This was about everyone in the program, from Gene Bleymaier on down, finding faith in their wet-behind-the-ears coach, the one players had pined for. It was also symbolic for another reason: Playing in the Big Sky, the Hornets were a glimpse into the past; a reminder of where the Broncos came from and what they had become.

It was also just the beginning.

After rushing for 83 yards on 13 carries in the first game, Ian Johnson, who had distanced himself from the other backs on the roster with his speed and elusiveness, would go on a tear throughout the rest of September.

In Week 2 against Oregon State, as the Broncos defeated the Beavers for the second time in four meetings—this time scoring 42 unanswered points to end the game—Johnson went wild. He rushed for 240 yards and five scores, including touchdown runs of 59 and 50 yards, while catching another from Zabransky. Over the next three games, he would rush for 385 more yards.

By the time the calendar hit October, he had amassed 714 yards and nine touchdowns, surpassing his previous year's totals in both categories.

The Broncos were 5–0, roughing up their opponents by 24 points per game, and after their 36–3 win at Utah on September 30, were ranked #22 in the country. It was the first time they had been ranked since the fateful trip to Georgia dropped them out the season before.

The emergence of Johnson was a welcome development; the drastic improvement of Zabransky was a Godsend.

Although his stats weren't blinding, Zabransky made it look like every interception, every fumble, every missed opportunity from the previous three seasons had been encapsulated in a tiny bottle and blown to pieces. He had thrown seven touchdowns and was completing 61 percent of his passes. Most importantly, he had just two interceptions.

After the Utah game, sweat-soaked and smiling, Petersen found himself surrounded by reporters. Buzz was beginning to swirl around the team; not only had they not lost a step in their post-Hawkins start—if anything, they looked more focused, more lethal, and more prepared than ever before to ascend to the next level.

With one sentence, Petersen quenched any postseason thoughts right there on the spot.

"Don't even ask me one question about the BCS."[8]

If Petersen did not want to talk about his team's odds of making it in, he was one of the few. Five games into the season, and with no ranked opponents left on their schedule, the Broncos had two ways of looking at their future: an almost surefire path to their undefeated season; or a schedule so weak that the BCS would remain a dream.

The Bowl Championship Series was a convoluted, disastrous concoction brewed up by analytical types. The ire the BCS drew from fans of college football was palpable; the "eye test," which had been the hotly debated, yet tried-and-true way of ranking teams for decades, ended after the 1997 season. It was replaced by analytics that included strength of schedule, as well as a review of other computer-generated data.

The formula had come under hell-fire during the 2004 season, when Southeastern Conference powerhouse Auburn Tigers were left out of the national championship game despite running the table with a 13–0 record. The Tigers finished the regular season ranked 2nd in both the Associated Press and the Coaches Polls, yet came in 3rd in the BCS, denying them a title shot.

For Boise State, all of the formulas would be irrelevant if they didn't win every game for the rest of the season. Schools from outside the "Power 5"—which consisted of the Pac-10 (at the time), the Big Ten, SEC, ACC, and Big 12—did not stand a chance with a loss.

From the BCS handbook, this is what the Broncos were focusing on, even if Petersen denied it:

> If there are fewer than 10 automatic qualifiers, then the bowls will select at-large participants to fill the remaining berths. An at-large team is any Football Bowl Subdivision team that is bowl-eligible and meets the following requirements:
>
> A. Has won at least nine regular-season games.
>
> B. Is among the top 14 teams in the final BCS Standings.
>
> No more than two teams from a conference may be selected, regardless of whether they are automatic qualifiers or at-large selections, unless two non-champions from the same conference are ranked No. 1 and No. 2 in the final BCS Standings.

Fresno State had stumbled out of the gate to a 1–4 start. John Lindsay, writing in the *Desert Sun*, gave the WAC a "D" score overall though five weeks—even with the Broncos' start, saying, "Fresno State's demise—along with the rest of the league's bottom-feeders—all but makes sure No. 19 Boise State won't get a BCS at-large bid if the Broncos go undefeated."[9]

After disposing of Louisiana Tech in Week 6 by 41 points (55–14), Boise State's Week 7 opponent, New Mexico State, was not going to improve the Broncos' overall standing, either. However, the Aggies *were* a viable threat on the field, bringing the nation's top passing offense. It was the Broncos' second game of the year televised on ESPN and their first as a ranked team. After their first appearance on national television in 2001, the Broncos had been on the network nineteen more times. Their record, 15–4.

By this point the WAC had fully succumbed to the idea of playing their games whenever necessary to get the most exposure. Because of that—and the major networks' insatiable appetite for around-the-clock football—Western Athletic teams oftentimes popped up on Tuesday, Wednesday, Thursday, and especially Friday nights. When the Broncos and Aggies squared off on Sunday night, October 15, directly opposite the Oakland Raiders-Denver Broncos NFL game playing on NBC, hardly anyone batted an eye.

The Broncos wasted little time in proving they belonged in the postseason discussion. Ian Johnson was locked in from the get-go, scoring four times in the first half, finishing with 192 yards, while Zabransky threw two second-half touchdowns. But New Mexico State, with that pass-happy attack, gave the

Broncos something to think about for the rest of the season. Aggies sophomore quarterback Chase Holbrock came into the game as the nation's leading scorer, and it was not hard to see why. The Broncos were giving up just 12 points per game coming into the contest; they gave up 28. They were allowing a paltry 166 yards per game through the air; Holbrock threw for 529, completing 50-of-66 passes.

Taking teaching points away from an otherwise ho-hum game can be a bit tricky, but Petersen knew exactly what his message was going to be once he got back to the locker room. If the Broncos weren't careful, a team like New Mexico State, or Idaho (the Broncos' next opponent) could jump up and snip them.

"The bulls-eye continues to grow the more we win," Petersen said as Idaho approached. "We've known that from the start."[10]

Dennis Erickson, who had coached the Idaho Vandals from 1982–1985, had returned before the 2006 season. His coaching run after Idaho included two national championships (University of Miami), relevancy to a downtrodden program (Oregon State), while also making stops in the NFL (with the Seattle Seahawks and San Francisco 49ers). Erickson came with a recognizeable name and an impenetrable coaching acumen.

The problem was, he inherited a terrible team, one in the midst of a six-game losing streak to Boise State. From the beginning, the rivalry had taken odd twists. Rarely, for the over forty years that the teams had been playing, was there a stretch of truly competitive football. In their 16 previous wins leading up to the 2006 game, the Broncos had defeated the Vandals by an average of 26.5 points; their 17 losses in the series were by an average of nearly 16 points per game. The matchup in 2006 looked like more of the same, despite the optimism surrounding Erickson's return to Moscow. The Vandals had gone a paltry 11–47 the five previous seasons, resulting in the dismissal of both Tom Cable and Nick Holt.

Erickson may have been a good coach in turning around Oregon State or maximizing talent at Miami, but Idaho was a different level of bad. Whereas the other schools had built-in advantages, such as fertile grounds or a hefty budget, the Vandals sported neither.

"Idaho had some good athletic directors in the 1980s and 1990s, but I don't think they had the money [Gene] Bleymaier could go out and get, especially the way the community of Boise began to get behind the school," says Bert Sahlberg, columnist for the *Lewiston Tribune*. While the Broncos had focused their efforts on building a brand and a stable stream of success, the Vandals had fallen by the wayside.

"I think Boise State had their eyes on a bigger picture," he continued. "Maybe they weren't being as successful as they would like to be [in the 1980s and '90s], but once they turned it on, everything was in place."

With five games remaining in the season, the Broncos found themselves at a crossroads. One of the downfalls of the BCS system was their emphasis on "quality wins." Since the WAC closely resembled a 4A high school league, they would get no help there; their lone out-of-conference win that could have carried weight, Oregon State, had stumbled out to a 3–3 start. The only way they could get those quality wins was to do the one thing no one wanted, but everyone knew was the right choice: if given the chance, the Broncos were going to have to start running up the score. A lot.

As in, dismantle a team, strip them down to their underwear in front of the gymnasium, and beat them again.

The higher the margin of victory, the more impressive it would look—especially when most of their games were on late at night when most voters, who were east coast-based, would not be watching. The final score would be the verdict.

As the game against the Vandals approached, the possibility of an intentional blowout was not lost on Erickson.

"Because of their schedule and all the things that are done in these rankings, that's something people look at," he said when the idea of Boise State running up the score was floated to him. "That's just how it is. Whether you're in the Mountain West or the WAC, any team that's not in the BCS [affiliated conference]. Those things happen."[11]

When the Broncos exited the locker room to 17,000 fans inside the Kibbie Dome in Moscow, their #18 ranking laid out a clear path to the BCS. One poor showing—even in victory— would spoil their dreams; overlook the Vandals, and the entire house of cards could come tumbling down.

Early on, that's exactly what happened.

When Steve Wichman capped off the Vandals' opening drive by hitting Wendall Octave for a 4-yard touchdown pass, the walls of the Kibbie Dome trembled. After Boise had tied the game on a 61-yard pass from Zabransky to Legedu Naanee, Wichman hit Luke Smith-Anderson for another touchdown, giving Idaho back the lead, 14–7.

After just one quarter, the Broncos had given up 14 points; only twice prior in the season had they given up more for the entire game. They were shaken. They were being bullied. For the first time during the season, they were facing a doomsday scenario, with a lesser opponent taking them for all they were worth.

They were also just getting revved up.

For the most part, Petersen had stuck to the script during his first year. With their impenetrable offensive line and the emergence of Ian Johnson, there was no need to overthink the offense; football was built off the concept of running the ball and playing solid defense.

Once they fell behind, the coaching staff went back to the basics.

The ball went back in Johnson's hands, and order was restored. He would score four touchdowns on the day—including three in the second half—when the Broncos outscored the Vandals 21–12. Johnson used every one of his 194 pounds in rumbling his way to 183 yards, upping his season total to 1,181 with 18 touchdowns.

"If a guy tries to arm tackle him, he's going to break that," Petersen said after the game. "If we give Ian a chance, he's always going to get positive yards."[12]

"It felt like a rivalry," said Zabransky, who had his worst day of the season, completing just 45.5 percent of his passes. "We knew they were gong to try and smash every hope we have."[13]

The 45–26 win was the smallest margin against Idaho since a 14-point win in 2003, but it was worth more than the margin. For the first time since they trailed 14–0 to Oregon State, the Broncos faced real adversity, and lived to play another day. With the win, they joined six other undefeated teams in the country—Ohio State, Michigan, Louisville, West Virginia, Rutgers, and USC—and remained alive in their fight for a BCS slot.

The final four games of the Broncos' season—Fresno State, San Jose State, Utah State, and Nevada—went by without a hitch. The school's second undefeated regular season was in the books. So, too, was the glass ceiling that they had butted up against in 2004.

On Sunday, December 3, the Fiesta Bowl (a BCS bowl) formally invited the Broncos. Unlike the Utah Utes two years prior, Boise State's opponent would be dripping with relevance. This program had national championships, Heisman trophy winners, and a serious case as one of the best teams in the country.

On January 1, 2007, Boise State would face the Oklahoma Sooners.

15

A FIESTA FOR ALL

"I wish I could recreate what it was that made us special for that Fiesta Bowl season; I can't really put my finger on it. We just had guys that wanted to win, guys that came up through the program together."

—Joe Bozikovich, Boise State, 2006–2008

THE OKLAHOMA SOONERS' traveling caravan is that of rock stars on tour. Everything about the program, from their seven national championships, forty-seven conference titles, to their six Heisman Trophy winners who adorn the walls announces the school's presence. When the Sooners claimed the Big 12 title on December 2, 2006, knocking off another perennial power in Nebraska, it set forth a chain of events that would go on to alter the course of not only Boise State, but arguably the entire college football landscape.

Nationally, the matchup was cliché fodder.

Big vs. Little. Behemoth against Runt. David vs. Golaith.

But inside the walls of the Boise State athletic department, a sundry attitude was brewing as the game approached.

"In terms of the intimidation factor, we didn't have it," says Nick Schlekeway, a defensive end, looking back. "It was, 'Yeah, you have good athletes. We have good athletes. Let's go compete. Let's see who can execute.'" Boise State players were well aware of the historical impact, as well as the imprint a school like Oklahoma carried with them. Without saying it aloud for the wrong hands to digest, they also knew what it could mean for the program and the perception of similar-sized schools when—not "if"—they won.

"We were all gathered around watching the Big 12 Championship game, and believe me: we were all rooting for Oklahoma. We wanted them," says Jeff Cavender.

Oklahoma had the size advantage, the speed advantage . . . whatever the category, they held the upper hand. Even so, the Broncos players weren't concerned.

"I'm one of the most un-athletic guys to ever play on the defensive end at Boise State, and I wasn't intimidated at all," says Schlekeway.

* * *

The airplane carrying the Boise State football team, complete with players, coaches, boosters, and media, left the tarmac on the morning of Tuesday, December 26, 2006. Christmas had come and gone, and Bowl games were in full swing around the country. When the contingent boarded the plane, the totality of the environment they were headed toward was still in the windshield, yet to be realized.

The ground in Boise was iced-over and cracked, the result of yet another harsh winter season; the wind whipping through could rattle the bones of the thickest lineman.

The site of the Fiesta Bowl—Glendale, Arizona—would be sun-splashed and warm.

The Broncos were heading into a different world, in more ways than one.

To help cement their status as the sideshow in the eyes of the Fiesta Bowl crew, the charter plane carrying the team landed in the wrong area of the airport, denying the Broncos the welcome moment that had been set up: a mariachi band, Fiesta Bowl volunteers, and pre-set fans ready to greet the team as they exited the plane. A reception befitting a BCS team.

Instead, they walked off to silence, the party seemingly miles away, rocking on without them.

They were outsiders to their own revelry.

Unlike years past when the overlook and disrespect was out of their hands, the Fiesta Bowl was an opportunity for the team to write their own ending. All they had to do was line up against arguably the greatest powerhouse program of all time, in a game no one expected them to be in, let alone win, and control the narrative.

"I do think other schools and people may have doubts about Boise State—us being from the WAC, which in other people's opinions has lesser schools," said linebacker David Shields before the game. "I really do think we have something to prove, which is why I'm so glad we're playing Oklahoma."[1]

The Fiesta Bowl's impact on the school at-large would be felt months and years down the road; for the locals of Boise that made the journey south, this was a time to bask in the glory.

"It seems like the whole city has rallied around the team, and the whole valley—the 500,000-plus that live in the Boise

Valley," said Petersen as the team headed to their hotel after arrival. "It seems like there are not many people from that area not coming to the game. I have never felt so much support toward this team since I have been here."

Petersen's opinions of his fan base echoed those he held about the players themselves.

"I've just been so impressed with our kids all year long," he continued. "No matter who we've played, they've stayed focused on the task at hand—taking every game as serious as the next; it didn't matter what the team's record was, good or bad. These guys have been very business-like all year long.

"It's going to be a challenge to play Oklahoma. They're like nobody we've seen all year or maybe since I got to Boise State."[2]

When Karl Benson, then the commissioner of the Western Athletic Conference, landed in Tempe, his near-giddy behavior seemed justified. As commissioner, he had been tasked with marketing an inferior product; now he could put his shiniest toy on the front display for all shoppers to see.

"I think this is significant in terms of the season the WAC has had. I'm proud that the WAC is currently rated by the computers as the seventh-best conference in the country,"[3] he groused. Benson, come hell or high water, was going to get in his digs.

When pressed on comments that he had made earlier that Boise State was the most dominant team in WAC history, more so than famed Arizona State (1975) and BYU (1984, co-national champions), Benson bowed up.

"I stand by it," he said. "What Boise State has done is more impressive that what Arizona State or BYU had done."[4]

The Fiesta Bowl was an opportunity for the program to make a statement on another level. Football results notwithstanding, the Broncos were now the face of underdogs everywhere. Where so often those folks don't get their true shot to conquer, the Broncos did. It was not lost on the players, many of whom had similar feelings of ineptitude which stoked their fire.

In a study put forth by the University of South Florida, titled "The Appeal of the Underdog," it was found that, "When people observe competition, they are often drawn to figures that are seen as disadvantaged or unlikely to prevail."[5]

On those grounds, Boise State's appeal made sense. So, too, did the family-like environment they were fostering.

"My whole career, from Pee-Wee through high school and at Boise, I had worn number 64," Pete Cavender says now. "My brother [Jeff, his twin] had worn 54. Before the first game of the season against Sacramento State, I crutch into the locker room. I was out for the season with an Achilles injury, and some of my teammates were telling me, 'Hey, have you checked out Jeff?' I look over to him, and he's wearing my number 64. It was a complete surprise; I didn't know about it. His thing was, 'If I couldn't be out on the field, at least my jersey would be.' It was a really touching gesture."

It was the 2006 Boise State team wrapped up in a moment. Together and unified.

* * *

"Mention Boise, Idaho, around the country and chances are most people would think of a backwater stop in the middle of nowhere."[6]

These words floated from the offices of the Associated Press on the morning of December 29, 2006, and in newspapers around the country. Agree or disagree, Bob Baum hit on perhaps the biggest misconception about the city of Boise—and a constant source of consternation among those who reside there. The perception was that they had arrived at the Fiesta Bowl by horse-and-buggy; that their place was "somewhere else"; that the program was not what it actually was, but a dreamt-up fable.

"The reason I am excited about this is not necessarily the game," Petersen said just three days before kickoff. "I am so excited because I want this momentum and fan support to grow and change our program. They are getting it done in Norman, Oklahoma; they are getting it done in Lincoln, Nebraska.

"Boise, Idaho, is a pretty special town, too."[7]

As the game drew near, there were natural ebbs-and-flows from the public buildup. Oklahoma entered the Fiesta Bowl as favorites, but both teams carried a particular weight on their shoulders: for Boise, they could now show the opportunity was deserved—"We know we've got to go out there and compete and show well," Petersen said, "or people will be saying, 'Yeah, they shouldn't have been there anyways'"[8]—and for Oklahoma, they were trying to avoid the dreaded letdown that their fans were fearing.

"It will not be hard for us to focus on this," Sooners' head coach Bob Stoops said at the time. "I look at people's track records. I look at what people have done over a great period of time, and Boise State has been excellent."[9]

Both sides, despite entering the game from opposite ends of the perception spectrum, were playing for the same purpose: pride.

As part of the week-long festivities, the teams held separate pep rallies; chances for fans, alumni, high-level boosters, and kids to circle together as one. As the Broncos' rally loomed, throngs of fans formed in front of the makeshift stage, boisterously chanting. The booze was flowing freely. The inhibitions were lowering. Months and years and decades of unrecognized success had built up to this week. When players and coaches took the stage, the top blew off.

After they had taken their place, Petersen grabbed a nearby microphone. As he prepared to speak, he paused. The surge of noise emanating from the crowd was overwhelming. Finally, after taking in the scenery, Petersen opened his mouth.

Six years prior, when he and his family had made the move from Eugene to Boise, the program Petersen had joined was far removed from the one he captained on this day. Dirk Koetter had gotten them close; Dan Hawkins moved them further. But as he stood on the stage, the setting sun and the dreams of every Bronco fan in front of him, he knew this moment was bigger than any one individual.

All that was left was to play.

"The guys have worked so hard," he began, easing in. "They're ready to go. And our question to you is . . . "

He stopped for another moment, long enough for the scene to reach its maximum potency.

"Are *you* ready to go?"

* * *

On the field, just moments before kickoff on January 1, 2007, Chris Petersen had a smile on his face, trending toward a smirk. A sly, all-knowing smirk.

As FOX sideline reporter Chris Myers was setting the stage for his introductory question, Petersen's eyes remained fixated on an outwardly figure.

When Myers uttered the following sentence, "Coach, your team, America's underdog, the little guy," the smirk on the coach's face grew.

It was all Petersen, mere seconds from the kickoff to the biggest game of his and his players' career, needed to hear.

"We're playing for a lot of things," he responded. "We're playing for the city of Boise, our university, the state of Idaho . . . anybody else out there who thinks they might not have a chance.

"We're playing for everybody."

For the Oklahoma Sooners, the return of star running back Adrian Peterson figured to be the emotional enhancement they needed. Peterson, a consensus five-star recruit out of high school, had been everything promised coming out of Palestine, Texas, three seasons before. During his freshman season in 2004, he had rushed for 1,925 yards and 15 touchdowns. Oklahoma finished 12–1 that season, 3rd in the country.

Peterson would be clipped by injuries throughout the following two seasons (in 2006, he had missed all but six games during the regular season, having not played since a win at Iowa State on October 14). When he put on his pads on January 1, his health remained the biggest question mark for both teams.

Was he healthy? Was he in any shape to play?

If he were both, then how would the Broncos be able to slow him down?

During the six games Peterson had played before his injury, "unstoppable" would be a flimsy and incorrect description of his play. He had rushed for 935 yards, including his 211-yard performance at Oregon. When healthy, no team—let alone an outsized Boise State squad—could slow him down.

On the first play of the Fiesta Bowl, the test for Boise State came. After Oklahoma quarterback Paul Thompson took the snap, he handed the ball to Peterson. Directly in front of him, Broncos defensive end Mike G. Williams had caravanned into the backfield, forcing Peterson to hop inside his intended hole.

Flying from his safety position, Gerald Alexander dove into Peterson's legs, taking him down for a nondescript 2-yard gain.

Intimidation factor, gone.

In one play, the question running through the mind of Oklahoma players of how the Broncos would react had been answered.

"They were amped up from the beginning," says Rufus Alexander, Oklahoma's all-everything linebacker. "They had that feeling of, 'We're the little team, nobody thinks we have a chance.'"

Peterson would gain nine yards on the next play, getting the Sooners a first down.

For the next 28 minutes of game action that followed, Boise State was in control.

On their first offensive possession, aided by a juggling, acrobatic catch from tight end Derek Schouman on 3rd and 5, the Broncos moved the ball with ease. The offensive line, holding hands as a measure to counter the noise made from the Sooner fans, was stone-like in giving Zabransky time to throw.

On first down, 49 yards from the end zone, with 9:16 to go in the first quarter, Zabransky found a receiver, Drisan James, streaking alone near the right sideline, untethered.

James, a native of Phoenix, had the first touchdown of the game.

"And the first stone, fired by David, hits Goliath right in the chest!" said Thom Brennaman, who was doing the play-by-play for the FOX broadcast.

With the Broncos fans in attendance causing the stands to vibrate under the weight of their screams, the Sooners took possession on their own 12-yard line.

On the very next play, the floodgates opened.

Broncos' defensive lineman Mike T. Williams broke through the line, sacking Thompson and forcing a fumble, giving the Broncos the ball on the Sooners' 9-yard line. Two plays later, Ian Johnson would score his 25th rushing touchdown of the season, giving Boise State a 14–0 lead.

Two touchdowns, one minute and thirty-eight seconds apart. A lifetime of frustrations unloaded.

Oklahoma would respond with a touchdown to cap off a 13-play drive, cutting Boise State's lead to 14–7 after the first quarter; they would make it 14–10 later in the second quarter, edging their way back in the fight.

Then, magic.

With 47 seconds remaining in the first half, 31 yards from the end zone, Zabransky, flanked by towering members of the Sooners' defensive line, escaped trouble, then tossed a lob across the field. After making the grab, James pivoted back toward the middle of the field, shed one tackle, and took off like a bolt of lightning. Splitting two more defenders, he dove into the end zone, giving the Broncos a 21–10 lead, eliminating any momentum the Sooners had built up over the previous 10 minutes.

As the final seconds ticked off the clock in the first half, with players from both sides exiting to their locker room, a distinct sound was emanating from the stands. This was not a clash of competing fanbases, both cheering their team on to the break. This sound was strictly from the throats of the fans clad in blue and orange: pure, unadulterated bliss.

Their team was just 30 minutes from immortality.

* * *

When Boise State was forced to punt on their first possession of the second half, the belief was that the Sooners had found their footing, and would begin the comeback that seemed so obvious (most likely after an ill-tempered halftime speech from their head coach Bob Stoops).

However, with 8:11 to play in the third and the score still 21–10, Broncos safety Marty Tadman stepped in front of Paul Thompson's pass at the 28-yard line and returned it for a touchdown.

The Broncos now led 28–10, with 23 minutes left in regulation.

"At that point, mentally, the offense was so into just putting the game away. The offensive line, as a group, we were really coming together. Everything was rolling really, really well," says Andrew Woodruff.

Outcomes of games can rest on the fate of a singular play. Whether it enhances momentum or steals it back to the other side, one play can alter the most lopsided of affairs. When the Sooners were forced to punt with just over five minutes to go in the third quarter, down by 18 and giving the ball back to a Broncos squad brimming with confidence, even the most devout and optimistic Sooner had to be worried.

Then, the "one play" came into effect.

As Tadman hovered near his own 10-yard line to receive the punt, waiving his hands for a fair catch, the ball crashed down at the nine and catapulted forward, hitting the leg of another Bronco player.

Live ball. Oklahoma recovery. Momentum, swung.

Two plays later, after Adrian Peterson galloped into the end zone, a stunned Broncos team looked on from the sidelines, questioning whether the scene playing out before them was real. In the blink of an eye, the lead was cut to 28–17.

After another Boise State punt, Oklahoma settled for a field goal, bringing the score to 28–20 as the clock struck zero to end the third quarter.

What followed is perhaps the most unbelievable final quarter college football has ever seen.

A series of punts and turnovers kept the teams at a stalemate until Oklahoma took over on their own 22-yard line, 78 yards from the end zone, with just 2:40 left in the game, trailing by eight.

Then, chaos.

A Paul Thompson completion moved the ball to the 35; another completion to Manuel Johnson took the ball to the Boise 47. After Johnson was tackled, Orlando Scandrick crumpled to the carpet with an injury, robbing the Broncos of their top defender.

After two more completions and a scramble run, Thompson hit Quinten Chaney in the end zone. The Sooners were a two-point conversion away from tying the game, one they were close to being blown out of earlier.

After all of it—all of the hype, all of the drama, all of the early lead and momentum-swilling plays—Boise State was in crisis mode. And, when the Sooners connected on their two-point conversion (after the first attempt was called back for defensive pass interferance and the second called back for illegal offensive shift), crisis turned to numbness.

On the first play of their ensuing possession, after putting forth a brilliant game and season, Zabransky threw an interception to Marcus Walker, who returned it for a touchdown.

After trailing for 59 minutes, Oklahoma grabbed their first lead, 35–28.

"I was really sick to my stomach," says Taylor Tharp, Zabransky's backup. "It felt like his career was going to be summed up by that."

Fortunately for Zabranksy and the rest of the team, Walker's pick-six left just enough time on the clock for one final attempt at history.

16

THE CIRCUS LEAVES TOWN

"Petersen's 'OKG' mantra wasn't just for the players; it went
for the coaches, too. You can see that with all of the turnover
he's had on his staff. He's pretty much a coaching factory. He
brings in guys, they become successful. He just has something
about him, where he can look into the soul of a person and see
what type of person you are."

—Aaron Tevis, Boise State, 2007–2011

THE SMILE THAT Taylor Tharp gives when describing the
play "Circus," which Boise State was set to run, makes sense
upon reflection.

When Jared Zabranksy lined up facing the now infamous 4th
and 18 play, with 18 seconds remaining in regulation, he was
staring down potentially the final play of his Boise State career.
If the Broncos failed to convert, it was done. His legacy would
start with the Georgia debacle and end with Marcus Walker
prancing into the end zone.

Luckily, Zabransky saw the same thing Tharp had seen when assessing the Oklahoma defense.

The Sooners, inexplicably, were giving Boise State exactly what they needed, having their safeties play too far back, leaving a wonderful pocket of space for the Broncos to work with. After taking the snap out of the shotgun at their own 45-yard line, Zabransky, with his feet chomping at the field as if running from prey, and his eyes permanently fixated downfield, cocked his arm back and unloaded.

When the ball landed in the arms of Drisan James, he was two full yards behind the first down marker. Surrounding him—one directly in front, one to his left, and one to his right—were Oklahoma defenders ready to tackle him just short of the first down and end the game. Had James maneuvered any other direction, the game would be over. Instead, he took three steps toward the middle of the field and slightly back in the wrong direction. There, crossing his backside, was fellow receiver Jerard Rabb, cutting back against the grain.

Before the Sooners defenders could process what was happening, James lateraled the ball to Rabb, who plucked it out of midair and turned upfield. One toss, one snag, and Rabb was gone, outrunning the entire Oklahoma secondary into the end zone, into immortality.

Into overtime.

* * *

When the Broncos won the toss in overtime, electing to go on defense first—a normal strategy—they put their hopes in a unit that had battled gallantly for the majority of the game. At best, they wanted to keep Oklahoma out, forcing a field goal.

Instead, on the first play of the extra period, Adrian Peterson took a handoff, cut to his left, and raced—nearly untouched—to paydirt.

One play. One decisive statement run from Oklahoma.

"It was like our defense was standing still on Peterson's touchdown run. It was like we weren't even on the field," says Schlekeway now.

The Broncos' main plot point had been foiled. The last thing they wanted was a second overtime; not with their team beat down and emotionally drained.

However, after the Sooners' touchdown, forcing a second overtime became the only thing left to do. In college football, each team starts their possession just 25 yards from the end zone. Oklahoma needed one play to score; Boise State took six plays just to get to the 6-yard line. Facing a 4th and 2, Chris Petersen again dug into his bag of tricks, pulling out a direct snap to wide receiver Vinny Perretta. With Zabransky flanked out as a decoy, Peretta rolled out to his right where tight end Derek Schouman—who already hauled in a pass on third down early in the drive—broke free and headed toward the back of the end zone.

Perretta's pass, as it had to be, was perfect. Touchdown.

The Broncos had pulled off the latest miracle. Still, they trailed by one point.

On the FOX broadcast, just seconds after Schouman's catch, Charles Davis, an analyst and former player, said, "They're going for two, guys, I'm telling you. They are tired. When you're Cinderella, at a certain point, you don't keep slugging with the big guy. They're going to try and win the football game right now."

Davis's prediction was correct—Boise State had come too far, overcome too much, and had too much to gain—to not try and push forward.

They were going to win or lose on this play.

"I think he [Petersen] knew he needed to win the game or not," Schlekeway says now. "When you're playing a team like Oklahoma, that really starts to show up in the fourth quarter. It shows up when you've got guys out there playing every single snap, and they have a second-string that is almost as good as their starters—especially on defense, and the defensive line."

After an Oklahoma timeout, Boise State lined up for the final time of their season, which was already in the books as the greatest in school history.

Zabranksy—with perfect execution—took the snap, turned with a twitch to his right, faked his pass attempt, and slung the ball around his back into the waiting arms of Ian Johnson, who saw nothing but daylight. The Statue of Liberty play, the epitome of trickery, had worked to perfection.

As Oklahoma defenders stood flat-footed in confusion, Johnson crossed the goal line, setting off celebratory tears across the state of Idaho. He flung the ball high into the stands, raised his arms, and attempted to jump. A collegiate athlete in the height of his physical abilities, his feet barely left the ground. The emotions, the physical toll, the enormity of the moment, was all too much.

The Broncos had pulled off the 43–42 win, a program-defining victory for the ages.

* * *

"Obviously the ending made it a lot more memorable, a lot more of a story, that we choked on our lead," says Schlekeway now. "I've talked to my teammates a thousand times, and I think I'm in the minority . . . they look at me, like, 'What the hell are you talking about? It was the best college football game in history.' From a fan's perspective it was; from a starting defensive lineman, I wish it had gone the way it had been going."

For Jared Zabranksy, a career that had catapulted from high-to-low-to-high, ended on the most surreal of notes. For his teammates, it was the perfect sendoff.

"It wasn't a surprise that his end happened," says Taylor Tharp now. "I lived through so much of his career as a backup—I'd seen every throw, every great throw, every mistake he had made—and I knew the plays he was making were just him being him."

Thanks to Ian Johnson, another magical moment was still to come.

* * *

By the time he made his way to the sideline, where he had galloped into history, media from around the globe had Johnson surrounded. There, he met Chris Myers to do the magnanimous interview, where he would spout coach-speak answers on his respect for the opposition, how the team never quit, etc. etc. etc.

With his arm around his girlfriend and cheerleader Chrissy Popadics, he did just that.

And then . . .

"I know you're going to propose to your girlfriend, so . . . " said Myers, a slip of the tongue that nearly spoiled one of the most iconic moments in college football history.

Try as he may, it didn't seem to matter.

Johnson stepped to the side, looked down at Chrissy, and proceeded to lower down to one knee.

The football hero got the girl.

It was so Boise State, that it was almost—almost—*too* Boise State.

17

FALL OUT BOYS

"There's a blue-collar, nobody is going to beat us attitude that has been evident from Lyle Smith, all the way to today."
—Brad Larrondo, Boise State Senior Associate Athletic Director

THE STREETS OF Boise, Idaho, were quiet on the morning of January 2, 2007. The party, which kicked off the moment Ian Johnson's foot crossed the goal line in Glendale the night before, went well into the night.

For the players, the night never ended.

"I don't think the city of Boise, or the kids that were there, or even the coaches, understood or appreciated what we were doing when we were doing it," says Ian Smart now. "But when you look back now, even the players go, 'Man, was that real?' Before we left Arizona, I was sitting in the hot tub with a few of my teammates, and we just looked at each other and said, 'Did that really just happen?'"

Overnight, Boise State was the most talked about school in the nation. Folks across the country, from the tips of the Pacific Northwest, through the midwest and up to the Eastern Seaboard, identified with the way Boise State carried themselves: the underdog, standing up to the big, bad bully, unafraid to punch back. They represented the best in everyone.

"Boise State upset the Oklahoma Sooners in overtime at the Fiesta Bowl Monday night. No one thought a small school could beat the winningest team in college football history. It was considered the surest sign yet the insurgency is spreading," said a passage in the *Norman Transcript* the following day.

After the triumphant victory, Chris Petersen had simple goals as it related to both him and his players: keep it there. Keep the perspective. Keep the attentive demeanor. Keep the focus.

"It's been tremendously easy," he said in the afterglow of the Fiesta Bowl, when life momentarily slowed. "What I think about is how the stage has been set for so many years for all this to happen. The players were so primed. We had all of those seniors. The blend of the new coaches, with the old coaches that stayed, was a magical combination."[1]

Petersen brought an understated confidence, which flew in the face of the rah-rah boastings of Houston Nutt, the introverted tunnel vision of Dirk Koetter, or the mind-melding tactics of Dan Hawkins.

Players could feel it.

"He'd say, 'You know what guys? This is going to be a hard game. If we do *this* well, we're going to win,'" said Derek Schouman. "And he stood by that. His confidence kind of overflowed onto everyone else, which I think was definitely part of our success."[2]

Bart Hendricks is the current president of the Varsity B, the school's alumni club for athletes. He had a front-row seat for the Fiesta Bowl and was one of the first to feel the effects that came from the win.

"The Fiesta Bowl changed everything. Not only in athletics, but across campus. The growth was just astronomical. From the amount of students enrolled, to the buildings being built, to the money that it generates for the economy in Boise . . . that game did it," he says now.

* * *

Before the Fiesta Bowl, *Good Morning America* was not a show you would have turned on to learn about the Boise State Broncos. Odds are, the hosts of the show had never heard of any of the players or coaches, nor could they even tell you the school's mascot. Their reputation among college football fans had been growing steadily for the better part of a decade; the rest of the sports world had started to take notice once Dan Hawkins began blowing the competition out of the water on a near-weekly basis.

But the general public was not yet hip to the game. You could walk down the streets of New York City before the start of the 2007 calendar year, corner 100 people, ask them any question about the Broncos, and you would likely receive 100 versions of misinformed, unintelligible answers.

Now, after Ian Johnson and "The Proposal," Boise State was suddenly in the lexicon of everyday life.

"It just snowballed. It was crazy," is how Ian's mom, Colleen, described the post-knee bend phenomenon, when her son and his bride-to-be were the talk of the country. "That shows the power of the moment."[3]

It was 6:01 a.m. on Tuesday, January 2, 2007, when the phone rang at the home of Chrissy's parents, Mark and Barbara Popadics. It was *Good Morning America*, trying to locate the most famous cheerleader in America. Once the phone started ringing, it didn't stop. By noon, Barbara had installed a caller ID in an attempt to suss out the intrusions.

For the locals, Ian's proposal was the opposite of normalcy.

By the time the dust had settled, Ian and Chrissy would visit the headquarters of ESPN, the studios of ABC, CNN, and the aforementioned *Good Morning America*. They received first-class treatment as they skipped through the streets of New York, to the Statue of Liberty, and onto the pages of *ESPN The Magazine* and *Sports Illustrated*.

"And may the football star and the cheerleader," Charles Gibson told his audience on ABC's *World News* during that trip to New York, "live happily ever after."

When Ian and Chrissy returned home to their formerly suburban lifestyle in Boise, celebrity status had overtaken their life. Where Ian was once a star football player and Chrissy a more innocuous cheerleader, they were known about town but oftentimes left to their own. They had a life. They had privacy. They had a charmed existence.

Because of the personalities of both Ian and Chrissy—quirky, but ultimately introverted—the change was palpable.

Nothing about Ian lent any belief to him becoming a national star.

"Very interesting thing about Ian . . . it was late at night, and I hear, 'Hey, Tuck, come check out this guy,'" says Robert Tucker. "We start watching Ian and I'm like, 'I love him.' We literally walked down to Hawk's office, and he says 'Let's offer him.' We go back, call, and offer him, and he committed on the spot. Done. He said, 'Coach, I'm in. You guys are the first to offer me, and I'm in. I'm a Bronco.' Almost at that moment, you think, 'Did we pull the trigger too fast?' But we had done our research."

Now, just a few days into January of 2007, less than two years into their relationship, they were no longer Ian Johnson and Chrissy Popadics. They were "that couple from the game." They were beckoned and harassed and mocked and cherished, oftentimes sometimes within a matter of moments. He was a black athlete in a predominantly white town; she was a white cheerleader. Some loathed the very thought of their relationship. Some sought them out as a sign of progression.

Some just wanted to spew their racial venom.

As the hoopla from the proposal died down and the wedding date came into focus for the summer of 2007, Ian and Chrissy were preparing for their big day. As expected, it was the buzz of the town; although the couple had kept a quiet profile once the initial media circus ended, they were still the state's most famous couple. And as the wedding crept closer, one underlying problem kept rearing its ugly head. At first it was a call here, or a letter there. Eventually, things progressed.

Ian began receiving death threats from bigoted civilians, angry about his marriage to Chrissy.

"You take it for what it is—the less educated, the less willing to change," Johnson told the *Idaho Statesman.* "But we're not acting like we're naive to all the stuff that's going on. We know what's been said. We're going to make sure we're safe at all times. It's an amazing day for us, and we'd hate to have it ruined by someone."

In all, Ian says the couple received phone calls, over thirty letters, and other forms of racial threats. The tension grew so much that the couple was forced to bring in enforcement for the wedding, staffing security in and around the venue. Their dream day, which had come about in the most unexpected of ways was, for a moment, trending toward a nightmare.

Ultimately, cooler heads prevailed. The wedding went off without a hitch—much like his proposal, which came with so many moving parts.

"I was glad to be a small part of it, but it was one of those crazy moments you had to be in to really realize what was going on. . . . It ended up working out and I'm glad they are still together and happy they have something very special that will last for a long, long time," said FOX's Chris Myers, who held the mic for the live proposal.

To this day, Ian and Chrissy are just that—Ian and Chrissy. They celebrated their 11th anniversary in 2018; they have a daughter. They live in Boise, where Ian is still the man he was back in 2007. He's a little older and doesn't have the same burst of speed or power he once had, but the couple is doing what was always their ultimate goal: living their life with roots set and a growing family.

Ian still looks back on that night with crystal-clear memory. "I remember there was a guy in a 41 jersey right behind me, and he was all obnoxious, and I was trying to entertain my thoughts and answer Chris's questions while knowing I am about to propose," he says. "When Myers said 'I'll let you propose,' Chrissy kind of backed up for a second and I said 'this is on live TV, you better say yes.' Obviously she did and it worked out pretty cool.

"I look back at it and it's just been a huge blessing for me and my family."

And, having done it on such a monumental platform, they will be able to relive it, anytime, anywhere, for as long as they both shall live.

"Just being able to share it with not only my Boise State family, but my daughter and wife, that's where this becomes something truly special for me. The ten-year anniversary, a perfect mark for everything," he says. "You couldn't have drawn up a better story. It's a perfect story, and I'm just blessed to have been on that team and in that game."

18

THE TRIFECTA

"All the stuff the school is doing now, with the equipment, the facilities, the type of players they're getting, it's all incredible to see. A guy like coach Petersen, with all of the success he's having now, it just goes to show you the culture he had at Boise State, it can go to a bigger place and work."
—Tad Miller, Boise State, 2004–2007

WITH THE FIESTA Bowl victory, Chris Petersen had accomplished the seemingly implausible. Less than thirteen months into the job, he had engraved his name in Boise State lore.

To think, it all could have been a dream.

"Back then [before he took the job], Pete was, like, 'Hell, I don't want to be a head coach; I don't want to deal with all of the media stuff. I want to be with you guys; I want to be working the X's and O's,'" says Donny Heck, who played under Petersen when he was the team's offensive coordinator.

The connection between Petersen and Dan Hawkins begins when they resided in the same state in the early 1990s, while Hawkins was at Willamette University, in Salem, Oregon, and Petersen was 90 minutes north at Portland State.

To trace the origins of their relationship, you have go back a few decades, head down to Davis, California, and look to a man that Boise State fans should thank with overwhelming veneration: Bob Foster.

Foster came to UC Davis in 1958 as a baby-faced freshman running back. After his playing days, he would go on to coach the linebackers, and eventually become the defensive coordinator under coach Jim Sochor for his alma mater.

Joining Foster and Sochor on the UC Davis staff, from 1985–1988, was an undergraduate student with a keen interest in the game of football by the name of Dan Hawkins.

One of the players Hawkins helped mold was a scrappy and undeterred quarterback named Chris Petersen.

In 1989, Foster took the head chair and convinced Petersen to stay on as his wide receivers coach.

Although Petersen had previously told his mother that he had no desire to join the family business—his father, Ron, had been a head coach at various levels for 21 seasons—because he did not want teenage boys to "determine my happiness," he couldn't let the game go.

That's a common theme among the three head coaches who have come to define the Boise State program—Petersen, Hawkins, and Dirk Koetter.

"A lot of [our mentality] came from our days at UC Davis, and what we learned there. How we coached people," says

Hawkins now, reflecting back on his and Petersen's early days together. "It was a place where guys came and got affirmed. It wasn't a negative place. That's not to say we couldn't coach guys hard, because we could. But it wasn't a beat guys down, treat them like a piece of dirt place. It was a build-em-up place."

Petersen joined Foster's staff at UC Davis under one condition: he was going to go to graduate school while he was on staff.

"It's good for the profession, it's good for the youth of America to have somebody like Chris Petersen to look up to and be coached by," Foster said later. "I feel like he could be a shining light in our profession."[1]

* * *

The Koetter era at Boise State gets lost in the shadows due to the success of Hawkins and Petersen. However, dismissing his impact is a mistake.

His ability to focus attention on his players, especially in the wake of the Houston Nutt regime, was an essential building block for the program, one that all successive coaches would mimic.

"Dirk was very focused," says B. J. Rhode, the Broncos' backup quarterback under Koetter and Hawkins. "One time I was walking by Dirk's office and he pulled me in. He said, 'Come here. What were you thinking on this play?' We went over a play or two, and he says, 'OK, have a good day.' A few years later, I'm walking by Hawkins's office, and he says, 'Hey, come here a minute.' And then something to the effect of,

'How's your family doing?' That shows the weird little dynamic of their two personalities."

Wes Nurse, a standout safety who came to the school under Koetter, eventually found himself under the tutelage of all three coaches. To him, the different personalities are what allowed players to get the most out of their time in Boise.

"Koetter was militant, a little bit, very straight forward. Hawkins was more philosophical. You had the mixture, where Petersen wanted everything done right, but then you had the Hawkins side, which was, 'Let's cut loose, have fun, let's go get this done.' So, it was a great dynamic between the three."

If you dropped in with no previous knowledge, Hawkins looks like the group's outsider. Koetter and Petersen take zero abstraction in looking like anything but a football coach; Hawkins, with his faultless hair, daffy smile, and sometimes incoherent ramblings, is all about perception. But he made it work, even if the wheels came off once he got to Colorado. His shtick was the perfect fit—while it lasted—following Koetter.

It was also the ultimate trickle-down.

"The staff [Hawkins] brought in was awesome. I have always thought Koetter was a genius; Petersen is just as much a genius as Koetter," says Jeff Cheek.

One trait all three coaches shared was an unwillingness to let a single player rise above the collective sum. There were guys who had seniority in taking leadership roles; however, if they had an attitude, it was quickly put to bed. The philosophy of the program was greater than individual attitudes, something that had been built, brick-by-brick, over time.

As Hawkins told *USA Today*, "There's a different vibe here than at a lot of programs. A lot of kids call me Hawk. I always tell them, 'I'm not your buddy, but I'm also not some deity that hangs out here in my office and you're my minion.' It's a family situation. We work on mutual respect. I discipline guys and have had to cut some of them loose, but we're sensitive to them as people and students."

The three coaches also had an affinity for offensive originality, which comes from sharing the same coaching tree. It also comes from the gut. These men were bred to be football coaches, and offense was their calling card.

"Dan was a little more 'Let's go out there and just punch them in the mouth, and let's let our emotions and our motivation help us,'" says Brad Allen, who played under both Koetter and Hawkins. "Dan would be more willing to give us freedom; Dirk was more 'By-the-book.' Same with Pete; he is like that, too. With Dirk and Pete, it was 'Do your job, or you're not going to play.' They had this lined out and this is what they expected you to do. And if you're not going to do your job, they're going to find somebody to do it, because I have ten other guys who are doing their job."

Great coaches rolled through Boise before "The Trifecta," but it wasn't until Koetter stabled everything with his hiring in 1998 that the program found their stride. Hawkins is quick to point out that what is happening today is a byproduct of the groundwork laid by Koetter.

"You look at what's gone on there, facilities-wise . . . during my time there was always something getting improved. We were in this little cubby hole," he says now. "When Dirk was there we got a quasi-football facility. Then they built the indoor facility. Then they built up the stadium. Then they built a brand-new facility, and now they have a new practice area. It was a combination—everybody getting in the boat and rowing together. When people do that, great things can happen."

Although Hawkins's reputation is the softest of the three, he was hardly a pushover. "It wasn't always warm and fuzzy; it wasn't always warm and fuzzy with my dad, either. But I knew he loved me and the things he had me do were for my benefit," he says now.

However, Hawkins's message, one that is contradicted by many who played under him, came to a conclusive finale among his players.

"I have the utmost respect for coach Hawkins, but I do think [by the time he left in 2005] that his voice had run its course a little bit," says Jeff Cavender, an offensive lineman. "I think it was a combination of things: going into the Georgia game in 2005 we were coming off a big year, and we had very high expectations, and I think maybe guys thought we were growing too fast outside of what we really were."

When Petersen slid in before the 2006 season, players knew the right decision had been made.

"It was one of those perfect storms. You have faith in the administration and the school; you have faith in the guys that are still playing; and coach Petersen stepping in and saying, 'Have faith in me. I've built a really good coaching staff.' It really was perfect. We needed to hit the reset button, I think, and that was the perfect time," says Cavender.

"Look at what Petersen has done for this program. If coach Hawkins had stayed, I'm not sure we make that first Fiesta Bowl [in 2006]. It was coach Petersen's twist on Hawkins's philosophy, which Hawk got from Koetter and so on and so forth. It was the evolution of not only football but Boise State football."

Andy Weldon goes one step further in dissecting the success of the coaches. The mindset put forth by the coaches, he says, was not for show. "These days, sayings like 'blue-collar mentality' and 'chip on the shoulder' are more lip service. Back in the early 2000s, under those guys, it was real."

Ryan Dinwiddie points to the similarities among the three as the binding tie.

"I think all of them [Koetter, Hawkins, and Petersen] had their differences, but the way they wanted to run the program, the structure, it was all the same," he says now. "Philosophy-wise, they're all different. Hawk is more of a father guy, rub your back. He'll scold you, but he's going to talk more, tell you your mistakes, what he expects of you. Philosophy. Religion. He's going to touch on a lot of things outside football.

"Dirk is very demanding, gets after his QBs," he continues. "He's a hard-ass; he expects a certain standard of football. He's almost like a professional coach; he wasn't really into building bonds with players, necessarily; he was more into running things the way they needed to be. He had to be demanding to get us going in the right direction, but I love Dirk. I'm a hard-nosed guy, too, so I always appreciated him. He was a breath of fresh air."

From 1998, Koetter's first year on the turf, through 2013, when Petersen left to take the job at the University of Washington, the Broncos put out one of the nation's most eclectic variations of offensive firepower and ingenuity.

Based on their results, and impact, it's hard to argue.

19

WANTING MOORE

"Physically, Kellen was kind of a goof-ball. But he could get
the ball there and dissect defenses; he knew what they were
going to do better than they did."
—Michael Choate, Boise State wide receiver, 2007–2009

FOR ALL OF the attention the Fiesta Bowl win brought,
going into the 2007 season, it was hard not to give a tip of
the cap to the teams who had come before. Since Chris Petersen
had taken over in 2001 as the team's offensive coordinator, the
Broncos had accumulated an astonishing 66–11 record. They
had been knocking on the door of relevance the entire time,
begging for a seat at the table. The lopsided loss to Georgia in
2005, unabashed and one-dimensional in its cruelty, took a pin
to their balloon. With the win over Oklahoma, the program was
back where it belonged.

"We've kind of been scratching and clawing the past five,
seven years, whatever it's been, to get people to notice us,"
Petersen told ESPN before the 2007 season began. "We've

been saying, 'Hey, look how many games we've been winning.' When you go on a national stage like we were on in the Fiesta Bowl, it gives you some legitimacy and credibility."

The biggest impact of the Fiesta Bowl would take place nearly seven months before the 2007 season kicked off. In February, Petersen and his staff brought in a recruiting class that would eventually leave as the winningest in program history, and one of the most successful in all of college football.

Shea McClellin, who would win a Super Bowl with the New England Patriots, was part of that class. "Boise State was, probably, the best time period of my life so far," he says now. So too were NFL stalwarts Billy Winn, Doug Martin, Titus Young, and Chase Baker.

Topping off the recruiting class was a compact, left-handed quarterback with the igniting smile by the name of Kellen Moore.

The impact of that class would be felt down the road. For Petersen and Taylor Tharp, who, after years backing up Jared Zabranksy, was finally getting his shot to start, the 2007 season was a chance to prove the Broncos' staying power. And they did just that, finishing the season with a 10–3 record. Tharp, for his part, was prodigious. After just 32 career pass attempts entering the season, he threw for 3,340 yards, completing over 68 percent of his passes to go along with 30 touchdowns.

The Broncos had successfully navigated the trickiest water: the step down from immortality into the real world.

Now, they could begin anew.

* * *

Chris Petersen was facing a major dilemma before the 2008 season; he knew there was a chance to set the program up for long-term success with one decision.

That one decision could potentially make or break his future. If he made it and it worked, he would be set. If he made it and it imploded, the entire base built up over the previous eight years could splinter.

Don't make it, and potentially look back, forever regretful.

Petersen needed a quarterback; he was down to two options. Bush Hamdan, a fifth-year senior who had given his all to the program; or Kellen Moore, the highly sought-after redshirt freshman who, by some accounts, was the most prized recruit the school had locked up to that point.

"I went to Boise in June going into my senior year, into the football camp, and there were a bunch of quarterbacks there. That was the time where it finally clicked that this place is awesome, first and foremost. I loved the people, and I thought, 'Maybe there's a chance.' Harsin was there. Pete was there. I grew up in a little town, five to six thousand people in Prosser. You walk into Bronco Stadium thinking, "this is cool, this is big-time football.' They offered me a few weeks later, and I committed in September," Moore says now.

Hamdan, a Gaithersburg, Maryland, native, was the anti-Boise State recruit when he arrived on campus in 2004. A Super 44 Prep and All-Metro team member in Washington, DC, during his high school days, he came out west, eschewing colleges closer to home, hoping to become the next Broncos quarterback to ignite the scoreboard. Instead, he was behind

Jared Zabransky for three seasons, followed by Taylor Tharp in 2007.

Despite his acclaim coming out of high school and his experience in the system, Hamdan routinely found himself stacked in the depth chart alongside guys like Nick Lomax, Mike Coughlin, and Tharp.

Entering his fifth and final season in Boise, he gave Petersen exactly what he was looking for in a quarterback: an experienced kid who wouldn't get rattled, especially with an early season game at Oregon looming. Unfortunately, as had been the case during his previous four years on campus, something was lurking around the corner.

This time it was the good-natured Moore. Kellen had savvy, instincts, and consistency. Kellen was otherworldly with his accuracy.

Kellen had . . . *something*. Something that Hamdan couldn't shake, and neither could the coaches.

On August 20, just ten days before the Broncos were set to open the season at home against former Big Sky foe Idaho State, Petersen listened to his gut, which was reminding him to follow what he believed to be true.

The decision was made. He named Kellen Moore the opening day quarterback.

"We've said all along, we'll play a freshman, we'll play a senior, whoever we think we can win with right now, that's the guy we're going with," Petersen said in his press conference. Sitting beside him, hands clasped on his lap, Moore looked on, his eyes far off in another world, a half-cocked smile on his face.

Petersen re-emphasized that naming Kellen the starter was not punting on the season, and building toward the future. Moore, baby-faced at just eighteen years of age, was the best option for the team to win immediately.

"We feel Kellen gives us the best chance," he continued. "Right now."

Luckily for the Broncos, the trip to Oregon to face the Ducks—Kellen's first true test—was still a month away. Idaho State, long in the rearview mirror from their competitive days with Boise State, would be a welcome warmup. The 2007 season had ended with a thud, including losses to Hawaii and East Carolina, which had cast a bit of a pall over the team. The loss to Hawaii kept the Broncos from claiming their sixth-straight conference title. It was fair to wonder: was a 10–3 season—still good by any measure, but a fall from their undefeated season— the norm, or an anomoly? Was handing the reins to Moore, despite their coach's insistence that it wasn't, an attempt to capture lightning in a bottle?

"We love to take a little bit of the underdog role," Petersen said after he announced Moore as the starter. "It's a lot easier to attack from that area. It's tough to stay on the mountaintop when everybody is gunning for you."

Idaho State would provide a soft landing spot for people seeking answers to those questions. Boise State could have played the game without a quarterback at all and likely won. Inserting Moore seemed a low-risk decision.

"I can't wait to watch him play, because I think he's got a tremendous feel for the game. We just feel this guy is extremely ready to go," Petersen said before the game.

It took less than one full game to see that Petersen wasn't going down a rabbit hole after all.

Moore was dynamic and in complete control from the moment he stepped onto the field. He was accurate. *Really accurate.* Passes didn't exit his hand as if shot from a cannon; they came out smooth as butter. They came out well before his receivers were open. They came out and landed directly in their chests.

Every. Single. Time.

He would complete 14-of-19 passes for 274 yards and two touchdowns in a 49–7 win. The only sweat he broke was from the blistering summer heat, which reached a sweltering 89 degrees. Other than that, Moore was cool as ice.

In their Week 2 win against Bowling Green, he was even better. Although the offense struggled to score points, Moore's accuracy and good decision-making were keys to the Broncos escaping with a 20–7 victory. He finished the game 18-for-23 passing for 180 yards. Although he didn't throw a touchdown, he also avoided throwing an interception. For a team whose defense was rounding into their stellar 2006-form, it was looking like that would be enough.

That would be tested in earnest the following week.

Eugene, Oregon. Autzen Stadium. An Oregon Ducks team that was an ACL injury to their quarterback away from playing for the national title the previous season. For any quarterback, regardless of experience or skill, their first road game brings about an extra set of nerves. Make that venue Autzen, a snakepit of noise and scattered bodies of victims past, and it can be almost too much to ask.

For Petersen, the trip to Eugene brought about fond memories—a homecoming of sorts—after his five-year stint in which he helped usher in a new era of Oregon football.

"They've done a great job," Oregon head coach Mike Bellotti said of Boise State before the game. "We have a good relationship with them because a lot of those guys have coached here, played here."

One of the guys who both played at Oregon and was now on the opposite sideline was defensive coordinator Justin Wilcox, who was a member of Oregon's secondary in the early 1990s. His father, Dave, also played two seasons at Boise State and two at Oregon. This game, one of the biggest in Boise State history, was an affair with more blood than water.

"They know how good Oregon is," Petersen said before the game. "The main thing is that the guys don't get too much anxiety about it."

Entering the September 20 contest, Boise still had one tick resting on their back that they could not rid themselves of: a road win over a BCS conference school.

Since the year 2000, Oregon had gone 41–12 at Autzen. However, entering the game against Boise State, they were a mess at quarterback, evening the playing field. The previous season, while heading to what assuredly would have been a national title appearance, their quarterback, Dennis Dixon, looked like the runaway Heisman trophy winner. Then, he crumpled to the turf in Tucson, Arizona, ending his season, his career and, ultimately, Oregon's season. Their second-, third-, and eventually fourth-string quarterbacks limped to a 0–3 finish on the season.

Through three games in 2008, not much had changed. Oregon entered 2008 expecting the fiery Nate Costa—who was knee-high-to-a-grasshopper—to start. A knee injury in camp changed those plans. Next in line was Justin Roper, a lanky 6-foot-6 kid who had led them to a bowl win the previous season against South Florida. However, he too had succumbed to injury before Boise State came to town. Now JC transfer Jeremiah Masoli had his moment. Chris Harper, a hyper-athletic freshman, was raw and not ready for the limelight. Darron Thomas, perhaps the truest quarterback on the roster, was in line to redshirt.

Entering hostile territory for the first time, just two games into his career, Moore looked like the grizzled veteran set to teach the young'uns from Oregon a thing or two about how to play the position.

When the game started, that's exactly what happened. Oregon boasted arguably the best secondary that Boise State had ever faced; three of their starters—Jarius Byrd, Patrick Chung, and T. J. Ward—would all have long NFL careers. Having Moore step into the lion's den and sling passes all day was not part of the gameplan. If it were, the odds of a disaster would be bountiful.

But on the first drive of the game, that's what they did. Two times Moore dropped back to pass. Two times the ball hit the turf. Less than 30 seconds into the game, the biggest of his young career, the youngster was already 0-for-2 passing, facing a third down with the crowd of nearly 60,000 leaning over him, hot breaths of vitriol in his ear.

Then, in a play that would sum up his career, Moore took another snap, dropped back . . . and tossed a dart. He hit Vinny

Perretta in the left flat for a gain of 10 yards and a first down. When the camera panned across his face, Moore flashed a capacious smile.

The first test had been passed.

Although they would be forced to punt before gathering another first down, the seal had been broken. Moore would not be wilting under the Oregon sun or their talented secondary.

Over the course of the game, the Broncos were able to keep the Ducks at arm's length. Even after Oregon inserted a new quarterback in Darron Thomas to interject life into the team, and rallied to within five points late, the Broncos would recover a late onside kick, securing their biggest road victory to date. The 37–32 win was the true introduction to the "Kellen Moore Era."

Moore would finish the game with 386 yards passing to go along with three touchdowns. He was brilliant from the opening kick, never once capitulating to the magnitude of the moment.

After the game, running back Ian Johnson, now a senior—who was held to 40 yards and one score on 19 carries—spoke of the confidence Boise State had entering the game.

"We came out here and didn't bow to Oregon," he said. "We came here to attack and show everyone what kind of team Boise State is now."

Despite stumbling during the Ducks' furious fourth-quarter rally, the Broncos' defense showed enough grit to give fans hope for the remainder of the season. Darron Thomas's near-rally was cause for concern, but the big picture—a season-defining road win—was complete.

"We wanted it back one more time," Thomas said after the game, reflecting on Oregon's onside kick that Boise State recovered, sealing the game. "We knew what we were capable of doing."

So did the Broncos. With the victory, they had proven to the naysayers, their fellow conference members and, most importantly, themselves, what they were capable of. It wasn't perfect, but it was a W.

"Their quarterback issues helped us," Petersen said in his postgame press conference. "But this is big."

* * *

Under Dan Hawkins, and now Petersen, the Broncos' recruiting had ticked upward at a steady pace. While they still failed to crack the Top 50 nationally, they took significant strides once Petersen took the head job.

During the final four seasons under Hawkins, according to scout.com, one of the country's most respected recruiting websites, the Broncos' class came in 73rd nationally on average out of 128 possible teams; in Petersen's first year, while putting together his staff, and having a short window after the departure of Hawkins, his class ranked 78th. The following season, with a full year's worth of time—and that Fiesta Bowl win to tout— Boise State's class ranked 57th, the highest in school history. The star power from that 2007 class—Kellen Moore, Billy Winn, Austin Pettis, Doug Martin, Titus Young, Brandyn Thompson, Shea McClellin—was already dripping with NFL potential, just two years into their time on campus.

And behind the guidance of an emerging superstar at defensive coordinator in Justin Wilcox, it was that group that was stealing the headlines. For decades the Broncos had relied on the development of unheralded and often undersized kids to fill in roster spots; that was most apparent in the trenches, where the Broncos used country-strong boys to overmatch their opponents. Now, they were reeling in the big boys. Winn, specifically, was a disaster for the opposition. He arrived on campus as a 6-foot-4 defensive end; by his sophomore year in 2008 he was a 288-pound defensive tackle, demanding double teams, disrupting plays, seeding blockers, and establishing himself as one of the most intimidating interior linemen in the country.

Despite his modest stats—he would finish with just 25 tackles (5.5 for loss) and 2.5 sacks on the season—the Broncos' defensive dominance, which started the week after Oregon when they beat Louisiana Tech, 38–3, started right up front behind the massive posterior of Winn. Along with veterans like Kyle Wilson and Jeron Johnson, Winn and the defense were the guiding light for the Broncos.

"You want these veteran guys to step up and make plays when it's on the line," Wilcox said. His guys were listening. After the Louisiana Tech game, the Broncos would hold their next four opponents—Southern Miss, Hawaii, San Jose State, and New Mexico State—to just 30 points combined. Those opponents were far from Murderer's Row, but dominance is dominance. Now in their third year under Wilcox, the Broncos had mastered his 4-2-5 defense, which was designed to get more speed on the field, making up for their lack of size. Wilcox was known for having defenses that thrived due to their truculent style of play, which often toed the line between aggressive and dirty.

"It's just the mentality we bring," said sophomore defensive end Ryan Winterswyk before the team's win at San Jose State. "Ever since spring ball we've been saying we have to be aggressive, we've got to get the ball."

The difference between the 2007 season, when the Broncos gave up 21 points per game—despite pitching two shutouts—was that aggressive nature: forcing turnovers, getting to the quarterback, fourth-down stops, and keeping teams out of the redzone.

"We're playing really inspired," Kyle Wilson said as the team headed into their Week 8 matchup against New Mexico State. "We're playing tremendous team football. Everyone is doing their jobs."

After the Broncos took care of their final four regular-season games, with wins against Utah State, Idaho, Nevada, and Fresno State, a Poinsettia Bowl matchup with TCU awaited. The Horned Frogs, another team known for their defense, were led by Gary Patterson, considered by many the guru of the vaunted 4-2-5 defense.

A second undefeated regular season was in the books, at 12–0. The Poinsettia Bowl beckoned.

Six of Boise State's regular-season opponents in 2008 would make bowl games; the Broncos beat those teams by an average score of nearly 40–17. Only Oregon and Nevada were close.

TCU finished their regular season at 10–2. Their two losses? The Oklahoma Sooners and a narrow defeat at the hands of the Utah Utes, both of which were in BCS games. The Utes would bludgeon the Alabama Crimson Tide in the Sugar Bowl, 31–17. Oklahoma was playing Florida for the national championship.

Not a bad resume.

Despite the Broncos' emergence defensively, that unit would take a backseat—in both reputation and performance—to the Horned Frogs. TCU came in with the number two defense in the country, allowing just 215 yards per game despite playing three Top-10 teams during the regular season. Although they played in the Mountain West Conference, the Horned Frogs were every bit their #11 ranking. Defensive end Jerry Hughes was the nation's leader in sacks, totaling 14 during the season. Hughes, and his ability to keep Kellen Moore uncomfortable in the pocket, was the central focus as the game approached.

Because of the bowl allocation system at the time, the Broncos missed out on another BCS bowl game; Utah, also playing in the MWC, finished the season with a tougher strength of schedule, giving them the nod. Both the Broncos and Utes went 12–0 during the season; both had wins over prominent Power 5 schools (Utah won at Michigan, versus TCU and BYU), and both sported top-level defenses.

Entering the game the Broncos were 35–3 over the past three seasons; two undefeateds sandwiched around 2007's three-loss campaign. Going out with a victory was something the school had bungled in years past. Bowl losses in 2004, 2005, and 2007 had tainted otherwise remarkable seasons. The Poinsettia Bowl was as much about setting the tone for the upcoming season as it was about finishing out the current one.

It was also about sending the seniors out in style—specifically, Ian Johnson.

Because of the youth in their offensive line and the superb arm talent of Moore, Johnson found himself in a different world just two years removed from his fairytale finish in the Fiesta Bowl. No longer were the Broncos reliant on his abilities to makeshift runs and get the team out of trouble. He was now a role player, a cog in an efficient machine. His 150 carries and 766 yards were the lowest since his freshman year.

The leadership Johnson displayed, and the example he set in practice and the weight room, had become more valuable to the team than what his legs did on Saturdays.

"Ian is obviously the poster child at Boise State; he'll probably be that for quite a long time after this," Moore said two days before the bowl game. "[He's] a guy who's been a great example of Boise State football, on and off the field."

As had been the case since his quirky personality first popped up in the Treasure Valley, Johnson approached his new role with the same smile, same passion, same charisma as anyone who knew him would expect. He was now splitting time with two speedy whippersnappers, Jeremy Avery and D. J. Harper. In his final regular season game as a Bronco, against Fresno State, he broke loose for 128 yards. It was his highest output since the middle of his 2006 season, when he rushed for 1,713 yards, scored 25 touchdowns, got the girl, become a national star, and took the school—*his school*—to heights unknown.

Now he was riding off into the sunset happy in his role as a mentor more than a star.

"The coaches knew I understood because I've been here for a while; I'm the old dog," he said as the bowl game approached. "I could see [a while ago] the writing was on the wall. The offensive line we had in 2006 was one where we were going to run the ball; we don't care what you line up in, we're just going to do it."

Johnson was one touchdown shy of breaking Marshall Faulk's Western Athletic Conference record of 57, a number he hit against Fresno State in the regular season finale as furious chants of "I-AN! I-AN!" rained down from the upper decks. Petersen inserted Johnson into the game one final time, watched him cross the goal line, and listened as the home crowd roared in approval.

"Will I settle for being tied with a Hall of Fame running back in Marshall Faulk? Of course," Johnson said when asked about his mentality heading into the bowl game. "But would I love to be outright? Oh yeah. Especially a game-winning or 50-plus-yard run."

His face and spirit were as content as his words. As the teams shuffled from charity event to community service to bowl-themed dinners and pep rallies, Johnson was just along for the ride, enjoying his swan song. Kellen Moore was the new face of the program; Petersen snagged the headlines and the attention of the media. Boisterous teammates like Winn stole the spotlight. Johnson had his wife, Chrissy, and, potentially, the NFL. He was happy. Despite being young, he and Chrissy were the old married couple in town, one that everyone knew and wanted to embrace. They were as much a part of the community as open fields, frigid winds, and victories.

"We love talking to people," Johnson told the *Idaho Statesman*. "We love talking to people and we understand that if we're going to go outside . . . this city has done so much for us, it's only right for them to want to come and say, 'Hey, how's it going?'"

To tie an even prettier bow on his quest for the record books, the bowl game would be played at SDCCU Stadium, where Faulk had played his college ball for San Diego State.

Johnson already had one fairytale ending in his career. Number two was waiting.

After the regular season finale against Fresno State, as ankle tape strung piled up on the floor of the locker room like pieces of muddy confetti, a realization washed over the Broncos like a net falling over unsuspecting prey.

They were champions yet again, undefeated, hungry, and bursting with anticipation to close the season with a bang. It was not the Fiesta Bowl, and TCU wasn't a prestigious program. Maybe that didn't matter.

This was once again about the Broncos, and their place in history.

Unfortunately, that place would have to wait. The Broncos' 17–16 loss to the Horned Frogs—the first of young Moore's career—came about from sundry moments and errors from both sides. Johnson would score one rushing touchdown, breaking the record, the lone bright spot in an otherwise forgetful evening.

With the loss, Boise State failed to secure the undefeated season they had fought so hard for, but the loss could not overshadow all that had been accomplished.

Moore had established himself as a star in the making. Although his play in the bowl game was subpar, it would propel him into the offseason with a sense of what could be and what needed to be fixed. In spite of the stumble at the end, his freshman season had been a rousing success.

Moore had thrown for 3,468 yards, 25 touchdowns with just 10 picks, completing 69.4 percent of his passes. It was unassailable in its dominance and effectiveness. His season was made even more impressive by not succumbing to the midseason wall that most freshmen hit; his worst game was against TCU, the toughest defense he had faced by a country mile. Outside of that performance—still a success by any measure—Moore had laid the groundwork for what was to come.

Everyone, including former Broncos who had seen the highest of highs, couldn't help but wonder what the ceiling was for their star quarterback.

"With Kellen in his third career start, in one of the toughest venues in the country—for three-and-a-half quarters, Boise State laid the wood to Oregon. They dominated them. To me, that is hands down one of the most memorable games I've seen," Pete Cavender, an offensive lineman who played under Petersen, says now.

The following September, in their season opener, the Broncos would have a chance to add to that list.

* * *

If you consider yourself one to have even a modicum of sports knowledge of events from the past decade, you've heard of "The Punch." It was impossible to avoid it. It was front page news around the country, the lead on *SportsCenter*, and brought into account racial lines and social lexicons. It was one of the more memorable and divisive moments the sporting world had seen in a long time.

It also overshadowed a monumental and significant win for Boise State, one that would be the catapult to a storybook season.

However, if you're not familiar with "The Punch," the synopsis goes as follows: after Boise State defeated the Oregon Ducks in the opening game of the regular season to start the 2009 season, a 19–8 win in a wire-to-wire defensive masterpiece, players from both sides spilled onto the field for the postgame handshakes.

After an emotional game played between the two schools back in the 2008 season, which saw multiple altercations, late hits, and flared tempers—in retrospect, the coming together of both teams on this night was the wrong decision.

Before the game, as the buildup for the rematch reached its crescendo, Oregon Ducks running back LeGarrette Blount, in an interview with *Sports Illustrated*, said that Boise State deserved an "ass whooping" after the previous season's game.

An ass whooping occurred to be sure; however, Blount's team had come out on the opposite end once again.

As he approached midfield, in a scrum of Boise State players and coaches, without warning, Blount's right arm swung violently, landing square on the chin of a Boise State player, Byron Hout, who then crumpled backward into teammates.

Blount, taunting the fallen player, was rushed off the field by a throng of Oregon coaches and officials. The Boise State crowd, many still in a euphoric state from the victory, ravished Blount as he was escorted to the locker room, restrained by coaches and security guards. It was a violent and unsettling scene, one that would tarnish the reputation of both players long after its conclusion.

To this day, the details are still not fully clear as to the flame that lit Blount's fuse. According to Hout, he made mention to Blount of the inaccuracies of his prediction that Boise State deserved the "ass whooping."

According to Blount, Hout "definitely said something way more harsh and disrespectful to me than what he said."

Regardless, the scene was a black eye on the sport; not just for Blount, who would be suspended for the majority of the season until his return in the team's regular season finale. Because the game was on ESPN between two high-profile teams, the moment magnified to an obscene level. Boise State, instead of basking in a vivid and prestigious win, was linked forever to Blount, to Hout, and to the punch.

"It was just something I shouldn't have done," Blount said after the dust had settled. "I lost my head."

Hout received no suspension from either the WAC or Boise State.

The incident would linger over the Broncos' heads for the majority of the season.

A season bereft of any other drama or contention.

Following the win over Oregon, their next closest game, a road win over Louisiana Tech, was still a 10-point victory. The Broncos did not steamroll their schedule, per se. Instead, they methodically took apart every single opponent.

Miami of Ohio? 48-point win.

Hawaii? 45-point win.

San Jose State? 38-point win.

The Broncos' excursion through the season coincided with a 35-point win over New Mexico State (42–7), giving them their second undefeated season in three years. Their average margin of victory, 25.1 points per game, conjured up talk that the Broncos could find boredom in their perceived dominance.

The Broncos were ranked #6 in the country after the win over New Mexico State, their highest end-of-regular-season ranking in school history. They also secured their second-ever trip to the Fiesta Bowl.

And just like the season prior, their bowl game would be against TCU.

* * *

On January 2, two days before his squad was set to face the TCU Horned Frogs, Chris Petersen sat down with Gene Bleymaier, grabbed a pen, and went a route few could have foreseen when he first took over in 2006: he signed a long-term deal to stay at Boise State. High-priced suitors could come, and they could go.

Petersen was all in.

"I kind of chuckle a bit when people talk about other jobs," Petersen said from Scottsdale, Arizona, before the ink was even dry on his contract. "Many people would give their right arm to be at Boise State, and that's why I appreciate where I am."

Before Boise State named Petersen head coach in 2006, he was a two-time Broyles Award nominee, given annually to the nation's top assistant. The feeling inside the athletic department was that Boise State had finally found itself on the path of least resistance; with Petersen, no longer would they need to chase the next coach who was looking for his springboard to a payday. With the program picking up steam toward its ultimate destination—a national championship—they simply needed to not rock the boat.

Despite the rankings of both teams entering the game—Boise State was ranked 6th in the country, TCU 3rd—Shea McClellin, the Broncos' star linebacker, couldn't help but feel the slightest bit disappointed to see TCU, once again, as their opponent. "Of course we wanted to play someone big, like an Alabama, or Ohio State, someone like that . . . but they put the two mid-majors together, of course. That's how they did us back in the day. No respect. That's the way I felt. I'm sure a lot of other guys did, too," he says now.

In many ways, TCU was viewed in a similar vein as Boise State. Despite having won two national championships (in 1935 and 1938), the Horned Frogs had toiled away in ambiguity for much of the past seventy years. They were formerly a member of the infamous Southwest Conference, alongside the likes of Southern Methodist, Oklahoma, Arkansas, Baylor, and Texas A&M, among others. After the conference folded, the Horned Frogs—despite their titles and the history of producing some of college football's all-time greats, including Davey O'Brien—struggled to find their footing. From the SWC they slipped down to the WAC in 1996; in 2001 they moved to Conference USA. Finally, by 2005, they had worked their way back to the MWC.

Respectability was back, too, in large part from the successful workings of their head coach Gary Patterson, who arrived in 2000 and had molded the team into one of the fiercest squads in the country. His 4-2-5 defense baffled opponents; their quarterback, Andy Dalton, was a fiery ginger who possessed an arm that the town of Fort Worth had not seen in ages. However, despite the juicy matchup on paper, the nation viewed the 2010 version of the Fiesta Bowl with a collective sigh; after the "Game of the Century" against Oklahoma, the matchup between Boise State and TCU lacked a certain . . . gravitas. Both schools were from outside BCS conferences, marking the first time a BCS matchup would pit two teams from smaller conferences. Still, it was an opportunity for both to send a message of superiority. It was, in a way, the de facto national championship for non-BCS schools.

Plus, it should be noted, both teams were really, *really* good.

"You never see a busted play or them giving up a big run for 20-some yards," Moore said when dissecting the Horned Frogs. "You just have to take positive gains on every drive. That's pretty much what everyone has to do against these guys."

The Broncos entered with the nation's top offense, scoring just a hair over 44 points per game; TCU brought the top defense, allowing a paltry 233 yards per game. It may not have worked from a marketing standpoint, but the chess match between two of the brightest coaches, and the strength-on-strength clash— not to mention TCU's outside shot at an Associated Press national title should they win—was rich with subplots.

"Every play is going to be competitive," said Bryan Harsin, the then-offensive coordinator for the Broncos. "There's always going to be a guy right beside you. It comes back to us more than anything. Everything you see in practice, all the little details, all the fundamentals, got to really stand out in this game because the speed and the type of player you're going up against."

Patterson was a bit more emotional. For him, TCUs arrival on the big stage had been an exercise in patience come to fruition.

"You probably think we have been waiting three weeks to get here," he said shortly after his team arrived in Phoenix. "I've been waiting twelve years at TCU."

To add another big-game victory notch to their belt, Harsin's unit was going to have to solve the Rubik's cube that was the Horned Frogs' defense. If they couldn't, they stood no chance. During the season, TCU's defense was a killing machine, ending every opponent who dared cross them. An early season trip to Virginia resulted in a 30–14 win; two weeks later, in one of the most hostile environments in all of college football, Death Valley in Clemson, they won 14–10. All season long the opposition tried and failed to crack the TCU code . . . no one came close.

During one four-game stretch, from a game at Colorado State through a trip to San Diego State, the Horned Frogs gave up just 25 points *total*. They were, without question, the toughest unit in football. Not just in the Mountain West— *all* of college football. TCU faced six teams during the regular season that would play in bowl games; they won those matchups by an average of 20 points. That they were from outside a BCS conference had no bearing on the totality of their talents.

Added Harsin, "I think for us, the matchup is great; they're the number three team, and the best possible team they could be playing."

Fortunately, TCU players could say the same thing about the Broncos.

After the opening night fiasco against Oregon, in which the Broncos mustered up just 19 points, Moore and company had morphed into a steamroller. From Week 2 on, the Broncos averaged 46.2 points per game, oftentimes with their starters resting for long stretches of the second half.

So it was with a bit of relief, some anxiousness, and a season's worth of excitement that TCU was their opponent. Finally, the two teams had found an opponent worthy of their full attention.

When 73,227 fans crammed into the Fiesta Bowl on January 4, 2010, a JV matchup in the eyes of the nation—but a heavyweight battle in the fight for supremacy for all involved—commenced. And when Boise State's Brandyn Thompson undercut a receivers route with 11:32 to go in the first quarter, intercepting Dalton's throw and returning it 51 yards for a touchdown, a new-era wrinkle to the Broncos repertoire was unveiled: a swarming, opportunistic defense. This team was no longer style over substance; trick plays over trenches-domination.

This team was going to beat you in whatever form necessary.

Not to be outdone, TCUs defense would play a major role in the game as well. The Horned Frogs were as violent as advertised. Moore entered as one of the nation's hottest quarterbacks; it took one possession for him to be reduced to a shell of who he had been during the regular season.

* * *

Chris Petersen's offense is an ode to synchronization. To hum along at warp speed, all moving parts must be timed perfectly. If a receiver is a split second slow getting into his route, the ball is whizzing by his head. If the running backs don't hit the hole the exact moment it opens, all other players' blocks downfield are meaningless. If the quarterback is rushed, it all falls apart.

With that knowledge, TCU's game plan was simple: spend as much of the game in the Boise State backfield as possible; blow by Bronco offensive linemen, burst through seams, or overpower them. Do that, and Moore and the offense would be befuddled.

It worked.

Every time Kellen dropped back to pass, a defender was bearing down. Moore, who is more of a statue than a gazelle, looked flustered from the opening kickoff; his passes floated, thrown from his back foot as he stumbled from pressure, only to see balls nosedive into the ground, rocket ten feet over a receiver, or float aimlessly through the air before finding awaiting turf.

A touchdown pass from Dalton to Curtis Clay just before halftime cut Boise State's lead to 10–7. After a Ross Evans field goal with 3:52 to play in the third tied the score at 10, the scene on the Boise State sideline was set. With the way their defense had been playing, one more touchdown would almost assuredly ice the game and their second undefeated season in four years.

Early in the fourth quarter, after Brandyn Thompson's second interception of the game, the Broncos offense once again stalled. In came Kyle Brotzman, Boise State's placekicker and punter, who had been one of the busiest players in the game due to the volume of punts. With 9:47 left and the Broncos facing a 4th and 9, Petersen, for the first time in the game, reached into his bag of tricks.

After Brotzman—lined up and ready to punt the ball away—received the snap, Kyle Efaw, a 6-foot-4 tight end, burst up the middle of the field, unguarded. A split-second after receiving the snap, the punter fired off a perfect pass, which landed softly in the arms of Efaw for a first down.

Four plays later, running back Doug Martin crossed the goal line, giving the Broncos the 17–10 lead. Neither team would score again.

TCU was the highest-ranked opponent Boise State had beat in program history. In doing so, they eliminated the Horned Frogs from a potential AP national championship.

Boise State's defense had been electric all night. TCU was ranked 27th nationally in third-down offense; they would convert just 1-of-12 opportunities against the Broncos. Dalton, who would go on to lead the Horned Frogs to the 2012 Rose Bowl and be a second-round pick of the Cincinnati Bengals, threw three picks, including the two by Brandyn Thompson. Boise State also held TCU to just 36 yards on 20 rushing attempts.

As Paola Boivin wrote in the *Arizona Republic* the following day, "the Boise State defense proved once and for all that Chris Petersen and his staff belonged at the upper-echelon of the college ranks."

And the fake punt, a symbolic moment for the school, was placed alongside the most memorable moments in program history.

"For us to run a fake like that is gutsy," said Brotzman, who was the Broncos' biggest weapon by pinning the Horned Frogs deep in their own territory on his punts. "That's Boise State football. For [Petersen] to call something like that and have faith in me to run and execute is awesome."

Afterward, Gary Patterson couldn't help but tip his cap to the Broncos for the masterpiece they had pulled off.

"Their defense's dominance spoke volumes about Petersen and his staff. Give them a month to get ready for the game, and they'll out prepare you."

And, of course, the trickery that snaked them in the end.

"The fake punt was a great call," he continued. "They outcoached us on that play."

With the win, Boise State had joined the 2004 Ohio State Buckeyes as the only 14–0 team in college football history. They had dismantled the Pac-10 champion Oregon Ducks, embarrassing the program in the process; ran through their conference with ease; and now, in front of the whole country, they had toppled the #3 team, winning on a night when the odds seem stacked against them and when their A-game was nowhere to be seen.

"I just know these kids have an unbelievable heart," an emotional Petersen said after the game. "We knew it was going to be a hard-fought game. A play here, a play there can turn the game. Our hats off to TCU. This game could have gone either way. We're lucky to have pulled it out."

For the second time in his four years as head coach, Petersen was undefeated. For the second time, his team was denied the opportunity to compete for a national championship. The Broncos had too far to climb, beginning the year ranked #14, with too few marquee matchups propelling them up the charts. But with the 2010 calendar year just four days old, something different was brewing. The core of the Broncos' team would again be returning the following season. Moore would be entering his junior year, the full playbook and a stable of skill players at his disposal. The defense would be just as nasty. Doug Martin was morphing into an all-timer at running back. And, perhaps as important as any, the Broncos would open the season in the biggest showcase game the school had ever seen.

The stars were aligned for Boise State to break through the final barrier.

20

A KICK SHORT

"We came out with the expectation that the nation is watching us, so we need to make some plays and do damage. We were chasing something bigger than the Fiesta Bowl."
—Chase Baker, Boise State defensive tackle, 2008–2011

OKLAHOMA SOONERS. OREGON Ducks, twice. TCU. Entering the 2010 season, Boise State's charmed existence as the upstart school that toppled the occasional powerhouse was beginning to fade. With each passing conference title and subsequent takedown of powerhouse BCS schools, the Broncos were beginning to bleed over into uncharted waters; suddenly, after a slow burn—and before anybody realized it was happening—they were now Big Time.

By knocking off almost every challenge that had come their way in recent years, it was time to take down one more. Insert the Virginia Tech Hokies, their lunch-pail mentality, #7 ranking, and their 80,000-plus maniacal fans on Labor Day weekend in Landover, Maryland.

Boise State entered the opening weekend matchup ranked #3 in the country, its highest in program history.

"Opening with Virginia Tech, it's one of the games why I came to play at Boise State," said Moore as the opening week crept closer. "Opportunities like this to play where we are playing in a big environment at FedEx Field [home of the NFL's Washington Redskins], these are the things you should be excited for and talking about at this point, and looking forward to them this offseason."[1]

Chris Petersen's prowess was a major part of the story as to how the Broncos had achieved this status. That part was obvious. But behind the scenes, a different reason for the coach's success was becoming apparent: his demeanor—soft-spoken, calculated, and focused—was viewed as the key cog in the program's success. As Jason Chatraw of the *Daily Press* wrote:

If you bump into the Boise State head coach in the Broncos' athletic department hallways, don't expect him to flash a smile, engage in a dutiful handshake and quickly dash away. Hastiness is not his style. Instead, prepare for him to stop, look you in the eye, and listen. And in that encounter, you capture Petersen's blueprint for success.[2]

Now in his fifth season, Petersen was 49–4 overall. He had 20 starters returning from 2009's 14–0 team, his second squad that had made it through a season unscathed.

But, most importantly, he had Moore. Two seasons in, the quarterback had blown the already sky-high expectations out of the water; his record (26–1) and quarterback rating (159.4) were both school records. He had thrown for 64 touchdowns to just 13 interceptions. Perhaps his biggest accomplishment was that he didn't allow the quarterback position to skip a beat—not after the uber-successful tenures of Bart Hendricks, Ryan Dinwiddie, and Jared Zabranksy. The inevitable fall-off that most programs face—especially those that don't reside in recruiting hotbeds, who are able to continuously stockpile their roster with 4- and 5-star kids—had been evaded, thanks in large part to Moore.

Kellen grew up in Prosser, Washington. He was the son of a coach, Tom Moore, who made sure his two sons—Kellen and his younger brother Kirby, who would play wide receiver at Boise State—were on the football path from day one. Kirby and Kellen were notorious in the neighborhood for always having a football in hand; Kellen was the leader of the neighborhood's infamous group of boys who occupied the streets. Only he and his crew weren't raising hell—they were playing ball.

Kellen was a natural born leader, adopting his father's coaching mentality from an early age. "He'd always have a little notepad with him; he was always taking notes," his father once said, and that studious nature was a large factor in his success. Kellen's body never caught up to his brain, as he topped out at 5-foot-11, 190 pounds on a generous day. His left arm never got close to that of, say, Michael Vick, who could flick the football 70 yards with ease. What Moore had was the "It" factor that other prospects lack.

He is also a notorious introvert—usually viewed as the deathknell for a quarterback, who needs to be the leader of the team. Jeff Cheek, who was a graduate assistant during Moore's sophomore campaign in 2009, remembers vividly the disappointment when he first stumbled upon Moore, who was much ballyhooed, but looked and acted nothing like a leader.

"He was this rising star, and I was extremely disappointed in him. Me, personally, I was like, 'This guy is some star quarterback?' He was kind of sheepish, didn't say anything at practice, or meetings, or anywhere. Doesn't get all excited. Just goes about his business," he says now. "He's not arrogant, he's not cocky . . . you would have no clue who he is. I was kind of pissed about it. I was thinking, 'Dude, be the quarterback. *Be the leader.*' It took me a while to figure out how he led and went about his business, but now I obviously have tremendous respect for him."

Now, he entered 2010 with his sights on every passing record the school counted. Helping matters was that with his small stature and lack of arm strength, Moore was a shoe-in to be at Boise State through his senior year. There was no threat of an early departure to the NFL. He gave Boise State a four-year package.

If Moore has gained legendary status from Broncos fans by his two wins over Oregon and the Fiesta Bowl triumph against TCU, Virginia Tech was an opportunity for the rest of the nation to take notice, with their rugged and physical style of play.

For all of the clichéd catchphrases thrown upon the Broncos over the years about their trickery and softness, the Hokies had the opposite reputation. Built under head coach Frank Beamer and defensive coordinator Bud Foster, they were Beamer-ball— outstanding speacial teams play—and Bruce Smith and Michael

Vick. The Hokies didn't come into a game and out-scheme you; they lined up, hit you in the jaw, stood their looking down as you melted into a pool of blood and tears, then stepped on your neck to finish the job. They were the antithesis of Oklahoma or Oregon; those schools would whiz by you. Virginia Tech would run through.

As Ralph D. Russo wrote the day of the game, "For all Boise State has accomplished—more wins than any major college team and two BCS victories—never before have the Broncos been a serious national championship contender. That changes if Boise State beats the Hokies at the home of the Washington Redskins in Landover, Maryland, a game far from neutral field, far away from the blue turf."[3]

Off the field, Moore was breaking out of his shell of reluctance. As he grew mentally, the team was following suit. Suddenly, the confident quips weren't coming from the opposition.

Boise State was now the one with the puffed chests.

"In the past it was always 'prove them wrong'; now it's a little bit of a switch," Moore said before the game. "The mentality can't change. I still think it's the same preparation needed and all those characteristics have to stay the same."[4]

Jeron Johnson, a Broncos safety who was going into his senior season, expressed confidence in the team's abilities, but cautioned to outsiders that it should not be mistaken for anything more.

"We don't have arrogance or cockiness or anything like that, but you have to go into every game with some bit of confidence," he said. "You can't have doubts going into any game. And we know [Virginia Tech] is a big game.

"The coaches haven't talked about it too much; there's no need for them to say anything, because as players we know how big of a game it is."[5]

Frank Beamer did not need a crash course in Broncos football; nor did he need extra convincing that the challenge awaiting his team was real. He had watched the film. He had studied the way Boise State conducted business. He saw their extremely talented yet undersized and overstimulated defensive line. He saw Moore's velvety passes fall into the waiting hands of his receivers. He saw Doug Martin pinballing between linemen, picking up yards most human beings could not get. He saw it all, and he knew what was waiting.

"I'm nervous about the game," he said.[6]

* * *

Countering the steady play of Moore was Virginia Tech's Tyrod Taylor, a dynamic playmaker who had guided the Hokies to a 10–3 record the previous season. Taylor fit the mold of former Hokies stars Michael and Marcus Vick; he possessed a big arm, but it was his legs and his ability to slither away from danger that kept the Boise State staff up at night.

Now a senior, Taylor started the 2010 season as a career 55.6 percent passer, below average for a starting quarterback on a championship-caliber team. However, he had accounted for 1,537 yards on the ground in three seasons, essentially giving the Hokies an extra-man advantage. Paired alongside Ryan Williams and David Wilson, they created a three-headed monster that was the perfect compliment to the Hokies' typically rugged offensive line. Neutralizing the run game was paramount if Boise State was going to walk away victorious.

"I can't really remember anybody having a backfield like they have, and the big physical line, which is scary," Petersen said before the game.[7]

Williams was the star, coming off a season in which he rushed for 1,655 yards. He was two tree trunks and a torso, standing a mere 5-foot-9, but a bruising 210 pounds. He came in the mold of an Ian Johnson, but wearing a more electrifying suit. Not only could he run *through* you, but given the slightest crease, he would run *away* from you.

Virginia Tech was 1–17 all-time against teams ranked in the Top 5; Boise State had never played a game when they were ranked in that range.

"I think both of us have reputations that were different probably from ten years ago," Beamer said the day before the game. "I don't think ten years ago anybody would have said Boise State-Virginia Tech was going to be the number one non-conference football game in the country. I don't think anybody would have said that."[8]

But now they were. And, for better or worse, something had to give.

"I remember thinking, 'OK, it's one of those Midwest, west teams that, you know . . . ' In my mind, coming from the south, the southeast, where the ACC and SEC go, to me those have always been the top conferences," says Virginia Tech's Bruce Taylor, a linebacker who made his first career start against the Broncos. "That game was tough."

* * *

The opening riff to Metallica's "Enter Sandman" is a recognizable and iconic song in the annals of music; the moment it hits, goosebumps cover your body like flags of defeat.

For that reason it is the chosen theme song that welcomes the Virginia Tech football team onto the field. From the first strum of the guitar, Hokie fans enter a state of delirium, eager to gobble up another victim. As a single camera caravanned over FedEx Field on the night of September 6 and the riff hit, 86,587 fans began to jump. And jump. And jump some more. They continued to jump until the infrastructure of the stadium felt as if it were going to give way. As an NFL stadium, FedEx Field was used to some noise; muttled cheers and boos were common things on Sundays during the fall. The pandemonium created by college football fans, the passion and commitment pouring like sweat from their insides, was a different story.

"You are looking live at FedEx Field in Landover, Maryland," legendary play-by-play announcer Brent Musburger announced as the camera took in the scene. "Where two Top-10 teams will battle for their national championship lives."

In an attempt to dilute the noise and, hopefully, suck some of the energy from the stadium, the Broncos won the kick and elected to defer to the second half. And, in a domino effect, force the near-rabid Hokies fanbase to swallow their howls as their team started on offense.

It was the perfect call.

On just the second play of the game, Taylor pulled out from under center, leaving the ball behind to fall to the turf. Boise State's lineman Billy Winn pounced.

Turnover. Broncos ball.

Momentum? Stolen.

Boise State had survived the initial test, with a little luck. Making the biggest—and most challenging—start of his career, Moore was gifted the ball at his opponents 31-yard line. Although the Broncos had to settle for a 44-yard field goal from Kyle Brotzman, the tone had been set—and the next two quarters were a testament to that. Once the initial jitters and turbocharged adrenaline subsided and both teams were able to settle into a rhythm, the similarities of the two squads began to shine through.

Boise State's 20–14 halftime lead felt both precarious and disappointing. For the better part of the game up to that point, they had outplayed Virginia Tech (leading 17–0 at the end of the first quarter). Missed plays here and there had kept them from extending the lead; with the firepower the Hokies had at their disposal, no lead was too large, either.

That's when Virginia Tech went to work.

After Moore was sacked, and then fumbled, with just over nine minutes to play in the third quarter, behind the running of Ryan Williams, the Hokies marched down and scored. After D. J. Harper responded for Boise State, scattering 71 yards for a touchdown to up the lead to 26–21, Taylor and the Hokies again went undeterred down the field. A missed field goal attempt by the Hokies was called off after a Boise State player ran into their kicker.

Gifted a first down, Taylor hit Jarrett Boykin for a touchdown on the next play. Once again Virginia Tech had popped ahead, 27–26.

Finally, with 1:47 left in the game, trailing 30–26, Boise State took possession on their own 44-yard line. Moore would lead a methodical drive, completing a succession of short, safe passes, until they reached the Hokies' 13-yard line.

With 1:14 to play, Moore took a snap, whipped around, and found a streaking Austin Pettis just as he crossed the goal line.

Game over. Final score: 33–30, Boise State.

"That was a true road game. Virginia Tech was so hyped, and Boise State was finally put at a level as peers from a poll standpoint. That was as impressive a win as we've seen," says Pete Cavender, who was doing color commentary for Boise State's radio network. "For me, that was the most enjoyable game I've called. It was so much fun to be at; the energy in the stadium was unbelievable."

The win over Virginia Tech had much more to do for the actual football side of things than the Oklahoma game four years prior. What the Fiesta Bowl did was put the program on the map for the outsiders; for those who had no interest in college football; for those who were looking for a cool story, or an anecdote to hang onto for inspiration. The win over Virginia Tech? That was for the football crowd, the ones that knew what the Hokies were.

"Coming into the game, I was, like, 'Do these guys really play football out there?' They definitely proved to me that all of those kids from out west . . . they made me a believer," says Taylor now.

If the Broncos made it through another season unscathed, there would be no denying their worthiness of inclusion into the topic of "best team in the country."

With the win, they planted their flag, right in the heart of the conversation.

* * *

When the final whistle blew, and the Broncos' most significant regular season win in school history was final, the immediate focus became, "What does it all mean?"

A look ahead on their schedule again revealed very few potential potholes; another undefeated season, this time with the head start of their high ranking, meant a trip to play for the national championship was not only within reach, but, in all likelihood, in the hands of the Broncos themselves.

Said Erik Smith of *USA Today*: "Part of the jubilation [Monday] was the dramatic ending, in what should be the toughest game for the Broncos this season. The rest was the relief of winning a game with such buildup and still having hope of being the first school from a league without an automatic Bowl Championship Series bid to play in the title game."[9]

The trip to Laramie to play Wyoming in Week 2 was a trap game, and a visit the week after from Oregon State, who finished second in the Pac-10 the year before, would pose some problems, but once conference play hit . . . well, the Broncos had not lost an in-conference game in two seasons. Survive and advance to Western Athletic Conference play unscathed, and all the stars would align. Finally, after years of slowly building up the program, Petersen and his staff were opening the seal.

And with the confidence and momentum radiating out of players after crashing Virginia Tech's season, they unleashed a tethered and cohesive onslaught.

Wyoming? Win, 51–6. Oregon State? Win, 37–24. They would win games by 59 points, by 43, by 48, 29, 35, and 51. They were steamrolling anything that came within ear shot; Moore was having a Heisman-worthy season; the defense had transformed into a suffocating unit, on par with any in the country. Over a seven-game stretch, from a home win in Week 4 at New Mexico State to a win against Fresno State in Week 10, the Broncos gave up just 55 points.

Nothing, it seemed, was going to penetrate their plan to lay claim as one of the best two teams in the country.

Nothing, except Nevada.

Nothing, except Colin Kaepernick.

* * *

Long before he took a seat, and then a knee; long before his stance on social injustice sparked a movement, altering the perception of the NFL; and long before his Person of the Year awards, Colin Kaepernick was a pistol quarterback under Chris Ault at the University of Nevada. He was part-man, part-cheetah, pencil-thin with a massive arm.

Coming out of high school, with few scholarship offers and even fewer believers in his ability as a quarterback, Kaepernick found himself headed to the desert with the opportunity to run Ault's system.

Entering the 2010 season, he had, like most teams in the WAC, found the Broncos to be a malevolent death star. He was

0–3 against Boise State, although his Wolfpack had arguably been their toughest foe. A 69–67 loss in 2007, after four gut-wrenching overtimes, had proven to be the high point in his rivalry with the Broncos. Two more close losses in 2008 and 2009 had been the final straw for the uber-talented Kaepernick who, entering his senior season, had found his way onto enough NFL scouts' radars to warrant considerable preseason hype. The two things that had evaded him—a conference title and a win over Boise State—now sat before him if the season broke correctly.

"Right now, they're the best," Kaepernick told reporters before the season. "They've been the best. I think, for us to become the best, we have to beat them."

On November 26, in front of 30,712 fans at a bursting-at-the-seams Mackay Stadium in Reno, Nevada, the stars had aligned. The Broncos still clung to their #3 ranking. Despite having risen to #2 earlier in the season and then falling back to #4, they entered the Nevada game as they entered the season: one spot outside the elusive Top-2 ranking.

Nevada had a 10–1 record, their lone loss to Hawaii, and was ranked 19th in the country. Kaepernick had been sensational all season long; through the team's first 11 games, he was completing 66 percent of his passes for 2,412 yards and 19 touchdowns. He had also amassed 984 yards on the ground, joining Virginia Tech's Taylor as arguably the toughest dual-threat quarterback in the nation.

The importance of the game for both teams was easy to understand.

"They have been playing football at Nevada since 1896; ask around these parts, they won't hesitate to say this is the most significant game ever here," said Joe Tessitore, who was calling the game on ESPN.

Boise State and Nevada would duel for nearly four full quarters in a spirited back-and-forth affair. This game—and the entire season—boiled down to the final moments for the Broncos.

With the score tied at 24, the Broncos took possession with 5:08 on the clock, 79 yards from scoring. Theory and logic told Petersen and the staff to put together a calculated drive, sifting away clock and keeping the ball away from Kaepernick.

Then, on the first play of the drive, lightning. Moore's screen pass to Doug Martin, who would zig-zag his way through seemingly the entire Nevada defense, resulted in a one-play touchdown, giving the Broncos a 31–24 lead.

It also left Kaepernick ample time to operate. He would lead the Wolfpack on a game-tying touchdown drive, which ended with just 13 seconds remaining in the game.

Then, all hell broke loose.

The Broncos, instead of taking a knee and succumbing to overtime, went against convention. On the first play of the drive, Moore launched a pass downfield, as far as he could throw it. Broncos receiver Titus Young—who had split two defenders along the left hashmark—dove, his outstretched body gliding through the cold desert night. As he landed, the ball settled into his chest as his body weight hit the turf.

Young, in a quick reaction, rolled over and called timeout to the nearest referee with just one second remaining on the clock.

Moments before, after the Wolfpack had tied the game, the stadium, rollicking all evening, nearly came off its hinges. In a manner of seconds, silence. Not a sound, aside from the few Broncos faithful who had made the journey.

With the ball resting on the 9-yard line, a 26-yard field goal stood between them and an improbable regulation win. Kyle Brotzman, who would end his career as the school's all-time leading scorer and one of the most prolific and accurate kickers in the history of the program, jogged onto the field. Ault, naturally, called for a review to make sure Young made a proper catch.

"It's a bit of a mind trip; when you go out, and the coach calls a timeout to ice the kicker, you kind of know that's coming. But in that situation, to me, clearly [Titus] was a catch and there did not need to be a review on that," says Brotzman now.

If Chris Ault and his Wolfpack were going to go down, they were going down swinging. Although an official review of Titus's catch was a necessity, the subsequent time it took for the referees to sort it out—almost three minutes in the frigid, windblown desert—made his decision to call for a review a masterful one. He had been at Nevada since 1979; had taken the Wolfpack to seven playoff appearances while members of Division I-AA; and had won the Western Athletic Conference in 2005, ripping it away from the Broncos. He was no spring chicken, and knew the exact moment to utilize the icing method.

It worked. Brotzman pushed the kick wide, sending the game into overtime.

The missed field goal exacerbated an already eerie night for the Broncos, one of those in which nothing came easy. As the teams headed for the extra period, Brotzman could very well get a shot at redemption.

In less than three minutes, he would. After Boise State picked up a first down, their drive in the extra period stalled at the 12-yard line, offering their kicker one more shot.

This time, in an overcompensation, he pulled it. No good, again.

Today, he chuckles a bit when recalling the night. While he has come to terms with the outcome and the fallout that came from it, there is a part of him—a small one, but still tangible—that can't help but wonder . . .

"I pushed [the first kick] to the right a little bit, but I still thought it was true. The refs thought otherwise, but end of story—they called it no good, and you have to move on from it."

Nevada would win the game a few moments later. A made field goal, of all things, ended the Broncos' national title hopes.

"We all started off hot, doing our jobs, but credit to Nevada," says Brotzman now. "They made the plays they needed to make, when they needed to make them, and we lost track of doing our job.

"We knew we were better than that, and we should have won that game."

In the Broncos' locker room afterward, silence loomed large. For Brotzman, it could have been the loneliest room in the world.

Instead, he found compassion and solace from teammates and coaches.

"It was quiet. Everyone just kind of couldn't believe what happened. From a big lead going into halftime, to giving that up. It's devastating," he says.

At 5-foot-10 and 190 pounds after a hearty trip to the buffet, Brotzman had made countless big kicks in his career, was in shock. The life of a kicker can take you on many paths; make the kick, and you will never have to buy a beer in town as long you live. Miss it, and life is miserable. There is no gray area; it's black or it's white. However, to his teammates, Brotzman was the same kid he was before the game. No one looked down on him. No one placed blame. If they won as a team, they lost as a team.

And, as he puts it, they were more than one game.

"That team clicked on all cylinders, with a staff that had everyone prepared, all season long. It was a special team, and a really good group of guys to be around.

"They helped me score a lot of points."

The Broncos would rebound and roll through Utah State, and then Utah in the MAACO Bowl, ending the season 13–1 and, once again, WAC champions.

It was the end of an era—the following season they would join the Mountain West Conference—and the beginning of the end for another.

The 2011 season would be the finale for the majority of the vaunted 2007 recruiting class. And, once again, they would kick off the season with a monumental showdown. They were headed back down south, to the Georgia Dome. And just like in 2005, they would open the season against the Bulldogs.

This time, things would be much, much different.

* * *

On September 3, 2011, in front of a predominantly pro-Georgia crowd at the Georgia Dome, in Atlanta, Boise State systematically took apart the Bulldogs. Although this was not one of the top-tier Georgia seasons—they would finish 10–4 overall—it was nonetheless a watershed moment for Boise State. This was their first win over an SEC team. It would also kickstart the senior campaign of Kellen Moore and his contemporaries who would finish their career with a record of 50–3 from 2008–2011.

The Broncos' 2011 season, with a 12–1 record, was the near-perfect exit for the class. A last-second loss—the lone home loss for those seniors—to TCU kept the Broncos, again, from a national title shot. It was the closest the program would get. The following season, a loss to Michigan State to open the year would bump them from consideration, leading to an 11–2 record.

In 2013, they started with a loss to Washington, leading to a five-loss campaign, the worst in Petersen's tenure.

Then, it was over.

* * *

After eight seasons, after an astounding 92 wins, including two BCS bowl games, Chris Petersen was leaving.

"The last few years I had no inclination to go anywhere or look anywhere. I really felt like growing that program and doing great things there," Petersen said. "But there comes a time when all things have a shelf life, and when the right things come at you."[10]

The lifespan of Petersen's time at Boise State often dominated offseason chats. When he didn't leave after his first season in 2006, it was viewed as an overwhelming victory. That his star continued to shine brighter after every season, and that he remained under the Broncos' employ, flew in the face of all preconceived norms.

The law of the land, as it had been all over the country, would have been for him to come into the program, work his way up to the head spot, win a bunch of games for the first couple of seasons, then high-tail it to a more lucrative spot.

But that's not who Petersen desired to be. In Boise, he and his family had found a home.

"Petersen put the biggest dent on where we were, and it's proven," says Rashaad Richards.

"Everything started with coach Petersen," says Shea McClellin. "The respect that he had for players, not just as athletes, but as human beings, allowed guys to buy into the program. And because of that, by 2010, 2011, bigger programs started respecting us, too."

It's hard to quantify the legacy that Petersen was leaving behind. The record, the trophies, and the evocation his tenure receives— all of it seems inconsequential to the totality of his work.

"I don't think there's one person in the program who doesn't believe Petersen is the best coach who ever walked through that program," Ryan Dinwiddie says now. "Petersen does everything the right way, by the book. He's not going to cut corners or recruit bad kids; he's not going to cheat. He's got standards, and if you're not doing what he expects, he'll kick you out, no matter how good you are. That's what he brings: structure."

With Petersen heading west to Seattle and the University of Washington, the program would turn back in time. Bryan Harsin, who lettered for the Broncos from 1996–1998, was back. After stints as Boise State's offensive coordinator, then to Texas in the same position, and later as the head coach of Arkansas State, Harsin would step into, arguably, the most difficult situation in all of college football. Replacing a legend is one thing; replacing one who had revolutionized the game, who had taken a program to heights heretofore unknown, and to do so while still being (mostly) in the good graces of a fanbase?

According to Harsin, it was the perfect challenge.

"We're coming home," he said the day of his hiring. "One of the hardest decisions we ever made was leaving Boise. We did that so I could become a better coach, so I could one day have the opportunity to return as head coach—that day has arrived."

21

OKGS AND MAINTAINING SUCCESS

"The offenses always got the credit, but they've had some dominating defenses. That's been a huge key for them, and now the talent pool has risen."

—B. J. Rains, *Idaho Press*

"**T**HE MENTALITY."

That phrase, oft used and dripping in propaganda, is rampant around the Boise State football program. Players from the 1950s, '60s, '70s, all the way through today, speak of "The Mentality." And to a Bronco, no matter what their record was at the time of their involvement, or how much they played, they speak of the mentality that Boise State played under: players were disrespected in high school; they were disrespected because they were at Boise State; they were disrespected because of this or that or something else perceived altogether.

"That was *our* mentality," they say. "We all had chips on our shoulders."

Shortly after Petersen was hired in 2006, he said that in order for the program to continue its upward trajectory, they needed to bring in OKGs—"Our Kinda Guys." That mantra took on a life of its own, but the line in the sand that he had set—no one player or coach is above the team—took the program from a 95 percent operational rate to 100.

The one- and two-star recruits turned to three- and four-star; Petersen and his staff managed to locate players who bore the physical gifts the coaches desired, but kept the mental edge that often slips away with pre-teen veneration.

"I always tell people, 'Guys like Kellen Moore probably wouldn't have came here if it weren't for the guys before him; Jared Zabransky wouldn't have come if it weren't for Ryan Dinwiddie,'" says Lamont Mikell now. "It trickles down, and [the program] just kept building, and building every year. It just kept getting better and better, until it was a powerhouse."

When Petersen left for the Pac-12 in 2013, he did so at a time when the infrastructure inside the program was too solid to crack. The bringing in of Bryan Harsin ensured the loyalists that even if the unprecedented run of success were to tail off a bit, the message would be the same. Harsin knew firsthand the struggles and glories of coaching the Broncos; if the mantras strayed too far off course, the essence of the program would be lost.

Nate Potter, an offensive lineman who came to Boise State in 2006, says the program's ability to build from the lines out—offensively and defensively—has been arguably the biggest key in toppling some of the sport's giants.

"I think one of the most underrated things about this program is the O-line tradition. I think the last five left tackles have been drafted? Something that people usually overlook when they talk about our success in that time frame was the talent that we really had, the players that they brought in. For those years [2008–2011], almost the entire defense played in the NFL. I know the entire secondary, the entire D-line, the entire receiving corps, the quarterbacks, the running backs—I mean, the NFL talent is just ridiculous. That can't be overstated."[2]

Potter is the poster child for the linemen that have waltzed into the program and gone on to the NFL, embarking on a long and successful career despite intially being viewed as undersized. He was tall, but significantly underweight coming out of Timberline high school, in Boise, stepping onto campus in 2006 at 6-foot-6, but just 250 pounds. He was a two-star recruit, according to *Rivals*, a national recruiting website.

Utilizing the Bronco Way, absorbing what he needed to absorb—food, strength, and knowledge—Potter ended up a 7th-round draft pick, and has been a quality NFL lineman since.

"A big part of that is the recipe, the formula. The coaches for a long time have known the type of players that they can get and can't get, and most of those five-star guys that are 300 pounds in high school and can move are not gonna come to Boise State. But the guys that grew up playing every sport, that are extremely athletic, that have the mentality, that are just undersized in some way, are perfect for Boise."[3]

Finding players who were undersized and turning them into Division I studs required more than just the proper weight room routine and a kitchen that was continually stocked.

It also took a unique approach in the recruiting, digging a bit deeper in a player's brain.

"We were kind of missed by a lot of these schools. That's what the coaches were looking for: does this guy have some fire in him? And is he coachable, in that he'll buy into what we're coaching him? Andrew [Woodward] was talented; Darren [Cooledge] was obviously very talented, and we have a process in place that can get these guys from Point A to Point B if they'll just buy in,"[4] said Zabransky, another guy famous for sliding under the radar.

Getting Zabransky from Hermiston, Oregon, required Boise State coaches to look past the measurables. Zabransky's frame may have pushed some schools away; he is barely six feet tall, thin, and came packaged with an elongated throwing motion. But he absorbed information, battled back from numerous adversities and miscalculations during his time . . . and, as it turned out, he benefitted from some of the brightest minds in the game.

"Shit, we had a bunch of psychologists as coaches. They recruited a bunch of guys that turned out to be pretty good leaders, guys that would buy into the system and lay it all on the line to win football games," says Zabranksy now.[5]

That system goes deeper than the coaches, back to the hallways with administrators, SIDs, etc.

"To this day, whenever I call the school and need anything, I've never been turned down. Again, I was just a kicker. I put in my time, my team voted me a captain my senior year, but still . . . they make everyone feel special," says Greg Erickson now.

"They've been doing this for a long time," said Gabe Rosenvall, Boise State's assistant athletic director for academic services.

"This team has done a great job over many years. It's part of who they are. They haven't got the publicity, but they've been close to records for years now. It's great to see them continue to build.

"Sometimes I'm even guilty of just expecting them to perform at a high level so I do have to stop every once in a while and say this is pretty unusual nationally to see this caliber of a football program compete at this level academically."[6]

Barry Every, who covered high school recruiting for *Rivals. com,* once assessed that "Boise State is the school that has to really hit the recruiting trail hard, because Idaho is, basically, void of D-I talent. I think Boise does a great job of identifying kids maybe a tad short or slow for "Big Six" schools to go after, but these same kids are legit, hard-nosed football players. A good football player, with the desire to succeed, will beat out a star athlete every time if the star athlete does not find the motivation to get better."

Perhaps Pete Cavender—who after a successful playing career has transitioned into the Broncos' radio analyst—sums up the program, and the people inside, best.

"When I was injured [in 2006], I was in the hospital for about four or five days. Coach Petersen was on family vacation that week—it was over the Fourth of July—and he called me every day from Hawaii," he says now. "That's just how genuinely good of a person he is. That's why people here in Boise, underneath our blue and orange, are wearing purple and gold [Washington colors]. I think the entire Treasure Valley would like to see him in a Rose Bowl and win it."

22

STATE OF THE PROGRAM

"The Oregon win in 2009 solidified what we could do. The previous year we had gone into Autzen and handled them, and they made a comeback. So all offseason we heard them saying it was a fluke, and they were going to come in and kick our ass. So that win solidified that we could compete with anyone."

—Chase Baker, Boise State, 2008–2011

THE BOISE STATE that exists today—hypnotic, relevant, thriving—evolved from decades of blood and sweat spilled onto "The Blue." The shade of blue that hits you, when you turn the corner from Chrisway Drive onto University Drive and spilling from the stadium, is indescribable to the unfamiliar eye. You cannot replicate it through osmosis or in fantastical dreams. The shade comes from the eyes of Gene Bleymaier and Lyle Smith and Tony Knap. The special tint is from the sacrifices and spirits of Duane Dlouhy and Paul Reyna and Pokey Allen.

To understand the nature of what Boise State is in the wide-ranging pantheon of college football and where its foothold rests, it takes far more that scanning random numbers. The history books will never give the Broncos their due. They will never reign supreme alongside the Alabama's, the Penn State's, the Oklahoma's, and the USC's. To understand the cultural relevance of the Broncos, from decade after decade of success to championing the "Little Guy" movement requires an open mind and a hint of the child-like wonderment we all lose over time. You have to locate the sharp lines of reality and expectation and look just beyond. That's where Boise State lives.

When Ian Johnson's foot crossed the goal line on January 1, 2007, he carried on his back the weight of those who came before him; the ones who were told they would not, could not, and should not succeed. He was Rudy, Hoosiers, and Buster Douglas in a 5-foot-9 frame, undeterred by life's laid-out plan. When the Broncos knocked out Virgina Tech in 2010, as millions of their fellow under-appreciated brethren looked on in awe, you could almost hear their faint screams from underneath the rubble they created, crying out for a morsel of the respect that still evaded them.

Boise State has embraced the "stepping stone" mantra, allowing them to consistently have young, innovative coaches. That's a huge part of their success.

"We have to realize that, when it comes to big-time college athletics, it is not an even playground. This isn't the NFL, where it's the best-of-the-best, and theoretically they have the same amount of money to spend across the board," says Bart Hendricks. "College athletes, you can spend as much as you want. So it's OK if we lose to some of these bigger schools; they have the money and resources to provide and do things that we just can't quite do yet. It's amazing what we have done with what we have."

With the untethered success, however, has come an issue that plagues many programs around the country. The attitude that once permeated throughout, one of toughness, and grit, when looked at by guys who once roamed the halls, is slipping.

"Whatever you want to call it . . . the entitled generation, the social media effect, people not being as hungry as they used to be, or being victims of their own success," says Nick Schlekeway. "I just know that the attitude and the edge that we had is not present anymore. It's not there. They can talk about it, and say 'blue collar' and all that shit all they want, but it's not there."

The natural tapering off is made more evident because for so long, the school avoided it. Even during darker periods, like the 1980s, where the standard of success dipped, the attitude among the people there never did.

"The guys that I played with, we were weird; we were a unique group of cats. Everybody that I played with had a chip on their shoulder about something. There were a lot of fights, and it was a rough crowd," Schlekeway continues. "We bonded as teammates and fought like only brothers can, and we brought that mentality to the field. . . . I just don't see that anymore."

The Cavender brothers, Jeff and Pete, who were instrumental to the program during the early years of Chris Petersen, point to the spreading of talent as perhaps a cause of the edge slipping. "The team was guys from small towns, or guys who had been overlooked and had a huge chip on their shoulder. I think that's the main difference between the old Boise State, and the Boise State of today," says Jeff.

Players entering the program now see one steeped in tradition. They don't know a Boise State unidentified with winning. It has been a great recruiting tool, and an obstacle the current coaches on staff have to fight off, daily, in an attempt to keep the edge.

"We were a little oblivious to what we were building [back in the day]," says Jeff Cavender. "What we knew was we were very talented, but there were a lot of other factors that went into our success."

* * *

In June of 1981, Boise State hired Eugene "Gene" Anthony Bleymaier as the school's athletic director, taking the reigns from Lyle Smith.

On August 11, 2011, in a move seen as both controversial, seismic, and, for the most part, bewildering, then-president Bob Kustra relieved Gene of his duties, ending his 30-year run as one of the most successful and innovative ADs that had ever presided over a university.

In between, he created magic. He created art and mystery, and fostered programs that transcended both expectations and realities.

After 30 seasons, which saw the Boise State program rise from Division I-AA power to Division I-A slug, to arguably the most successful mid-major of all time, Gene was out. A blink of an eye, a stamp of approval, a lifetime's worth of accomplishments, gone.

"I was surprised and disappointed, very disappointed," Bleymaier said. "I didn't expect this."[1]

"I did not come to this decision lightly," Kustra said in the press release following Bleymaier's dismissal. "After a careful management review and discussions about the future of the program, I determined that new leadership will be needed as we commit ourselves to the highest level of attention and enforcement of NCAA standards, and also continue to move Boise State athletics to the next level of success."[2]

However, Bleymaier's time was not without its dark moments. Minor recruiting violations have popped up from time to time, and an incident involving a former player, Sam Ukwuachu, rape allegations, and what the school did or did not disclose before his transfer, stuck out like sore thumbs.

"The program as a whole has gone from a small university to a true power program, and as things have changed and grown there are things that come along with it. If you're not tuned to it and cannot forecast and project, it can be tough," says Pete Cavender. "I think that was one of the challenges Boise State has faced. It's nothing against Gene by any means, but Boise has grown, and there are more and more challenges."

Bleymaier had a propensity for lurking in the shadows, making him an odd figure among the Bronco regime. As athletic director, in-tune fans knew that he was the one pulling the strings. However, because he lacked the bombastic personality, his role and impact often went overlooked.

"To me, Gene was always available, and that's what I appreciated about him. If you needed something, he was there," says Jeff Cavender. "He is just a good person, and I think he saw the value the football team brought to the university."

In the overview of his stint at the school, it is hard to tap down Bleymaier's largest accomplishment. One could easily look toward his ability to assess coaching talent in myriad sports.

The blue turf, which has morphed into the calling card for the university, is hard to top as the talisman of his impact.

"Gene took a big chance on putting that blue turf in," Cavender continues. "He had to understand how much of a risk that was, being a young athletic director, and seeing the confused looks he probably got when talking to boosters. But he did it."

When Bleymaier's dismissal was announced, it coincided with "major recruiting violations" in their women's basketball program, along with minor violations in four other sports, including football. The violations involving the football team, which included impermissible housing, transportation, and food and meals involving prospective students, took place, it was announced, between the 2005–2009 seasons. The amount of the benefits totaled $4,934. In the big stakes world of collegiate athletics, it was a drop in the bucket.

For Kustra, it was enough to see that Bleymaier's time at the school would be no more. Despite the school leading the investigation nearly two years before the NCAA violations became official, it was too little, too late.

It's unknown whether the violations had more to do with Bleymaier's exit or the sometimes-contentious relation between he and Kustra. Rumors swirled internally for periods of time that the two had a frosty relationship, with Kustra being jealous of the praise heaped on Bleymaier for the school's success.

Regardless, it was announced that Bleymaier's last day as the AD of Boise State would be September 8, 2011.

Shortly after, he would return to the state of California, where he took on a similar role with the San Jose State Spartans.

During his time there, Bleymaier's challenges were more difficult than what he had faced during his time in Boise, even when the situation was at its leanest.

"I think the thing he quickly learned at San Jose State was that the level of support was not what he was used to and expected," says Jimmy Durkin, who covered the Spartans for the *San Jose Mercury News* at the time.

* * *

Through it all—the coaching changes, the rise to immortality, and the inevitable stabling that has come with it—Boise State has managed to avoid the ignominious falls. Where black eyes appear in almost all successful collegiate programs, the Broncos—save a red splotch here and there—have come out relatively unscathed. They climbed to an unfathomable height in an era that was designed to keep that moment from happening.

From May–August 2016, over 25,000 people, from all over the globe, visited Boise State and the blue turf. What started out as a sideshow has turned into a tourist destination for fans and non-fans alike. The blue turf could have easily been an amalgamation of horrifying concepts. At the time, in 1986, the program had yet to establish its true footing. In 1980, when the school won the national championship, ESPN was barely a year old. The impact of the worldwide leader was light years from where it would end up. Schools like Boise State, and all others of their ilk, did not yet benefit from the 24/7 cycle of content.

Luckily, for all involved, but perhaps for Bleymaier most, the blue turf worked. "The Blue" became a symbol of pride and of stability. It meant standing out among your peers, not afraid to be different; not afraid to be who you are, reputations and assumptions aside.

It worked. That is, after all, the program's state of mind.

EPILOGUE: IN THEIR WORDS

IN ORDER FOR this book to come together, it took an immense amount of cooperation and sacrificing of time from individuals whom I had never met, and who had no reason to believe what I was doing was real. When I started the process of interviewing former players, coaches, administrators, opponents, fans, and media members, I approached them with the notion that, someday, *maybe*, this would be a book.

The process of writing a book does not come about without its share of mistakes—the biggest of which was losing the first interview I did, after a voice recorder malfunction. But speaking with Harry Hedrick allowed this to take off; his passion and glowing review of his time in Boise made me realize I was taking on the correct project. Thank you, Harry, for confirming my beliefs.

From the first person I contacted to the last, Marty Tadman, the outpouring of stories, reflections, memories, tears, laughter—

all of it came from a common place: the people I talked to, the ones who were so generous in helping me realize my dream, carry a torch for the Boise State program unlike any I have ever seen. That's why this epilogue is dedicated to them; in the process of writing this book, some people's contributions didn't make the final cut. But their stories and tidbits helped shaped the final product in ways I could never explain.

For that, I felt it very important that everyone gets the proper credit they deserve. Because of that, this section is for you. These snapshots of our conversations, while only a glimpse, went a long way in helping me understand what makes the university—and the football program, in particular—so unique.

Thank you.

* * *

Dennis Brady, Boise State, 1978–1982
"Practices were a lot of times harder than the games. You go in expecting to work really hard, but you go in expecting to win, too."

* * *

Steve Despot, Boise State, 1982–1985
"The rivalries between Boise State and Nevada, Boise State and Idaho stand out . . . but when you're playing football, you're focused; the memories when you get done are more about the guys you played with."

* * *

Jake Hamar, former radio host, KTIK
"When they beat Oregon, both times, in 2008 and 2009 . . . that was a true, 'Wow, this team has arrived.'"

* * *

Toots Kaahanui, Boise State, 1974–1975
"The best part of the Samoan community in Boise, is that we didn't just rely on football. We would go out, grab a bite to eat, just be together as a family."

* * *

Eric Andrade, Boise State, 1983–1987
"Lyle Setencich was a defensive genius; I don't know if he ever got the right offensive coordinators in there. If you talk to Lyle about things he could have done differently, I think he would have opened things up more offensively. He was old-school."

* * *

Steve Svitak, Boise State, 1968–1969
"Lyle Smith took care of me like a son. He took me under his wing; when I would slip up, he would encourage me in a nice way. Not for selfish reasons. Just to help."

* * *

Jeff Caves, Boise State, 1980–1983
"Life as a BSU player was a rock star existence. Recognition, booster support, and fan appreciation were very evident in the smaller Boise community. We were important to the city and we knew it."

* * *

Paul Buker, sports reporter, *The Oregonian*
"Pokey knew we were on deadline for some of those late games, so Pokey would let us reporters walk down the stands, onto the sidelines, and start interviewing players in the middle of the fourth quarter to make sure we got their quotes in for the Sunday paper."

* * *

Brian Smith, Boise State, 1991–1995
"Pokey taught me two things that stand out: you control your effort and your attitude. He taught us how to fight through adversity; you might not reach the goal you set out for, but you'll reach success by striving for a higher goal."

* * *

Scott Baker, Boise State, 1981–1984
"Football saved me. The way I was going, I was going to be a semester short of making it. Coach Criner did that by giving me a scholarship. Ninety-five percent of keeping me on track had to do with the program, and I owe them a lot."

* * *

Dane Oldham, Boise State, 1999–2003
"Off the field, we had a lot of fun. Too much, sometimes, but we all made it through. When it came down to it, Bart Hendricks and Ryan Dinwiddie were oil-and-water, but both knew how to lead."

* * *

John Charles, Portland State, 1989–1992
"Pokey was so humble; he let the other coaches run their part, and he trusted them. A couple times we had practice, and we're wondering where coach is, and he's at lunches and dinners promoting the program, and he'd show up halfway through practice like at the other coaches, and say 'Where are we?'"

* * *

Terry Heffner, Boise State, 1987–1990
"As both us and Idaho made the jump to Division I, you could tell that one program, Idaho, was doing so with both hands tied behind their back, from an economic standpoint. I think people in the area miss that rivalry a little bit."

* * *

Chris Wing, Boise State, 1994–1996
"You thought about Pokey; when he came back [in 1996] it was tough to see him that way, but I'll tell you—he coached. And the game he returned, the magic popped right back into us for that game."

* * *

Lance Sellers, Boise State, 1982–1986
"After I graduated, my academic counselor called me one day and said, 'Hey, you need to come down to Boise State. Bring your workout gear.' I get there, Channel 7 News puts a microphone on me, and they tell me I'm going to do an *American Gladiators* segment. So, I did it."

* * *

Matt Slater, Boise State, 2007–2010
"The second time we played Oregon [in 2009], we weren't just thinking, 'Hey, we're excited to be here.' We were there to kick their ass. Now it's our time to shine."

* * *

Tierre Sams, Fresno State, 2000–2001
"We were going into that game thinking, 'We're going to kill these guys, these Boise, blue-turf dudes.' We went into that game kind of cocky. Then they hit us right in the mouth."

* * *

B. J. Rains, reporter, *Idaho Press Tribune*
"Chris Petersen always let us watch every practice during fall camp and spring practice, which was unique. Bryan Harsin knows what he's doing; he learned so much from Petersen."

* * *

Tim Foley, Boise State, 1992–1995
"It's such a testament to the city itself, but so many guys who come to Boise State to play football ended up staying and living there. They come and start to realize it's such a great city, it supports its program. The veterans are still brought in today to talk to new kids about how this is a longer tradition than just recent success."

* * *

John Kilgo, Boise State, 1981–1984
"I was close to being an Idaho Vandal. My best friend was a Vandal. But as a team, we hated them. Idaho week, we all put a 'DAV' sticker on our helmets the first day of practice: Dog Ass Vandals. Beating them was everything."

* * *

Michael Atkinson, Boise State, 2009–2012
"Our defense always had chemistry. There was no bullying, no hazing. Coach Petersen was so good at keeping us unified; everyone felt comfortable. You never went into a practice thinking, 'If I screw this up, I'm going to get yelled at.'"

* * *

Jim Belin, Boise State, 1990
"Being an African American in Boise, coming from California, it almost seemed like a fairytale. It didn't always seem real; it was just easy living. There was no place I would rather have gone to school."

* * *

Rocky Atkinson, Boise State, 2001–2004
"At the time, the big wins energize you; it makes you more confident in what you can do. You can't necessarily see the shift of how you're improving when you're there in the moment. Now we can reflect back over and see the changes."

* * *

Bryan Johnson, Boise State, 1996–1999
"Pokey getting sick was emotional, but I think, at the same time, at our age you don't really understand. They tried to protect us and not tell us everything."

* * *

Jason Rosen, Boise State, 1988–1989
"Blood, sweat, and tears . . . everything I needed to do, I did while I was there. I wanted to compete, and I did."

* * *

Vince Watson, Boise State, 1994–1995
"Boise, Idaho is a place where I can honestly, and genuinely, say I never really felt racial tension. Everyone knew who we were; I'm in the 6-foot-2/6-foot-3 range. People knew, 'He's probably not playing tennis.' We had our own community within ourselves, guys from all over the West Coast."

* * *

ACKNOWLEDGMENTS

IT HAS BEEN roughly 732 days since the first blip of this idea popped into my head. It was August of 2016, and it was amidst that dry spell (I believe) all writers go through, especially ones who do not have the comfort of a full-time paycheck to fall back on. I was freelancing where I could, but between my regular job, and our (at the time) three-year-old daughter and three-month-old twins, I was running on fumes (quite literally, actually; occasionally a light, but tangible, stream of smoke would emanate from my ears).

It was this point, all those days ago, that I had the asinine thought that I would take my writing career into my own hands. For some reason, "I'll write a book. That'll show 'em" is a real thought that went through my brain (again, fumes). After some internal banter, the first idea that had come to me, the true story of how the Boise State football program evolved into a mid-major juggernaut, won out over the rest.

Without a second thought, I was off. However, before I began, I wrote myself a letter; in it, I vowed that this would be different from ones in my past, ones that had seen me start with the best of intentions, only to falter soon after, either by circumstances of a lack of follow through on my part.

Next, I called my friend Casey Hedrick, at the time the only person I knew who had any association with the program (and who later, alongside his fiancée, Sarah, would welcome me into their home on my voyages to Boise and be huge assets themselves). Casey led me to his father, Harry, a former offensive coordinator for the Broncos, and my first official interview for the book. Harry would introduce me to Skip Hall and Scott Criner; the rest, as they say, is history.

The process of actually writing the book was a trying one; the real joy came in all of the conversations I had with former players, coaches, media members, etc., ones who took me on wonderful journeys down memory lane. So many of those conversations involved tears of joy, of sadness, or of the realization that they were a part of something special.

One hundred and ten interviews later, you hold in your hands the truest emotions of the people who made the story what it was; I was simply the brush to paint the picture.

It would be silly for me to name all those here who deserve it; every single person who took the time to speak to me—friends in my life, folks I have encountered who left an impression— you will never know what it means to me. Without you, this is not happening. However, there are those who stand out for their continued support, extra efforts to help guide me, or for various other reasons.

Taylor Tharp was the lone interview I did in person, and he was an absolute pleasure. During a busy recruiting weekend, he took an hour out to sit and talk through the biggest game in program history, painting an illustrious picture. His recollection drove the initial narrative, and set the stage for the outline of the entire book.

Monte Burke, a phenomenal author, hinted to me the idea of writing a proposal for the book, long before any such thing had entered my brain. That proposal would go on to land me the contract with Sports Publishing. To this day, reading the email offer from the man himself, Jason Katzman, is the hardest I have ever cried. I know how that sounds; I don't care. My wife and kids understand.

Speaking of Jason: I don't have the words to say just how amazing you have been. The amount of times you had to begin a conversation with "Joel, chill out . . . you're fine," when I would ramp up my fears . . . I'm sure you thought of screening my calls. I don't know where our paths will take us from here, but you will always be my editor and friend.

Jason Payne, Vince Watson, Greg Erickson, Bart Hendricks, Kenneth Phillips—some people just stick in your brain after you speak with them. These gentlemen fall into that category. Their stories, their kindness, their networking for me—all of it was essential. John Kilgo may have been the best promotions man I have encountered. His love of Boise State and desire to see this book come to fruition—and to do well—gives me goosebumps to this day.

Boise State University could not have been more helpful. Brad Larrondo, from the moment I reached out, was as courteous and forthcoming as I could have hoped for. He set the tone for everyone that I reached out to inside the program. Joe Nickell as well deserves major credit.

David Diehr, a longtime friend, is the scariest human being I have ever encountered when he's dissecting your work. David's genius with language is without question, and I asked him to edit my proposal. When he returned it, and I noticed all of the remarks, I decided to quit writing (kidding). Through his honest feedback, David pushed me, and his critiques are the number one reason my proposal was accepted.

The fellas at *The Cauldron*—Jamie O'Grady, Jim Cavan, and Andy Glockner—gave me my first foray into the big-time. It was short-lived, but, gentlemen: you ignited a confidence in me that still burns (flickers?) today. Through them, a dream came true when I got to work with a man I have idolized, Joey Harrington. The work Joey and I did forced me to look in the mirror and say, "You can do this. Push."

Joey—you may not realize, but to this day you are a huge inspiration, and every time I leave my office I see the autographed picture of our work and smile.

My parents have been my biggest cheerleaders since the first time I mentioned writing. Although my life took many paths along the way to get here, no matter the direction I went, they were there to keep me from derailing. Jackie, Ron, Keith—I don't know what else to say. You're the absolute best. My in-laws, Sandy and Hugh, have joined in on the fun of cheering me along. Thank you both.

My step-siblings (Kristina, Keith, Eric) never made me feel as if "step" was part of my title. Siblings through the in-law route (Melissa and Jake), the same goes for you. From day one you brought me in.

ACKNOWLEDGMENTS

My children—wow. There is no way to describe the drive you three give me. Isla, watching you make books out of paper, saying you're doing it "to be like daddy," brings up feelings I didn't know existed. Nash and Stella—someday you'll understand why I spent so many hours up in my office, diligently crossing out words with red pen. It won't erase the nights I was working, but, hopefully, it will give them meaning.

To my wife: the biggest influence in my life. The person who pushes me hardest, keeps me motivated, encourages me to be my best. You are my sounding board, cheerleader, and partner. You have the most amazing eye, and took this book from a raw, disorganized mess, to the final product. I cannot imagine doing this without your vision and sense of language. This book is dedicated to so many, but you sacrificed the most to see that I finished. Without your unwavering enthusiasm for my passion, this is not real.

To every person who talked, edited, listened, watched, and now read—thank you.

SOURCES

Chapter Two: Tony Knap, and the Second Round of Dominance

1. "Boise State coach aims for heights," Wayne Cornell, *Idaho Free Press*, February 16, 1968.
2. "Prep grinders sign with Boise State," UPI, *Daily Herald*, April 10, 1969.
3. "Big Sky enthusiastic about new expansion," UPI, *Daily Herald*, November 26, 1969.
4. "Boise's Knap has views on expansion," AP, *Idaho State Journal*, November 26, 1969.
5. "Boise St. coach wants 1970 game with Idaho," AP, *Great Falls Tribune*, November 27, 1969.
6. "Getting out just in time," John Killen, *Lewiston Morning Tribune*, August 8, 1982.
7. "Broncos: Spoiler role eyed," James E. Shelledy, *Daily Inter Lake*, August 30, 1971.

8. "Boise wins first grid title," AP, *Independent Record*, November 12, 1973.

9. "Autele hurls winning pass," AP, *Idaho State Journal*, November 12, 1973.

10. Ibid.

11. "Boise wins first grid title," AP, *Independent Record*, November 12, 1973.

12. "Big Sky teams hope to save face," UPI, *Daily Herald*, November 15, 1973.

13. "Boise State scores big win," UPI, *Daily Herald*, November 19, 1973.

14. "Knap sees tougher test in Wichita Falls game," AP, *Idaho State Journal*, December 3, 1973.

15. Ibid.

16. "La. Tech faces irresistible force in Pioneer Bowl," Gerry Robichaux, *The Times*, December 8, 1973.

17. Ibid.

18. "Broncos await semifinal battle," AP, *Ogden Standard*, December 6, 1973.

19. "Duron-to-Carr wins it for Tech," Gerry Robichaux, *The Times*, December 9, 1973.

20. Ibid.

Chapter Three: Four Horsemen Gallop to Title

1. "Broncos, Bengals tab new football coaches," AP, *Missoulian*, February 14, 1976.

2. "Boise State taking dead aim on Big Sky and National titles," George Geise, *Great Falls Tribune*, September 3, 1980.

3. "Big Sky Squads Stun Football Powers," AP, *Great Falls Tribune*, September 8, 1980.

4. "Idaho State 'encouraged' despite defeat," *Great Falls Tribune*, September 15, 1980.

5. "It All Started with Utah," Scout.com, August 22, 2010.

6. "Defense keys Boise St. win," *Great Falls Tribune*, December 14, 1980.

7. "Boise St. stymies Grambling, 14–9," *Statesman Journal*, December 14, 1980.

8. "Second title would be great thrill for Gus Parks," *Advocate-Messenger*, December 16, 1980.

9. Ibid.

10. "Boise State Awaits Bid," *Daily Spectrum*, November 25, 1980.

11. "The oral history of Boise State, college football's moneybag," Bill Connelly, *SB Nation*.

Chapter Four: Turning Blue

1. "Griz, Nevada-Reno favored in conference race," Robert Mims, *Great Falls Tribune*, July 30, 1990.

2. "UNI will open 1-AA playoffs at Boise State," Dan McCool, *Des Moines Register Guard*, November 19, 1990.

3. "Boise State stops UNI in playoffs," Dan McCool, *Des Moines Register*, November 25, 1990.

4. Ibid.

5. "Boise State relishes home field against No. 1 Blue Raiders," AP, *Missoulian*, November 30, 1990.

6. Ibid.

7. "Boise State up for MTSU challenge," Mike Organ, *Tennessean*, December 1, 1990.

8. Ibid.

9. "Boise St. fakes way past MTSU," Mike Organ, *Tennessean*, December 2, 1990.

10. Ibid.

11. "Now, it's on to Statesboro," Joe Santoro, *Reno Gazette-Journal*, December 9, 1990.

Chapter Five: A Man Named Pokey

1. *Pokey: The Good Fight*, Pokey Allen and Bob Evancho. Bootleg Books, 1997.

2. Ibid.

3. "Boise State courts Allen," *Statesman Journal*, John Millman, December 2, 1992.

4. *Pokey: The Good Fight*

5. Ibid.

6. Ibid.

7. Ibid.

8. Ibid.

9. Ibid.

10. Ibid.

11. Ibid.

12. Ibid.

13. Ibid.

14. Ibid.

15. Ibid.

16. "Big Sky coaches pick Griz to go like the Dicken(son)s," Bob Mims, *Montana Standard*, July 23, 1994.

17. "UM, MSU Big Sky rivals appraised," AP, *Montana Standard*, August 26, 1994.
18. Ibid.
19. "K.C. Adams emerges as Boise State's star," Mark Anderson, *Reno Gazette-Journal*, September 13, 1994.
20. Ibid.
21. "Wolf Pack bombs in Boise," Mark Anderson, *Reno Gazette-Journal*, September 18, 1994.
22. Ibid.
23. "Pokey Allen wishes Cliff Hysell the best, but not just yet," Scott Mansch, *Great Falls Tribune*, October 20, 1994.
24. "Boise blasts Bobcats," AP, *Montana Standard*, October 23, 1994.
25. "Intrastate feuds to heat Big Sky race," AP, *Montana Standard*, November 18, 1994.
26. *Pokey: The Good Fight*

Chapter Six: In Sickness and in Health

1. *Pokey: The Good Fight*, Pokey Allen and Bob Evancho. Bootleg Books, 1997.
2. Ibid.
3. "Allen works his magic at Boise State," *Statesman Journal* news services, *Statesman Journal*, December 8, 1994.
4. Ibid.
5. *Pokey: The Good Fight*
6. *Blue Magic: Boise State's Inspiring Journey to a Fiesta Bowl Win*, Chadd Cripe and Brian Murphy. *Idaho Statesman*, 2007.
7. *Pokey: The Good Fight*

8. Ibid.

9. "Boise State rallies to make finals," AP, *Great Falls Tribune*, December 11, 1994.

10. "Boise St. turnabout fair play," AP, *Daily Press*, December 14, 1994.

11. "Youngstown rolls to crown," AP, *Courier-News*, December 18, 1994.

12. "Big Sky allegiances don't hold for 'Big-Dog' Boise State," George Geiss, *Great Falls Tribune*, December 15, 1994.

13. Ibid.

14. Ibid.

15. "Allen's cancer treatments can't dampen his spirits," AP, *Missoulian*, January 22, 1995.

16. Ibid.

17. Ibid.

18. Ibid.

19. "Broncos best Big Sky again," Kim Briggeman, *Missoulian*, February 11, 1995.

20. Ibid.

21. "Oregon hires Borges to guide offense," AP, *Statesman Journal*, March 2, 1995.

22. Ibid.

23. "Boise State has talent to repeat," Quane Kenyon, *Missoulian*, August 24, 1995.

24. "Boise State coach's cancer yet another foe," Paola Bolvin, *Arizona Republic*, October 5, 1995.

Chapter Seven: The Passing and the Nutt

1. "Allen's cancer retreats," AP, *Missoulian*, December 23, 1995.

2. "Boise State coach has faced tougher battle than Division 1-A," AP, *South Florida Sun Sentinel*, August 4, 1996.
3. "Pokey Allen ill again," AP, *Missoulian*, August 7, 1996.
4. "Surgeons fail to get all of Allen's cancer," AP, *The World*, August 16, 1996.
5. *Pokey: The Good Fight*, Pokey Allen and Bob Evancho. Bootleg Books, 1997.
6. "Boise State coach anxious to return," AP, the *Statesman Journal*, August 31, 1996.
7. *Blue Magic: Boise State's Inspiring Journey to a Fiesta Bowl Win*, Chadd Cripe and Brian Murphy. *Idaho Statesman*, 2007.
8. Ibid.
9. "How Holtz measures up the hurrying Husky signal; Calling at Air Force and Bama; Pokey Allen's return," Christian Stone, Tim Layden, Cheryl Rosenburg, *Sports Illustrated*, November 25, 1996.
10. *Blue Magic: Boise State's Inspiring Journey to a Fiesta Bowl Win*
11. Houston Nutt biography, olemisssports.com
12. "Bowling Green coach seeing red," Gary Klein, *Los Angeles Times*, September 28, 1997.
13. "Dutton delivers; Boise bounced," Mark Anderson, *Reno Gazette-Journal*, November 9, 1997.

Chapter Eight: Dirk Koetter's Third Time Is the Charm

1. *Blue Magic: Boise State's Inspiring Journey to a Fiesta Bowl Win*, Chadd Cripe and Brian Murphy. *Idaho Statesman*, 2007.
2. "Oregon loses coach to Boise," Quane Kenyon, *The World*, December 11, 1997.

3. Ibid.

4. "The oral history of Boise State, college football's moneybag," Bill Connelly, *SB Nation*.

5. "All-American running back Wedemeyer dies at age 74," AP, *Santa Cruz Sentinel*, January 27, 1999.

6. "Big West's parity trails Nevada, Idaho," Steve Sneedon, *Reno Gazette-Journal*, July 31, 1999.

7. "Boise State coach boots one, punishes four other players," AP, *Reno Gazette-Journal*, August 12, 1999.

8. "Toledo: Life more important than football," AP, *The Signal*, September 4, 1999.

9. "Hendricks airing it out for Boise State," Dash Robinson, *Reno-Gazette Journal*, August 23, 2000.

10. *Blue Magic: Boise State's Inspiring Journey to a Fiesta Bowl Win*.

11. "Next stop Boise for older, probably wiser Cards," Jody Demling, the *Courier-Journal*, December 26, 1999.

12. "Boise State's biggest loss came on practice field," Jody Demling, the *Courier-Journal*, December 29, 1999.

13. Ibid.

14. Ibid.

15. "Boise St. successful in first bowl appearance," AP, *Tampa Bay Times*, December 31, 1999.

16. Ibid.

17. Ibid.

Chapter Nine: Ignition

1. "Anxiety vs. Eagerness," Tommy Trujillo, *Santa Fe New Mexican*, September 1, 2000.

2. "Boise State named pre-season favorite," Wire Reports, *Daily Spectrum*, July 28, 2000.

3. "Hendricks airing it out for Boise State," Dash Robinson, *Reno-Gazette Journal*, August 23, 2000.

4. Ibid.

5. "Lobos have something to make up for," Dennis Latta, *Albuquerque Journal*, September 2, 2000.

6. Ibid.

7. *Blue Magic: Boise State's Inspiring Journey to a Fiesta Bowl Win*

Chapter Ten: End of the Beginning, Birth of the Hawk

1. "Potent offenses to clash in Humanitarian Bowl," AP, *Arizona Daily Star*, December 28, 2000.

2. "UW's Petersen brings unique approach," Pete Thamel, *Sports Illustrated*, August 11, 2014.

3. "Husky coach Chris Petersen is a perfectionist with a personal touch," Adam Jude, *Seattle Times*, August 27, 2014.

4. Ibid.

5. *Blue Magic: Boise State's Inspiring Journey to a Fiesta Bowl Win*, Chadd Cripe and Brian Murphy. *Idaho Statesman*, 2007.

6. Ibid.

Chapter Eleven: Taking Flight

1. "Bulldogs toughen up for the title run," Scott Sonner, *Honolulu Advertiser*, August 13, 2001.

2. "WAC touts its new stability," Stephen Tsal, *Honolulu Advertiser*, July 29, 2001.

3. "Broncos renew rivalry with Pack," Chad Hartley, *Reno Gazette-Journal*, August 19, 2001.

4. "Boise State won't adjust habits for USC," Rick Scoppe, *Greenville News*, August 31, 2001.

5. "Holtz says Boise State is a threat," AP, *Index-Journal*, August 28, 2001.

6. "Boise State won't adjust habits for USC," Rick Scoppe, *Greenville News*, August 31, 2001.

7. "Holtz doesn't want to talk about last year," AP, *Index-Journal*, September 1, 2001.

8. "SI gets on Fresno State bandwagon," Scott Beder, *News-Star*, September 13, 2001.

9. "Boise State hurt by several injuries," Scott Beer, *News-Star*, October 11, 2001.

10. "Owls offer different challenge for Pack 'D,'" Chad Hartley, *Reno Gazette-Journal*, October 17, 2001.

11. "Boise St. Stuns No. 8 Fresno St.," AP, *Reno Gazette-Journal*, October 19, 2001.

12. "Bulldogs hope to benefit from bowl game, exposure," Jimmy Watson, *The Times*, January 2, 2002.

13. "Police probing Boise State quarterback," *Amarillo Globe News*, November 25, 2001.

14. "Boise State replacing AstroTurf at stadium," Stephen Tsai, *Honolulu Advertiser*, July 23, 2002.

15. "Quote Corner," AP, *Gettysburg Times*, November 8, 2002.

16. "The oral history of Boise State, college football's moneybag," Bill Connelly, *SB Nation*.

17. "Arkansas tries to avoid being Boise State's big prize," Douglas Pils, *Springfield News-Leader*, September 7, 2002.

18. "Kentucky discovers its defense, while LSU left reeling after loss," David Climer, *Jackson Sun*, September 4, 2002.

19. "Benson tries to find silver lining in WACs 0–9 effort," Chad Hartley, *Reno Gazette-Journal*, September 10, 2002.

20. Ibid.

21. "'Leave no doubt' motto paying off for Boise State," Chad Hartley, *Reno Gazette-Journal*, October 22, 2002.

22. Ibid.

23. "Boise St. pounces on Spartans, 45–8," AP, *Santa Cruz Sentinel*, October 27, 2002.

24. "Boise State going for perfect mark," Dave Reardon, *Honolulu Star-Bulletin*, November 22, 2002.

25. "Boise St. coach sees game as life lesson," Chadd Cripe, *Statesman Journal*, September 17, 2003.

Chapter Twelve: The Explosion

1. "Poumele ahead of Ilaoa," Dave Reardon, *Honolulu Star-Bulletin*, July 30, 2004.

2. *Out of the Blue: A Film About Life and Football*, Iron Circle Pictures, Priddy Brothers, Appaloosa Pictures, 2007.

3. *Honolulu Star-Bulletin*, September 5, 2004.

4. *Out of the Blue: A Film About Life and Football*

5. "Boise coach mixes X's, O's with ABC's," Michael Grant, *Courier-Journal*, December 30, 2004.

6. *Out of the Blue*

Chapter Thirteen: Georgia on My Mind

1. "AU, UGA face upsets, experts say," Tony Barnhart, *Anniston Star*, August 15, 2005.

2. Ibid.
3. Ibid.
4. *Out of the Blue: A Film About Life and Football*
5. "A journey back 'between the hedges,'" John D. Lukacs, ESPN
6. "New age style boosts Boise State," Christopher Smith, *Chicago Tribune*, September 3, 2005.
7. "Shockley leads Georgia to rout of Boise State," Paul Newberry, *Tennessean*, September 4, 2005.
8. Ibid.
9. "Leave dramatics in real world," Greg Hansen, *Arizona Daily Star*, September 8, 2005.
10. "Beavers seek to avenge loss to Boise State," Gary Horowitz, *Statesman Journal*, September 10, 2005.
11. Ibid.
12. Ibid.
13. "Beavers rally; Ducks roll," Gary Horowitz, *Statesman Journal*, September 11, 2005.
14. Ibid.
15. "Fresno State overcomes Broncos," Greg Beacham, *The Signal*, November 11, 2005.
16. "Fresno State takes down WC powerhouse Boise St.," Greg Beacham, *Reno Gazette-Journal*, November 11, 2005.
17. *Out of the Blue: A Film About Life and Football*
18. "Colorado closes in on Boise St. coach," AP, *Palm Beach Post*, December 16, 2005.
19. "Boise State hoping evolving door of coaches ends with Petersen," Tim Booth, AP, December 30, 2005.

Chapter Fourteen: All, Aboard!

1. "Petersen replaces Hawkins at Boise State," AP, *Missoulian*, December 17, 2005.
2. "Boise State hoping evolving door of coaches ends with Petersen," Tim Booth, AP, December 30, 2005.
3. "Under a new direction," Keith Fidler, *Missoulian*, August 20, 2006.
4. Ibid.
5. Ibid.
6. "New coach, same old Broncos," Dave Reardon, *Honolulu Star-Bulletin*, August 23, 2006.
7. "Boise making smooth transition," AP, *Honolulu Star-Bulletin*, April 24, 2006.
8. "Ohio State will rule BCS," Mike Huguenin, *Orlando Sentinel*, October 2, 2006.
9. "SEC grades high at halfway," John Lindsay, *Sun Desert*, October 11, 2006.
10. "Boise State struggles to beat New Mexico," Wire Reports, *Tulare Advance-Register*, October 16, 2006.
11. "No. 10 Notre Dame awaits Bruins," Beth Harris, AP, *Desert Sun*, October 17, 2006.
12. "Johnson rumbles for 183 yards, 4 TDs for Boise State," AP, October 21, 2006.
13. Ibid.

Chapter Fifteen: A Fiesta For All

1. "Boise State arrives for its first BCS party," AP, *Cincinnati Enquirer*, December 27, 2006.

2. "Petersen: Broncos maintain focus as attention intensifies," Dan Hinxman, *Reno Gazette-Journal*, December 19, 2006.
3. Ibid.
4. Ibid.
5. "The Appeal of the Underdog," Joseph A. Vandella; Nadav P. Goldschmied; David A.R. Richards. University of South Florida.
6. "Boise State no longer small-time program," Bob Baum, AP, December 29, 2006.
7. Ibid.
8. "BSU gets their shot," AP, *Honolulu Advertiser*, December 4, 2006.
9. Ibid.

Chapter Seventeen: Fall Out Boys

1. *Blue Magic: Boise State's Inspiring Journey to a Fiesta Bowl Win*, Chadd Cripe and Brian Murphy. *Idaho Statesman*, 2007.
2. Ibid.
3. Ibid.

Chapter Eighteen: The Trifecta

1. *Blue Magic: Boise State's Inspiring Journey to a Fiesta Bowl Win*, Chadd Cripe and Brian Murphy. *Idaho Statesman*, 2007.

Chapter Twenty: A Kick Short

1. "Boise Right On Schedule," Jason Chatraw, *Daily Press*, April 11, 2010.

2. Ibid.

3. "Stakes have never been higher for Boise State," Ralph D. Russo, *Great Falls Tribune*, September 6, 2010.

4. Ibid.

5. "Boise right on schedule," Jason Chatraw, *Daily Press*, April 11, 2010.

6. "Stakes have never been higher for Boise State," Ralph D. Russo, *Great Falls Tribune*, September 6, 2010.

7. "Broncos face stiff test," Norm Wood, *Orlando Sentinel*, September 6, 2010.

8. Ibid.

9. "Boise hopes victory start of big run," Erik Smith, *USA Today*, September 8, 2010.

10. "UW's Petersen brings unique approach," Pete Thamel, *Sports Illustrated*, August 11, 2014.

Chapter Twenty-One: OKGs and Maintaining Success

1. "Boise St. stuns Koetter," Kent Somers, *Arizona Republic*, January 3, 2010.

2. "The oral history of Boise State, college football's moneybag," Bill Connelly, *SB Nation*.

3. Ibid.

4. Ibid.

5. Ibid.

6. "Academic success continuing at record pace for Boise State Football," B. J. Rains, *Idaho Press-Tribune*, July 9, 2017.

Chapter Twenty-Two: State of the Program

1. "Man behind Blue Turf, Boise State growth, Gene Bleymaier terminated as AD," Tom Fox, *Idaho Press*, August 11, 2011.
2. Ibid.